GAFFERS

GAFFERS

50 YEARS OF
IRISH FOOTBALL MANAGERS

TREVOR KEANE

MERCIER PRESS
Irish Publisher – Irish Story

MERCIER PRESS

Cork

www.mercierpress.ie

© Trevor Keane, 2010

© Foreword: Darren Clarke, 2010

ISBN: 978 1 85635 666 4

10 9 8 7 6 5 4 3 2 1

A CIP record for this title is available from the British Library

Printed and bound in the EU.

CONTENTS

Dedicated to my wife Oonagh, my son Seán, my mother Noreen, sister Deirdre, and in loving memory of my father, Jim.

ACKNOWLEDGEMENTS

This book has been a long time in the writing for me, but I could not have done it without help from a lot of people. I would like to thank Mercier Press for giving me the opportunity to write a book I have always wanted to write. Thanks to my family and friends for listening to me go on and on about the book, especially my wife Oonagh, who not only listened, but also supported me through its writing.

I would like to give a very special thank you to Pat Whitty, who helped me at the start, answered every email, and gave me some wonderful contacts and advice; I bet he will be happy to see that the book is finally finished.

I spoke to a lot of footballers in the writing of this book, and I want to thank them all for taking the time to help and to talk to me. Their stories were fantastic, and it was great to witness the passion that they have for the game, especially the game in Ireland.

Special thanks as well to Terry Phelan and Craig Johnston – it was great to talk to two players who I hold in such respect – while anyone who is fortunate enough to have a chat with Turlough O'Connor about football is a lucky person indeed.

League of Ireland footballers may not get the same exposure as their English counterparts; however, the time they give to the game in Ireland is unparalleled, and their passion for football is infectious, and I thank each and every one of them for their help.

Although the book is full of interviews with players and managers, none of these would have been possible without the help of the administrative staff who work at clubs in Ireland, England and Scotland. I would need another book just to name you all, but I appreciate everything you did for me. I would like to give special thanks, however, to the staff at DC United, especially Mark Simpson, who helped me out so much with stories, emails and photographs.

Thanks to the Football Association of Ireland (FAI) for arranging the Giovanni Trapattoni interview for me. Thanks as well to the FAI's director of communications Peter Sherrard, who, without realising it, gave me a real confidence boost when he laughed upon hearing my proposed title of 'An Englishman, an Irishman and an Italian'; this small chuckle gave me the belief that I could impress people in footballing circles.

Thanks also to Liam Kelly from the *Irish Independent* newspaper for allowing me to take his hard work researching the earnings of various managers and to reproduce it throughout the book, as well as providing me with some helpful tips on interviewing people.

I would also like to thank Donal Cullen for sending me his only surviving copy of *Ireland on the Ball*, which details all Ireland's games from 1926 to 1993 and is a great encyclopaedia for Irish football. His book helped me form the basis of the statistics that form part of the book. I will return it, I swear. I would also like to say thank you to Con for putting me in touch with Dave Langan.

Thanks as well to Eugene McLaughlin, whose website Awaythelads.com has wonderful pictures of Ireland's managers and of teams in action, some of which can been seen in this book.

FOREWORD

When I was asked to write a foreword for Trevor's book, I must admit I was baffled – he does know I'm a golfer, doesn't he? Then I thought, sure, why not. Even though I am a golfer, I do enjoy watching and attending a good game of football, so maybe there is a link after all. I am, of course, a big Liverpool fan, and a fine round of golf cost me my place at Cardiff for the 2006 FA Cup final when Liverpool beat West Ham.

When I was growing up in Dungannon in County Tyrone, Liverpool were the team of the time, while George Best was the footballer. For me, he will be forever remembered as the most talented footballer ever to come from the island of Ireland, and it is such a shame that his skills failed to grace the biggest stage of them all at a World Cup.

That Liverpool team of my youth was so successful and had some of the best players who ever played the game, Kenny Dalglish and Kevin Keegan springing immediately to mind. But as I started to think about what I would write, my thoughts turned to the large number of Irish players who have played for Liverpool during the years since I have supported them, real household names and genuine stars of the game. Liverpool and Ireland are closely interlinked, with the city enjoying a large Irish population, and, of course, the first ever Liverpool manager, John McKenna, was a County Monaghan man. And, over the years, Liverpool have helped provide the Ireland team with some of the finest players ever to wear the shirt – or maybe that should read Ireland have helped fill the Liverpool team with some of the finest players ever to wear their shirt. In the 1970s, the Reds' Steve Heighway raced down the flanks for Ireland, while in the 1980s and early 1990s, when I really started to support Liverpool, the team was filled with some of the biggest names ever to play for Ireland – players such as Ronnie Whelan, John Aldridge and Ray Houghton. These players were big names and enjoyed massive success with Liverpool, but for many people, and I include myself, the lack of any form of success for the Ireland team on the pitch meant that we just thought of these players as Liverpool players.

Northern Ireland enjoyed the thrills of a World Cup in 1958 and 1982. For a small country, this is a great achievement, and to this day they remain the smallest nation to have reached more than one World Cup. Things were about to happen for the Republic of Ireland, though, as in December 1985 an Englishman by the name of Jack Charlton came along and changed the face of Irish football forever, and for years to come Jack Charlton's legacy will endure with fans of the game everywhere. Not just in Ireland, but also in his native England, he is a hero of the game, having won everything you can imagine, including the trophy of dreams, the World Cup.

For the Republic of Ireland, the tournament that changed everything was Euro '88 in Germany. Suddenly, everyone was following what Ireland and Jack did. They captured the imagination of people not just in Ireland, but around the world. Then, success at the Italia '90 and USA '94 World Cups had the whole island, both north and south, in a whirl. It was some achievement, considering the size of the country, but it's no surprise when you think about it further, because Ireland has always had a history of producing fantastic sports people. Whether in golf, boxing, rugby or soccer, Ireland has always managed to produce sportsmen and women and results that belittle the fact that we are a small country.

As in all other sports, football is nothing without its fans, and Ireland boasts some of the best supporters you will ever come across. As a golfer you can rest assured that no matter what event you are playing at you will always see a green, white and gold flag waving in the distance. The support at the Irish Open is always amazing, as it was at the Ryder Cup when it was held in Ireland, and the Irish really get behind their teams.

Brian Kerr, Steve Staunton and, more recently, Giovanni Trapattoni have all tried to emulate Jack and his successor Mick McCarthy. Ireland under Trapattoni seems like a team on the up, and the confidence he has instilled in the players is good to see. It's great that results are improving again and once again the country is behind the team. Let's hope this success continues.

Of course, there is another good reason to buy this book, aside from the interesting stories about the men who have managed Ireland. There is also the fact that a percentage of the royalties are going to the Diabetes Federation of Ireland. I know through my own work with the Darren Clarke Foundation, how important it is to give something back no matter what the cause is, and I am delighted to be able to offer my support to this worthwhile charity.

Enjoy the read.

Darren Clarke

INTRODUCTION

You hear it in almost every football interview nowadays: the gaffer told us this and the gaffer told us that. The word 'gaffer', footballing slang for the boss or manager, has become part of modern-day football culture. This book, then, is intended to be a celebration of Ireland's gaffers, and of what they have achieved in football, especially with the Republic of Ireland, over the last fifty-seven years.

If, like me, you are only old enough to remember Irish football from Euro '88 onwards, you might mistakenly think that Jack Charlton was the first Ireland football manager. Jack seems to be the benchmark that all managers past, present and future will have to measure up to, and I have found that just about everybody has a Jack story and that they feel almost honoured to share it with people. It was with great difficulty, then, that the book did not turn into a celebration of Jack, such is the esteem in which he is held by the players he managed and by the general public. This is a measure of the man and of the role he played in the development of international football in Ireland. The respect people have for him is not surprising, as 'Big Jack' led Irish football on a glorious trail of success.

It is very easy to get caught up in reminiscences about the

Charlton era and forget the other men who managed our national team. However, there can be no doubting the popularity of the game in Ireland well before the arrival of Big Jack, and although he might have built the walls, the foundations were laid well before his arrival. Since the late, great Johnny Carey managed the side from 1953, a total of fifteen men have sat in the dugout, either as manager or as caretaker manager, for the Republic of Ireland.

Ireland is a small country, so the impact we make on international sport is amazing. We have a fantastic sporting history and an equally extraordinary fan base. Irish supporters do not limit themselves to one sport, and whether Ireland is playing soccer, football, hurling, rugby, golf or even cricket, the country will come out in force and try and push the players on that extra inch. I cannot think of any other set of fans that gives as much to their national teams as the Irish do – or maybe I am just biased.

While most Americans who were around at the time can tell you where they were when John F. Kennedy was shot, and most English people of a certain age can remember where they were when England won the World Cup, I am sure everybody in Ireland who is old enough can tell you where they were when Ronnie Whelan scored a goal against the Russians, where they were when a certain Glaswegian put the ball in the English net, not to mention the Italian net, and more recently, where they were to witness the 'Hand of Gaul' which cruelly robbed Ireland of a place at the World Cup in South Africa in 2010.

A brief history of Irish football in the early days is a good starting point for any discussion of the managers. Before 1921 Ireland had a single national football team. In those early days, players were selected from both the north and south, but an event occurred in December 1920 that paved the way for the modern team we have today – the country was officially divided by the Government of Ireland Act. A year later, the FAI was formed and in 1923 was recognised by FIFA as the governing body of Irish Free State football.

The new Ireland team made its international debut at the 1924 Olympics, where it reached the quarter-finals. Between 1924 and 1936 the team competed as the Irish Free State and made its World Cup debut in 1934, where it drew 4–4 with Belgium in a qualifier at Dalymount Park, the national stadium at the time. That game saw one of the first Irish footballing heroes emerge, Paddy Moore, who became an instant legend and record maker when he scored all four Irish goals in that draw. His feat still remains in the record books, as he is the only player to score four goals in a World Cup qualifying game.

In those days, even though the Irish Free State had been established, players could pick and choose who they played for, and confusion reigned over selection rights. After twenty years of puzzlement, when players regularly played for both Ireland and Northern Ireland, some clarity was achieved in 1953 when FIFA ruled that Northern Ireland and the Republic of Ireland were to be considered separate teams with their own pool of players. This proved to be necessary after the near-farcical spectacle at the 1950 World Cup when four players turned out for both Irish teams in the same tournament.

To this day, this remains a controversial topic, and fans of modern football and politics alike will be aware of the case of Manchester United's Darron Gibson. He is a very talented player and was wanted by both the Northern Ireland and the

Ireland teams. He ended up being at the centre of a disagreement between the Northern Irish governing body, the Irish Football Association (IFA), and the FAI over the eligibility of players born within Northern Ireland to represent the Republic of Ireland. In normal circumstances, players not born within the country or territory of the association they wish to represent must demonstrate to FIFA that they have a valid connection with that country or territory in terms of either ancestry or residence. However, the exceptional constitutional position of Northern Ireland means that Irish citizenship is the birthright of every person born there if they so desire. This meant that Gibson was eligible to play for the Republic of Ireland at international level. As a result, Gibson was approached to represent both Northern Ireland, whom he played for at Under-16 level, and the Republic of Ireland at international level. Gibson chose to play for the Republic of Ireland and has played at Under-17 level as well as captaining both the Under-19 and Under-21 teams. To date, he has five caps. So, to some extent, it is still the player's choice which part of Ireland he decides to play for.

The Republic of Ireland has always had great players and great teams. In 1956 Ireland beat West Germany 3–0 at Dalymount Park. This was a German team that had beaten a Hungary team containing the legendary Ferenc Puskás 3–2 at the 1954 World Cup. There were seven players from the League of Ireland in the team that day, including Ronnie Nolan and James 'Maxie' McCann, who won his only cap that day and scored a goal. Then, in 1957, Ireland drew 1–1 with a great England team at Dalymount. England only managed the draw through a late goal scored by John Atyeo, so the foundation for success was there, even if Ireland was a small country with small resources.

The management structure was limited in those days: a committee of selectors chose the team and on occasion a coach or team manager was appointed. For example, Val Harris and Bill Lacey were managers of the national team when it was known as the Irish Free State team. And before the appointment of Johnny Carey in 1953 to the newly formed Republic of Ireland team, Doug Livingstone and Alex Stevenson managed the Irish team in the early 1950s. However, the role of the Irish manager evolved over time as the power of the committee became weaker and weaker.

It was not until 1969 that an Ireland manager was able to pick his own side. Before that a panel of selectors were responsible for team selection. To put Ireland's situation into perspective, Walter Winterbottom became the first full-time manager of England in 1946, while Andy Beattie became the first Scottish manager in 1954, a difference of twenty-three and fifteen years respectively. This lack of a full-time manager definitely cost Ireland, particularly as you get a sense, when talking to League of Ireland players of the late 1950s, 1960s and early 1970s, that those years were a golden era for Irish football. The League of Ireland was booming and people were spilling through the gates to see their teams in action, as former Ireland international and Bohemians player Tony O'Connell recalls: 'Football in Ireland in the 1960s was booming, and if ever there was a time for the League of Ireland to go professional, it was then. It would of course have helped the national team no end, too. The crowds were huge, and the gates could have supported the clubs. Irish football was innovative in those days and was often ahead of the English game. I can remember my company Jodi sponsoring Bohemians in 1973 and it was the first time in

Ireland, Scotland, Wales or England that a club had a sponsor on their jersey. [Liverpool were the first English side, in 1978, to have a sponsor on their shirts.] In those days there was not a lot between the League teams. I sponsored Bohemians until 1978 and then things changed. Football in Ireland seemed to go downhill from there. Everyone wanted to fly over to England to see a game. The profile of the game slipped away. I know Johnny Giles tried to resurrect it in the 1980s, but it was too late by then – the boom had passed.'

The success of the League and the national team never seemed to be interlinked, however, as while the League was doing well, the national team, despite supplying England with an abundance of talent, was still not qualifying for major tournaments. The Ireland team, much like their modern counterparts, had been a star attraction, with 40,000 and more often packing into Dalymount Park to watch them play, but from the 1970s soccer in Ireland seemed to slowly lose its momentum. Diehard fans aside, the majority of football fans can be a fickle bunch who require success and entertainment to maintain their interest in a team. Despite the progress that was being made with the backroom staff and set-up of the international team, the results were not up to the standard of previous decades and for the fans to start believing in the ideas of the FAI and the players, success was a big pre-requisite. Regardless of the fantastic footballers that Ireland was producing, the lack of qualification on the international stage slowly saw the popularity of the sport fall behind in the eyes of the people. The traditional Irish sports of hurling and Gaelic football, which had always had a strong following, became even more popular, and the national rugby team also started to reap the rewards of success on the international stage.

The League of Ireland fell a little by the wayside, and standards and attendances began to drop. Until the mid 1980s, soccer was not the first choice sport of youngsters or supporters. Football was in a recession, as was the country as a whole, and it needed something major to happen to kick-start its resurgence. Jack Charlton was that catalyst. His demeanour, not to mention his success and the brand of football he advocated, epitomised the era and saw soccer enjoy a pre-Premiership boom in the hearts of the Irish. However, the late 1980s and early 1990s was also the beginning of the commercial era for football. The game was changing, and Ireland's footballers were part of that change.

Irish stars of the past did not enjoy the coverage their modern-day counterparts do today. Television and newspaper coverage, not to mention Internet coverage, make the modern-day Ireland international instantly recognisable to the majority of people. The Ireland football stars of today adorn the front and back pages of the domestic papers, not to mention participating in some of Ireland's top-rated television shows, on which Irish viewers have witnessed appearances by Jack Charlton, Robbie Keane and Niall Quinn. However, players from years gone by perhaps had more of an aura about them, given the exclusivity that came with seeing them play. Fans of football did not have the money to travel to England to see their heroes play week in, week out, and had to rely on home internationals to watch their favourite players in action. The number of actual attendees at these games was often understated in the reported attendance, as many fans claimed they climbed the walls of Dalymount to watch Ireland play – the emphasis on health and safety in those days was not what it is today.

Mick McGrath told me that when he used to get off the

Irish squad team bus to head into Phibsborough stadium, he would be inundated with requests for tickets. Nowadays few people have the pleasure of getting that close for an autograph, never mind having the audacity to ask for a ticket. In those days fans would write letters to the FAI, and these letters would be passed on to the players, who would choose which ones to respond to. Requests were generally for a signed picture of the player, although Mick told me about a Cork fan to whom he sent his socks from each game he played.

Football has changed considerably from those days, and the modern-day footballer and manager is a different breed from the older generation. The media interest in the game nowadays ensures that players and managers are big news, and, as a result, their actions have greater consequences. Although the squad and management are heroes in their own country through their profile with their club teams, they are also instantly recognisable to football fans all over the planet – the game is now well and truly a global phenomenon.

Over the years Ireland has had some fantastic footballers, from Johnny Carey, Tommy Eglington and Peter Farrell to Noel Cantwell, Charlie Hurley, Johnny Giles, Mick Meagan, Liam Brady, Paul McGrath, Kevin Moran and Packie Bonner, right through to Mick McCarthy, Steve Staunton, Andy Townsend, Roy Keane and the current legends of Shay Given, Damian Duff and Robbie Keane. Ireland has a fantastic habit of producing terrific footballers, and every generation has a player who sticks out in the mind. However, players need managing, and this book charts the last fifty years of Ireland football managers, tracing their early careers on the pitch to their moves to the dugout.

With the exception of Johnny Giles, the older generation of

manager did not enjoy, if you can call it that, the same profile that the modern manager has to contend with. This changed with the success of Jack Charlton. If there ever was a turning point for Irish football and the profile of its managers, it was Euro '88, and while Jack and the boys got all the kudos, lady luck can also be credited with changing the face of the game in Ireland. Ireland's fiftieth game in the history of the European Championship saw them beat Bulgaria 2–0 and finish with eleven points in group seven, but this was not enough to secure immediate qualification and the Ireland team was left relying on other results to help them secure their qualification to the European Championship finals. With two games in hand Bulgaria had their destiny in their own hands – wins over Luxembourg and Scotland would see them instead of Ireland make it to Germany. A 3–0 win against Luxembourg saw the first hurdle passed, leaving a must-win match at home with Scotland. With eighty-seven minutes gone the game was evenly matched at 0–0 when Scottish midfielder Gary MacKay made himself an instant Irish hero, scoring the goal that secured a win for Scotland and ultimately started the Irish footballing odyssey, by giving them that dreamed-of place in the European Championship finals.

Pulling on the green shirt of Ireland is the ultimate footballing honour for a player born on these shores, or for that matter a player born on foreign shores with a legitimate claim to play for this country. I can only imagine the feeling that is experienced by a player as he pulls on the Ireland shirt for the first time. Likewise, if playing for your country is the ultimate honour for a player, the managerial equivalent is to have charge of your national team, and while there are eleven players on the pitch and five substitutes, there is only one manager. And over the last fifty years, Ireland has had some fantastic managers in the dugout.

One of the most interesting facts to emerge from researching this book is that all of the Ireland managers enjoyed tremendous success as either players or club bosses before taking on the job of managing the national side. Johnny Carey was a Championship winner and an FA Cup winner with Manchester United, Noel Cantwell lifted the FA Cup for Manchester United, Charlie Hurley was an important part of the Sunderland side of the 1960s, Mick Meagan was a League winner with Everton, Seán Thomas had massive success in League of Ireland football, Johnny Giles won almost all the titles the game had to offer at Leeds, Alan Kelly became a successful coach in the USA, Eoin Hand enjoyed League success with Limerick FC, Jack Charlton was a member of the same team as Giles, Mick McCarthy was a Scottish League and Cup winner with Celtic, Brian Kerr transformed St Patrick's Athletic to League champions in his time, Steve Staunton won trophies with Liverpool and Aston Villa, while Giovanni Trapattoni won the Italian League and titles in Portugal, Austria and Germany, as well as European trophies, one of the true measures of a top-class manager. While the success they have endured in the Ireland job has been mixed, the calibre and pedigree of the men cannot be questioned.

I have observed through the writing of this book that the older generation of footballers are more open in their communication and for me, being a first time writer, as I was researching the modern game the opportunity for contact and interaction with today's footballers seems to have diminished. I do not mean this as a gripe, nor is it a criticism of the players – I was thrilled to speak with those I did get to interview. The reason for this lack of access may be that the demands on the modern-day footballer far exceed those of previous generations. The media scrutiny of players from all levels of football has increased as the popularity of the game has expanded, and when they are not on the training field, the players are often sitting in press rooms discussing football. Therefore, it is perhaps a bit easier to understand that these footballers need a break from football and football talk from time to time. I imagine it can be draining on them.

When speaking with today's players I noticed how media savvy they are and how well-trained in public relations they are. It is a surprising trait, especially after speaking to a much more open generation of footballer from an earlier era. Moreover, today's player can be reluctant to share the smallest of stories, as it can have a negative impact on their career. But I spoke to a lot of footballers for this book, and each and every one of them was fantastic and so helpful. No amount of words can thank them enough for their time. I could sit and listen all day to each of them talk about the game they clearly love.

Of course, there is another aspect to this book, and that is to raise awareness of diabetes. As a result, a portion of the royalties from this book will be donated to the Diabetes Federation of Ireland.

So I hope you enjoy reading *Gaffers*, and I wish to thank you for helping me to support a worthwhile cause.

1

JOHNNY CAREY

Figurehead: a person nominally having a prominent position, but no real authority.

Collins Concise dictionary

Johnny Carey, was Ireland's manager for a twelve-year period from November 1955 to February 1967 and is also regarded by many as the first big-name Irish footballer. With his success in the English League, he paved the way for footballers from Ireland to make it in English football. A natural leader on and off the pitch, Carey is a Manchester United legend and still ranks as one of the greatest players to have ever played for both the Red Devils and Ireland. A natural sportsman on the pitch, he was a charismatic gentleman off it and was fondly referred to as 'Gentle John'. Before Carey, Alex Stevenson, one of only three players born in the Republic of Ireland to have played for Glasgow Rangers, presided over the team, but he, like Johnny after him, had very little input into team selection. During Stevenson's stint as manager, from 1953 to 1955, Johnny Carey was the captain of the team.

As a Manchester United player Carey played in an incredible nine different positions, including goalkeeper, and won all the English game had to offer at the time. As a manager he had spells with Blackburn Rovers, Everton, Nottingham Forest and Leyton Orient and he was the first high-profile English-based manager to coach the Irish national soccer team. A truly modern and versatile footballer, who was revered in Ireland, the role of coaching the national side was made for Johnny, with the pipe-smoking Dubliner staying at the helm for twelve years.

EARLY LIFE

Born in 1919 in Dublin, Carey was an all-rounder when it came to sport, playing minor Gaelic football for Dublin and junior football for Home Farm. And in his formative years Carey was a keen swimmer, as well as being a ball boy at tennis matches at the Fitzwilliam Lawn Tennis Club. The skills he learned in those early days, whether it was the concentration and ball-watching skills he acquired from being a ball boy or the sheer strength of mind he gained from swimming, formed the basis for his successful career in football – nothing he learned was wasted.

It was a swimming race that gave an early glimpse of the determination that was to become a hallmark of Carey's career. Entered in a 100-yard contest by his father at a time when the young boy could only swim forty yards, Carey delayed the start of the next race while he slowly but determinedly finished the full course.

Football and Gaelic soon took over Johnny's life. However, in those days soccer was considered to be a foreign game, so Johnny was banned from Croke Park and effectively forced to choose one sport over the other. Thankfully for Ireland and Manchester United fans, he chose soccer and moved on from Home Farm after signing for St James' Gate in 1936 at the age of seventeen.

In 1936, after only a few weeks with the St James' Gate team, Johnny's talent was spotted by Manchester United. The story goes that the Red Devils' chief scout and general fixer Louis Rocca was in Dublin to cast his eye over another young player but instead found himself focusing on the young Carey, who even at such a young age was head and shoulders above all the others on the pitch. The renowned talent-spotter wasted little time in agreeing a £250 fee with St James' Gate.

Apparently when Johnny arrived in Manchester, he saw a newspaper banner that read 'United Sign Star' and he uncharacteristically jumped to the conclusion that he must be the subject of the article. However, on buying a paper he found out that the 'star' in question was Blackburn Rovers' Ernie Thompson, and a mere two lines at the bottom of the page were devoted to the acquisition of Johnny Carey. As it happened, despite the low-key arrival of Carey and the big fanfare for Thompson, it was Carey who left the biggest impression on Old Trafford, while Thompson's United career was over almost before it began.

Johnny made his League debut on the left of midfield in September 1937 and that season celebrated promotion with Manchester United to the First Division. He also made his international debut in what was a momentous first year in English football for the young man. But just as his career was really taking off and gathering pace, the Second World War broke out, and he was faced with a very big decision. Hailing from Ireland, which was and is a neutral country, he had the right to go home if he wished, but the highly principled Carey reckoned that as he earned his crust in Britain he should stay and fight for the country, so he joined the British army.

Carey continued to play football during the Second World War, appearing in the wartime regional leagues, a league competition that replaced the football league from 1939 to 1945. The league divided England into three sections as travel was limited, with a Northern League, a Southern League and a London League. During the war a lot of football stadiums actually became military bases and when players were not fighting they were free to guest for any team in the league. Carey appeared in 112 games, scoring forty-seven goals. His impressive skills could be seen on the field as a guest player for several English clubs, including Liverpool, Manchester City, Middlesbrough and Everton, and he played a number of times for Shamrock Rovers as well as in a League of Ireland XI. Carey served with the British army in Italy and the Middle East, and he also played football as the guest of a number of Italian sides. He received several offers from clubs to remain in Italy, but although his feet might have left Manchester, his heart never did, and he returned to United when the war ended.

It 1945, when something like normal football service was resumed, change was afoot. A new era was dawning at United with the arrival of Matt Busby, a manager who would change the face of football in Manchester. Busby was quick to recognise Carey's natural authority and leadership skills, so he decided to make him club captain. But Busby was not only impressed with Johnny Carey's leadership qualities, he was also impressed with his versatility. Carey was a great passer of the ball, and he was ahead of his time in terms of positional play. Having played in all positions for United, under Busby he found his home and made the right-back slot his own.

The club soon reaped the benefits when Carey captained the club to the 1948 FA Cup final, United beating a Stanley Matthews-inspired Blackpool 4–2, despite being 2–1 down at half-time. Carey's half-time team talk was said to have laid the groundwork for the team to turn things around and win.

In 1952 Carey achieved his ultimate reward. Having finished as runners-up four times between 1947 and 1951, Manchester United were finally crowned First Division champions. In all, Carey played 344 games for United and scored eighteen goals. He finally retired as a player in 1953. He will always be remembered as the first non-UK footballer and the first Irishman to captain a winning team in an FA Cup final and to win the First Division title.

INTERNATIONAL CAREER

Carey began his international career in 1937 when there were in effect two Ireland teams, chosen by the rival associations. The IFA and the FAI claimed jurisdiction over the whole of Ireland, ensuring that Carey was a dual internationalist, not only playing for but also captaining both Ireland teams. In fact, such was the set-up at the time that several notable players played for both teams. Amazingly, in 1946 Carey played for the IFA XI in a 7–2 loss to England before facing them again three days later for the FAI XI in a more morale-boosting 1–0 loss. In 1947 he also captained a Europe XI that played a Great Britain XI at Hampden Park. In 1949 he was voted Footballer of the Year and that same year captained the FAI XI to a 2–0 win over England. In doing so Ireland became the first non-UK-based team to beat England on their home soil.

In all, Carey appeared for the FAI on no fewer than twenty-nine occasions between 1937 and 1953, scoring three goals. He made his debut against Norway in a World Cup qualifier that ended 3–3, while his first goal came in a 3–2 win over Poland in 1938. He captained Ireland no fewer than nineteen times, with his last game for the FAI's national team coming in 1953 in a 4–0 win over Austria.

During the period 1946 to 1949, Carey played nine times for the IFA's Ireland team, helping them to finish runners-up in the British Home Championship of 1947. There were seven players from the Irish Free State and four from Northern Ireland making up the team. A 0–0 draw with Scotland secured the runners-up spot.

CAREY THE COACH

Following his retirement in 1953, Carey accepted the role of Blackburn Rovers manager and, after narrowly missing promotion four times, he took them to the top division in his fifth year in charge. Mick McGrath, who played twenty-two times for Ireland and was signed for Blackburn by Carey, recalls: 'I first came across Johnny Carey when I was living in Dublin and playing for Home Farm at the age of eighteen. Johnny was in the stand, he would have been manager of Blackburn at the time and he was over scouting for players. The match he was watching was the All-Ireland Under-18 final played in

Dalymount Park and I was in the Home Farm team that day and we were playing against Tower Rovers from Cork. I must have made an impression on him as a few days later he signed me and three others from that match.

'We travelled over to Blackburn, and Johnny took us into a room, told us we would earn £9 a week and gave us a list of rules and regulations. He told us to respect people. That was a big thing with him.

'When Carey took over at Blackburn Rovers, he set about changing what was an old team. He brought in Brian Douglas, who was eighteen when he came into the first team, and he also promoted Ronnie Clayton, who would go on to become a club legend. Clayton had made his debut in 1950 but was still a young player when Carey took over. He also made some shrewd signings, bringing in experienced players such as Frank Mooney and Bobby Langton. Carey managed to draw performances from us that we did not know we could achieve. We became known as "Carey's Chicks". The average age of the team was twenty to twenty-one.

'I know people talk up the team that won the Premier League in 1995, but if you speak to older generations of fans, they will tell you that the team that Johnny Carey built was one of the best ever.'

Despite steering Blackburn to promotion, Johnny did not hang around to help them in Division One, as he accepted a role with Everton, who at the time were among the also-rans of the League and a mid-table side. The move did not last long, however, for despite leading the club to their highest post-war position of fifth place in 1961, Carey was sacked at the end of the season. The chairman of the club was the Pools magnate John Moores, who had backed the club financially in the transfer market and expected more from the team and manager than a fifth place finish. The actual sacking of Carey took place in the back of a taxi. His replacement at Everton was Harry Catterick, who led Everton to the title two years later.

Carey continued his development as a coach with Leyton Orient, whom he led to promotion to the First Division in 1962, to this date their only season in the top tier of English football. But his greatest success as a manager came with Nottingham Forest, whom he guided to the runners-up spot in the First Division, finishing behind his beloved Manchester United. That season he also led Forest to the FA Cup semi-final where they lost to Tottenham Hotspur.

During this time, Carey was also the manager of the Republic of Ireland's national team. He served as the boss of the national side from 1955 to 1967. However, as was the case with his predecessors, Carey was not responsible for the picking of the side during this period. His reign started with a 2–2 draw at home to Spain in November 1955, and in his second game in charge Ireland travelled to Rotterdam to beat Holland 4–1. Good times, it seemed, were on the way. In fact, Carey enjoyed three wins and a draw in his first eighteen months in charge, but he and the team came crashing down to earth with a 5–1 loss to England in May 1957 in a qualifying game for the 1958 World Cup.

Mick McGrath remembers that 'from about 1955 onwards, Johnny managed both the Ireland team and the Blackburn team. However, when we were at Blackburn, there was no mention of Ireland. A couple of weeks before a game, the FAI would contact Blackburn and give them the details of Ireland's game and a list of where we were to go and meet. Even though Johnny was the manager, the squad was picked by a committee.

'In those days, Ireland games were played on a Sunday, so you would play your club match on a Saturday at 3.00 p.m. – there were no Sunday or Monday games – and when the game finished, you made your way to Liverpool to catch the mail boat over to the North Wall. The conditions at that time meant you could hardly sleep on the boat, and you arrived in Dublin at 7.30 a.m., where you then made your way to the Four Courts Hotel down by the Liffey. That was where we stayed back then. You would then grab a couple of hours' sleep before you met up with the team at 12 noon in the Gresham Hotel, which was a major hotel in those days. There you would meet up with the League of Ireland lads – some of them you would have never met before.

'There was no chance for training or practice. We would have a light meal – some lads would have steaks or a poached egg with toast, but I generally had toast and tea – then we would head up to a room and discuss the game. Johnny would generally start by saying he did not know much about the opposition. That was the way it was then. We had to focus on what we had. He would tell us to work hard and to support each other. He would have his pipe in his mouth and he would be puffing away. He would then go to each individual and tell them what their job was.

'I got my first call for an Ireland squad for a match against Poland, but I didn't get on that day, and, in fact, I got my first cap against Austria. I was very nervous before the game but was still looking forward to it. We lost 2–0, but I got some decent press.'

That campaign saw Ireland finish runners-up to England. Denmark were the cannon fodder in the group, with Ireland managing to beat them twice. Dermot Curtis was the star of the Irish campaign, with three goals.

A highlight of Carey's career was presiding over the Republic of Ireland team during a historic era for football. The game was going through a period of evolution, and with the game growing, the European Championships were created for the cream of Europe. Ireland were drawn against Czechoslovakia in a qualifying round for the first tournament in 1960, which was referred to in those days as the Nations Cup. Ireland won the first leg at Dalymount Park 2–0, with goals from two future Ireland managers: Liam Tuohy, scorer of the first ever goal in the history of the European Championships, and Manchester United's Noel Cantwell.

Despite conceding an early penalty in the away leg, the Irish performed well and retained the advantage until a twenty-three-minute spell in the second half when they conceded three goals, eventually losing out 4–2 on aggregate. Czechoslovakia went on to qualify for the finals, finishing in third place after being beaten by the ultimate 1960 European Nations Cup winners, the Soviet Union, in the semi-final.

The year 1962 saw the Irish team reach a low point when they suffered a humiliating 7–1 loss to Czechoslovakia in a World Cup qualifying match. This result remains Ireland's biggest competitive defeat. The team managed to put that disastrous result behind them, but in the European qualifiers of 1964, Ireland lost out to eventual winners Spain.

Tony O'Connell was with Dundalk when he was called into the Ireland squad under Carey: 'I remember we met at the Gresham Hotel, as was the norm for the time, and he did not say one word to me. I had caught his eye in a League of Ireland XI that had been beaten 4–2 by Scotland. Joe Haverty had called off for the game against Spain, and I was drafted in. There was no discussion before the game, and I remember just giving it my all. The game finished 0–0. I would not get another cap till four years later.'

Paddy Mulligan looks back at the era and remembers what it was like to be part of the Ireland squad at that time: 'I was first called into the Ireland squad in 1966 when the team was under the management of Johnny Carey, although Noel [Cantwell] and Charlie [Hurley] were big influences, even in those days. I travelled with the team to Austria and Belgium for a double-header. It was amazing. I was surrounded by players I grew up idolising. There was Alan Kelly, Mick McGrath, Tony Dunne and Johnny Giles, all amazing players, not to mention the two managers – I mean Charlie Hurley, who was at Sunderland, and Noel, who was at West Ham and then Manchester United – so to be involved was a great honour. They all had a presence about them. I was in awe, but they all were great and welcomed me into the squad with open arms.

'I remember we played Austria on the Sunday and lost 1–0. We were very unlucky, too, but that was the way it was for Irish football in those days. A short pass from Mick McGrath back to Alan Kelly led to the winner for Austria, although I remember that Mick Meagan twice had to clear the ball off the line.

'Then, a few days later, we played Belgium and got a great result, winning 3–2. Noel Cantwell scored twice that day. I did not get on the pitch in either game, but to be involved was just fantastic. I had played for a League of Ireland selection XI, which was made up of players that only played in the League of Ireland, against Scotland and England, but to be in the Ireland team was altogether different.'

Carey's final game in charge came in February 1967, when

Ireland lost to Turkey 2–1. In all he was Ireland manager for forty-six matches. Many people thought that he was too relaxed to be a manager and often left the players to decide the tactics. He never challenged the status quo of the era and was happy to go along with the decisions of the FAI. According to Mick McGrath, 'Carey was a very quiet man. He spoke to you like you were his equal, but you definitely knew he was the boss. He was very shrewd. You have to remember that Johnny was trained in the school of Sir Matt Busby from his time at Manchester United, and he was of a similar footballing mind. He would tell us that even if we were losing, we should still play good football.'

Eric Barber recalls the early days in his career when he was in a couple of squads under Johnny Carey: 'I remember that it was Noel who would speak to us. He would tell people to pull their weight and to watch certain opposition players. The first time I was in the squad, I was sitting in the hotel and Johnny Carey looked at me and asked, "Who's that?" Someone told him I was Eric Barber. Another time we were in Milltown, training before a game and a civilian, dressed up in all the gear, came out and trained with us. The players knew, of course, but Johnny Carey did not know who he was.'

Carey's hands were tied a lot of the time. Despite being a big name in the world of football, many people thought he was too laid-back to use his name and the power associated with it to make changes within the Irish game. According to Mick McGrath: 'The players wanted change, though. I remember we travelled to Poland for a game, and there were fifteen players in the squad on the flight but twenty FAI officials. It was mad really. We would often have a midweek game, and I would head out to Shamrock Rovers' pitch to train, but there would be no one there. Then, ten minutes later, someone else would come along. There was no organisation to it. Everyone went by their own tune, it needed someone to step up and arrange things better.'

Frank O'Farrell says Johnny Carey was a player whom everyone within the set-up had great respect for: 'He was a wartime player, and we all knew that to play under him was a big honour. That said, he did very little in terms of team preparation. He would give the pre-match and half-time talk. Things were not as thorough as they are today. The system in those days was very strange.

'Looking back at my own time in the green shirt, I only got nine caps for Ireland over the course of seven years. After playing for West Ham, I transferred to Preston North End in a swap for 'Busby Babe' Eddie Lewis and was probably playing the best football of my life, yet I wasn't called into the squad. It was very strange. Still, it was a great honour to play for my country.

'I made my debut for Ireland against Austria in a 6–0 defeat, although we won the return fixture 4–0, and I scored. In those days you could be called into one squad, then left out of the next and then called in again – there was no consistency. Johnny had no involvement in the squad and team selection. It was not like it is today, where the squad is named and then on the day of the game the team is named; in those days the selectors announced the team straight away, with only one or two subs named on the bench.

'Johnny was a good manager to the younger players, though. He gave us good advice and told us to mind our money, not that we had a lot. Not only that but he pushed us to challenge for a place, and I would not have played at the level I did if it were not for him. You see, I was in the youth team and reserve team at Blackburn, and there was a lad in the first team who played wing-half who broke his leg, so Johnny said to me there was a spot if I wanted it and was hungry enough to be a regular in the team, which I was.

'Football then was not what it is like now. Money has, to an extent, changed the game. On the pitch the basics remain the same. But off the field there are more distractions. I laugh now when I think back to a meeting we had with Johnny. He was trying to keep us level-headed. There was one lad in the team at that time and he had twenty-six shirts. Johnny said to him, "What do you want with twenty-six shirts?" He did not understand it, and I don't think he would understand the footballers of today.

'I still keep in touch with people from Blackburn Rovers, and I hear stories of sixteen- and seventeen-year-old players earning as much as £4,000 a week. It's crazy money, especially when you think about what we were getting.

'I was a workhorse of a player. I won the tackle and passed the ball to the more creative players. It was the donkey work, as you might call it. But I grabbed the opportunity and never looked back.'

Like many Irish footballers, Mick Leech started his career as a fan of the team that Ireland had under Carey: 'I started supporting Ireland when the likes of Peter Farrell and Tommy Eglington were in the team. They were at Everton, who were a big club at that time. I remember going over with my dad to see them play. We wanted to be back for the St Patrick's Athletic game on the Sunday, so we would watch the game on the Saturday in Liverpool, then come back on the mail boat. I remember seeing both Peter and Tommy on those mail boats when they were coming back for internationals. It was the same for my generation of footballers in England and Scotland. There were no private jets or planes to get you around the country, but you did it because you loved playing for your country. These were great footballers and big names at the time. They were involved in the Ireland set-up at the start of Johnny's reign.'

Johnny Carey was a great player, but, sadly, he was only a name as a manager. Alfie Hale recalls: 'He was handed the team sheet on the day and told to sort out the positions, and even then that was sorted for him. His role was not befitting for such a great man. All he had to do was give a pep talk to the players.

'Looking back, it was hard to understand the selection committee's teams at times. I remember that two of the best players never to get capped by Ireland were my own brother, Dixie Hale, and John O'Neill, and I think both players suffered because they did not go to England. Dixie had been chased by Arsenal but was a bit misadvised by my father, I think, as he stayed in Ireland and played for Shamrock Rovers. He was capped at youth level and also at inter-League level, as was John, but neither got full caps. It was a travesty, and for me it shows that the system had its flaws.

'If you played in England, it seemed to guarantee you a cap. Before I went over to England, I had played amateur football in the League of Ireland and had made it to inter-League level but had never got a call-up. Then I was at Villa and struggling to establish myself in the first team, yet I won my first international cap for the Republic of Ireland. I hadn't even been there twelve months, but I had received some good write-ups, so I was called up to the Ireland team.

'The committee in those days picked the squad, and you could say they were made up of a dozen wise men. You were either a victim or you were lucky. I got fourteen caps, and I can tell you I didn't deserve half of them, but there are ones I missed out on that I should have got. You were at the whim of the selectors.'

A lot of people will not be over-familiar with some of the players that Ireland had in the 1950s and 1960s. Johnny Carey is the obvious name that springs to mind when you think about that era, but as you delve into the history books you realise that Irish players were having a big impact in England at the time. Arthur Fitzsimons was one such player. An old-school inside-right, he had a magnificent career, playing for Middlesbrough, Lincoln City and Mansfield, as well as coaching in Libya during what were difficult times in the Middle East.

Arthur also played for ten years for the Republic of Ireland, six of them under the guidance of Johnny Carey. He is a living legend of the Irish game, an FAI hall of famer whose career in English football began when he signed for Middlesbrough in 1949. But Arthur's life as a footballer began down in the Ringsend area of Dublin when he played in the minor league with Johnsville, who were managed by the legendary Jim Kennedy. After progressing to League of Ireland football with Shelbourne, Arthur was soon spotted by David Jack, who was Middlesbrough manager and also the first man ever to score at Wembley. Following the mandatory couple of years that most young players require to settle in, he finally made the breakthrough into the first team and then got the call-up to the Ireland squad.

'In those days the FAI contacted the club and told them that you had been called into the squad and that the details would follow. I was based in the north-east at that stage and had the furthest to travel of any of the players in the squad. I remember playing a game on the Saturday and then getting a train to Darlington, where I changed for Liverpool and then, finally, I had to get the B&I ferry home to Ireland.

'Peter Farrell and Tommy Eglington were based in Liverpool in those days, and they would often get the earlier ferry. On the odd occasion, they would say to the head man that I was on the way and ask him to keep a cabin for me because we had a big game the next day and I needed the sleep. It was lovely to get a cabin, and I felt a lot better for the game.

'I would arrive in Dublin at 7 a.m., and then I would pop home to see my mother, get a half an hours sleep and head to Mass before the team all met up in the Gresham at 12 noon for lunch. Johnny Carey would give his talk to the players and tell us what position he wanted us to play in. He was a great ambassador for Ireland and Irish football, and there was a lot of respect for him amongst the players and the FAI.

'Even though Johnny would give you direction, it was often very difficult to carry out. You see, sometimes you had to follow the way a game was going and get on the ball and dictate the tempo. At the end of the day, it was about winning matches.

'I think one of the finest collective performances ever by an Irish team came in the 1–1 draw with England in 1957. England had beaten us 5–1 in London two weeks earlier and only needed a point to secure their place in the 1958 World Cup finals, while if we won, we would have had to beat Denmark to force a play-off [Ireland beat Denmark 2–0 the following October]. Everyone gave it their all that day, and we were 1–0 up through Alf Ringstead. The crowd were unbelievable and really got behind the team, the noise in the stands was unreal.

We thought we had won when deep in stoppage time England scored.

'We were so disappointed. We had given it everything. We were all blaming each other in the changing-room, but Johnny just told us he was very proud of us. It was a super bunch of players in the team that day. There was great team spirit, and we all used to have great craic together.

'I had played at inside-right in the game we'd lost in London, with the late Liam Whelan at inside-left. Johnny was concerned that Duncan Edwards might get too much respect from Liam in the second match, so he moved me to inside-left and Liam to the right. It worked a treat, and Duncan barely got a look in. This showed how aware of the game Johnny was. He had great football knowledge, although he was very relaxed. It was the finest game I ever played in. Sadly, both Liam and Duncan later died in the Munich air disaster. It was such a shame, as they were two fine players and two fine men.

'I was a constant member of the panel and played twenty-six games for Ireland. However, it was not like nowadays, when there are a lot of games in a season. In those days you really had to work hard to accumulate your caps.'

Al Finucane played in Johnny Carey's last match in charge, a 2–1 defeat to Turkey: 'He said nothing to us at the end of the game, and it was not until we read it in the papers a couple of weeks later that we found out that he had resigned from the role.

'I had been called into the squad at the last minute. Manchester United's Tony Dunne had pulled out because of injury, so Mick Twomey, who was the Limerick FC chairman in those days, got a call from the FAI, and he in turn rang me and told me to make my way up to Dublin. I had played well in an Ireland Under-23 match against France, and this is what must have impressed the selectors.

'When we got over to Turkey, I was under the impression that I would be on the bench, but then I found out that I was starting. Johnny just told me that I would start. He said nothing more to me, no bit of advice or anything. We just had a team meeting, and he named the starting XI, and I was to play at the back.'

When his life in football ended, Johnny went on to work for a textile company and then in the treasurer's office of Trafford Borough Council. The influence he had on the game still prevails today, and the fact remains that Johnny Carey is one of Ireland's greatest-ever players and will forever be remembered as a legend for Manchester United and for Ireland. Carey passed away in August 1996 at the age of seventy-six.

JOHNNY CAREY'S CLUB MANAGERIAL HONOURS RECORD:

No management honours

JOHNNY CAREY'S IRELAND RECORD:

Total number of games in charge: 45
Total number of wins: 17 (ratio 37.78%)
Total number of draws: 7 (ratio 15.55%)
Total number of losses: 21 (ratio 46.67%)

Biggest win: 4–1 *v.* Holland, 4–1 *v.* Norway
Biggest defeat: 1–7 *v.* Czechoslovakia
Longest run without defeat: 5 games

JOHNNY CAREY'S RESULTS AS IRELAND MANAGER:

Date	Home/ Away	Opponent	Score	Result	Type of Fixture
27/11/1955	Home	Spain	2–2	D	Friendly
10/05/1956	Away	Holland	4–1	W	Friendly
03/10/1956	Home	Denmark	2–1	W	Competitive
25/11/1956	Home	West Germany	3–0	W	Friendly
08/05/1957	Away	England	1–5	L	Competitive
19/05/1957	Home	England	1–1	D	Competitive
02/10/1957	Away	Denmark	2–0	W	Competitive
14/03/1958	Away	Austria	1–3	L	Friendly
11/05/1958	Away	Poland	2–2	D	Friendly
05/10/1958	Home	Poland	2–2	D	Friendly
05/04/1959	Home	Czechoslovakia	2–0	W	Competitive
10/05/1959	Away	Czechoslovakia	0–4	L	Competitive
01/11/1959	Home	Sweden	3–2	W	Friendly
30/03/1960	Home	Chile	2–0	W	Friendly
11/05/1960	Away	West Germany	1–0	W	Friendly
18/05/1960	Away	Sweden	1–4	L	Friendly
28/09/1960	Home	Wales	2–3	L	Friendly
06/11/1960	Home	Norway	3–1	W	Friendly

03/05/1961	Away	Scotland	1–4	L	Competitive
07/05/1961	Home	Scotland	0–3	L	Competitive
08/10/1961	Home	Czechoslovakia	1–3	L	Competitive
29/10/1961	Away	Czechoslovakia	1–7	L	Competitive
08/04/1962	Home	Austria	2–3	L	Friendly
12/08/1962	Home	Iceland	4–2	W	Competitive
02/09/1962	Away	Iceland	1–1	D	Competitive
09/06/1963	Home	Scotland	1–0	W	Friendly
25/09/1963	Away	Austria	0–0	D	Competitive
13/10/1963	Home	Austria	3–2	W	Competitive
11/03/1964	Away	Spain	1–5	L	Competitive
08/04/1964	Home	Spain	0–2	L	Competitive
10/05/1964	Away	Poland	1–3	L	Friendly
13/05/1964	Away	Norway	4–1	W	Friendly
24/05/1964	Home	England	1–3	L	Friendly
25/10/1964	Home	Poland	3–2	W	Friendly
24/03/1965	Home	Belgium	0–2	L	Friendly
05/05/1965	Home	Spain	1–0	W	Competitive
27/10/1965	Away	Spain	1–4	L	Competitive
10/11/1965	Away	Spain	0–1	L	Competitive
04/05/1966	Home	West Germany	0–4	L	Friendly
22/05/1966	Away	Austria	0–1	L	Friendly
25/05/1966	Away	Belgium	3–2	W	Friendly
23/10/1966	Home	Spain	0–0	D	Competitive
16/11/1966	Home	Turkey	2–1	W	Competitive
07/12/1966	Away	Spain	0–2	L	Competitive
22/02/1967	Away	Turkey	1–2	L	Competitive

2

NOEL CANTWELL

Over the years, Cork has produced some of Ireland's best soccer players, with Roy Keane and Denis Irwin as two who stand out. However, long before my time watching football, the names of Charlie Hurley and Noel Cantwell were the cherries on top of the cake that was Irish football. Noel and Charlie were fantastic players and played at the highest level, while they were obviously proud of their Irish heritage and played their hearts out when they put on the green shirt of Ireland. Both men were natural leaders, and it was no surprise that they had such a standing in the game. When Johnny Carey stood down from his managerial role with Ireland in 1967, the FAI, lacking any clear direction in which to turn, approached Noel and Charlie to become the figureheads of the national team and co-manage the side for a double-header against Czechoslovakia. Whether either man wanted this or not is not clear; however, when the FAI asked them to be player–coaches, such was their love of the national team that they could not say no. The FAI eventually opted to appoint Noel as sole manager in October 1967.

As former Ireland international Alfie Hale put it: 'After Johnny Carey, Noel Cantwell and Charlie Hurley had come in and taken control of the team, but they had no real power. They did their best with what they were given, but the power was still with the selectors. Not much had changed. All they did was marshal the team on the day, but they lobbied the FAI for change. Both Noel and Charlie tried to make a big impact on the FAI.'

Noel Cantwell was a true leader and a natural sportsman, who was respected by his fellow footballers, managers and fans alike. Along with Roy Keane and Johnny Carey, he is one of the legendary Irish captains of Manchester United and Ireland. However, Noel was not content with just enjoying success with one of the biggest clubs in world football or with captaining his country, he was also an all-rounder and could have played any number of sports to a high level. While in Cork, he played for Cork Bohemians Cricket Club, making it to the Ireland team as a left-handed batsman and a right-arm, medium-pace bowler. He played five times for his country, making his debut in what was his only first-class match, against Scotland in Edinburgh in 1956, scoring 31 and 17 not out in a game that ended in a draw. In 1958 he was the top scorer for Ireland in a game against New Zealand. His last match for his country was against Lancashire in July 1959.

However, football was his first calling, and such was his knowledge of the game that Cantwell was a rare breed of footballer, a man who believed in tactics and strategy. He wanted to play good football based on the way the game was played in Europe and Brazil. While a member of the Ireland team, he championed the rights of the players and wanted better conditions for his fellow teammates. His time with United earned him respect, while his role with the Professional Footballers Association (PFA) in England gave him the clout and political diplomacy that were needed to push the boundaries of the committees operating within Ireland.

Such was his standing at Manchester United that he was at one stage being tipped to take over from the legendary Matt Busby as manager of the famous Red Devils. However, determined not to live in someone else's shadow, Cantwell showed the footballing world that he could be his own man when he turned his back on Old Trafford. He was involved with the Ireland soccer team on a part-time basis from October 1967 to May 1968, but although he had championed the rights of his fellow professionals as a player, as a manager he did not have the same power and his efforts to improve the Irish team's performances did not produce the desired results.

CANTWELL'S EARLY YEARS AND THE EAST END OF LONDON

Born in the Mardyke area of Cork city, Cantwell started playing as a full-back for Western Rovers; however, it was with Cork Athletic that he came to prominence. Frank O'Farrell, who would later be Cantwell's teammate at West Ham and with Ireland, actually grew up with Noel and remembers him well: 'I knew Noel from when he was nine years old. I played with his brother Frank, who was also a full-back, for Western Rovers in Cork. Noel would come to watch us play and to collect the kit. We used to call him "Skippy", because he was always following us around.

'He was a small, thin lad in those days, and he suffered from adenoids which caused him a lot of discomfort. He managed to overcome it and grew up to be a big, strong man and a fine footballer. Even at a young age, he had great skill.

'I joined West Ham in 1948. I remember it well. At the time I was working on the railway and playing semi-pro for Cork United. My father had also worked the railway, driving the express between Dublin and Cork. It was a good life, and if I had not made it in football, I would have been happy working for the rail company. When West Ham came in for me I had to decide whether I could turn my back on the railway and make the move to London. It was a huge decision, one Noel would also have to make later on. I didn't have to wait too long before I met up with Skippy again, because Noel signed for West Ham four years later in 1952.'

In that time Cantwell had grown up to be a strong athlete and with his movie-star looks he was destined for the top. The transfer came about in the second half of the 1952–53 season, Cantwell having caught the eye of West Ham's manager Ted Fenton. After joining the club, Cantwell settled into London and made three League appearances. The following season saw him progress further, and he secured a regular place in the first-team squad, making twenty-two appearances.

As his confidence grew, Cantwell fashioned an inventive full-back partnership with John Bond. Neither man was an old-fashioned, stagnant, physically imposing defender. Instead, both were very attack-minded, using every opportunity to become involved in the build-up play and relishing making overlapping runs into attack.

Cantwell became known for his versatility, easily switching

to centre-half or centre-forward, and he emerged as one of West Ham's key men. His importance to the side became apparent very quickly, and he was soon appointed captain of the team. His greatest moment was when he led the side to the Second Division title in 1958 and back to the big time after a twenty-eight-year absence. Then, having helped the team to secure promotion, he contributed to the Hammers consolidating their position in the First Division.

While at West Ham, his stature continued to grow, and he soon found himself tasting European football for the first time when he was selected in the London XI side that competed in the first Inter-Cities Fairs Cup final on 1 May 1958. The Inter-Cities Fairs Cup was a precursor to the UEFA (Union of European Football Associations) Cup and was a tournament that mixed football with trade shows. The first competition was to be held over two seasons to avoid clashes with national League fixtures. However, because it was also planned to correspond with international trade fairs, in the end it ran over into a third year, the tournament commencing in 1955 and eventually finishing in 1958.

The first competition included a group stage and also featured some representative teams instead of clubs, hence Cantwell's appearance for a London XI managed by Chelsea chairman Joe Mears. They reached the final after topping a group that included a Basel and Frankfurt XI, and also the Swiss club Lausanne-Sport. Their eventual opponents in the final were a Barcelona XI. Unlike the London team, Barcelona was effectively made up of players from FC Barcelona, with one player from RCD Espanyol. After a 2–2 draw at Stamford Bridge, Barcelona won the return 6–0. The London XI only competed in the first tournament. All future Inter-Cities Fairs Cups would be contested by individual clubs from London instead.

Cantwell only played one game in the tournament, and that was the final itself, and he did not feature in the first leg that ended 2–2, instead appearing in the 6–0 thrashing in the return leg. His future Ireland playing and coaching partner Charlie Hurley also featured in the tournament, playing in the group stages in a 3–2 victory over Frankfurt.

Between 1953 and 1960 Cantwell made 245 League appearances and scored sixteen League goals for West Ham. His performances began to get noticed and such was his level of skill and versatility that he caught the eye of one of the greatest managers ever. Matt Busby knew a good player when he saw one, and in November 1960 he shelled out £29,500, then a record for a defender, to sign Cantwell. Manchester United were in a state of rebuilding at that time, following the tragedy of the Munich air disaster, but the club was slowly moving forward again.

In a seven year spell with United, Cantwell made 144 appearances and scored eight goals, playing alongside some of the greatest players ever to pull on the red jersey, including Denis Law, Bobby Charlton and George Best. The highlight of his time with the club was undoubtedly the 1963 FA Cup final, the first trophy won by United after the Munich disaster, making it an important building block on the road to recovery. Leicester were the favourites to win the match, but he led the club to a 3–1 win. Cantwell himself acknowledged the turmoil of those times when he commented on the number of captains the club had had that season, but the Cork player was the man of the day and even had time to cause some ructions of his own when he hurled the famous FA Cup in the air.

That win was a turning point for United. The season after, they finished runners-up to Liverpool, and they went one better the season after, winning the League. At that stage, though, Cantwell was not a regular starter on the side, only providing cover for Tony Dunne, Bill Foulkes and Shay Brennan. They won another League title in Cantwell's final year in 1967, although by that point he was playing even less and only made four appearances during the Championship-winning season. However, such was his stature at United that in the season they won the League and Cantwell was on the periphery of the team, he still retained his role as club captain.

THE INTERNATIONALIST

Cantwell made his Ireland debut against Luxembourg in October 1953, and over a fourteen-year period he became a permanent fixture in the team, playing in almost every outfield position. He eventually took over the captaincy in 1957. He was a natural leader, and as Mick McGrath, the former Blackburn defender, points out: 'Noel was a great public speaker and not afraid to tell the committee that ran the show what he was thinking. He would often have a natter with Joe Wickham, who was an official at the FAI, asking him, "How come we can't have lighter shirts like the England team?" Our shirts at the time were very heavy, and it did not help on the pitch, especially if it was raining. But it was all about money – or the lack of it. It was the small things that needed changing. For example, the England players would get a cap a game, and we would get a cap a season. They would write the fixtures you'd played in on the cap. Noel highlighted this sort of thing on behalf of the players.

'There were a lot of hangers-on in the Ireland set-up at that time. The committee was made up of the local committees from Limerick, Cork, Galway and Dublin. But Noel was great. He wanted to see some changes. We were frustrated with the old socks and shirts and the lack of tracksuits. He wanted us to be professional, and he pushed for what these days would be considered the basics.'

However, it was on the field that he was most invaluable, proving to be surprisingly assured in front of goal for a defender. In the 1960 European Nations Cup, Ireland was drawn against Czechoslovakia in the qualifying round. Ireland won the first leg 2–0 at Dalymount Park, with Cantwell getting the second goal. The return leg saw Ireland lose an early penalty, but they were still in with a chance of qualification until three goals in a twenty-minute spell in the second half saw them limp out.

The qualification for the 1964 European Championship saw Cantwell net four goals, including two against Iceland and a further two in a 3–2 victory over Austria. His second goal was a last-minute penalty that sealed a quarter-final place against Spain, which the team lost 7–1 on aggregate.

As with a lot of Ireland's greatest players of that generation, while they tasted success with their clubs in England, a lack of success with Ireland was a sore point, and the 1966 World Cup in England was the closest that Cantwell and his compatriots came to qualifying. Ireland had been drawn with Spain and Syria, who later withdrew when they backed a protest by the African countries over their allocation of places in the finals, in group nine. The protest by the African countries was based on the FIFA rule that the winner of the African zone was required to play a play-off against the winner of the Asian or the Oceania zone for a place at the 1966 World Cup. Syria supported the African stance and promptly withdrew from the qualification campaign as a result. With Syria now out of the picture it was a straight fight between Ireland and Spain. Ireland won the home match in Dalymount with a 1–0 win courtesy of an own goal; however, they lost the second leg 4–1.

Cantwell was the most experienced Ireland man on the pitch in Spain, with thirty-one games under his belt – five players that day had less than ten caps, and there was a distinct lack of experience in the team. In fact, and bear in mind that this was a qualifier for the World Cup finals, Eric Barber, a striker, made his debut for Ireland that day: 'I remember I was called into the squad for the match against Spain in Seville. I was with Shelbourne at the time and had received some good press coverage and was in good shape. We were flying over on the Monday, three days before the game. I woke up that morning and had the worst toothache and my jaw was swollen. We were leaving at 12.00 p.m., and I figured I had time to get into Mercer's Hospital and have someone have a look at it. I told the doctor the situation and was given an injection to help the pain, but it made me pass out.

'I only woke up at 12.10 p.m. I panicked and rushed out of the hospital to get a taxi to the airport. Little did I know that the team had held the plane back for me. I actually spoke to Noel first and not Johnny [Carey]. He asked me, "Did you not get the itinerary?" and I explained what had happened. I was petrified, and I don't think he believed me. Even though Johnny was in charge, Noel was the captain and a real leader in the Ireland set-up.

'I was on antibiotics over there, and they had a bad effect on me. I was not feeling the best, and, looking back, I don't think I should have played, but I was eager to be involved. We lost 4–1, and I hardly had a touch. I think Johnny Carey should have maybe taken the decision not to play me, but I don't think he had the heart to do it.

'Both Noel and Charlie played in the match, and they took turns in the changing-room before the game to speak to us. Noel and Charlie were big men of the game and very influential players. Charlie was a 6-foot 3-inch centre-half, and he could head the ball almost to the halfway line. Noel was a tough man, a bit like Roy Keane, although maybe not as outspoken. He liked to do things his way, and he had very little time for the officials who were involved with the FAI at the time.'

Despite the defeat, it was not all doom and gloom. These days qualification for a major tournament often hinges on the difference between goals scored and goals conceded, especially when the teams finish level on points. As both teams had won a game each it was decided that they would meet again in a play-off match. The play-off was to be held in a neutral venue – initially it was decided that the game would be played in London, but then it was decided to play the game in Paris. This move to Paris ensured that there were more Spanish than Irish in the stands, although the crowd had little bearing on the outcome. Ireland put on a credible show and came close, before losing 1–0.

In all Cantwell won thirty-six full international caps for Ireland and scored fourteen goals. He made his final appearance for his country away to Turkey in a European Championship qualifier in February 1967. It was fitting that in his last game of international football for Ireland he scored a penalty in the final minute, although sadly for him he did not end his career with a victory, as Turkey won 2–1. The match also marked the end of Johnny Carey's reign as manager.

MANAGER

During Cantwell's time with West Ham, the club was a hotbed of future thinking, led by Ted Fenton. While his peers, managers and fans thought of Cantwell as a shrewd and intelligent footballer, he was not alone at West Ham, surrounded as he was by players who all understood how the beautiful game should be played.

His time at West Ham was also the beginning of his integration into a group of players who were all destined to become managers. He played alongside John Bond and Malcolm Allison, who would later lead Manchester City to success, as well as Frank O'Farrell and Dave Sexton, who both went on to manage Manchester United.

In those days, the coaching of the kids at West Ham was the responsibility of one or two of the senior players, most notably Noel and Malcolm Allison. In fact, the pair were instrumental in the development of a young Bobby Moore, encouraging the manager Ted Fenton to introduce him to the first team. Those early years allowed Cantwell to develop the skills that he would later hone at Coventry, where he helped to shape a squad of talented players.

When training had finished for the day, Cantwell, Allison, Sexton and Bond would spend hours after training at a local café talking football and tactics, using the condiments of the café to work out their strategies. O'Farrell would also join them on their coffee trips, and he remembers this time as laying the foundations for their managerial careers: 'I remember after training each day we would go to Casatori's Italian café near the ground and talk football. This was around the time that the famous Hungarian national football team came to England and surprised everyone with their skills and tactical ability. Malcolm Allison was the main organiser of the get-togethers. He had done some national service with the English army and had seen the difference in the footballing skills between the footballers of Eastern Europe (where he was based) and their English counterparts. Dave Sexton, John Bond, Noel Cantwell and I would move spoons and salt cellars around and argue over tactics.

'Ted Fenton, the manager of West Ham at the time, was very open-minded, and he would allow us to practise some of the tactics we came up with in training. In those days Noel was a very forthright character with a lot to say. He knew how to get his point of view across, too.

'The conversations that took place between us were to inspire a golden period of entertaining football, with Allison the first to put his money where his mouth was when he inspired Manchester City to the League title, the FA Cup, the Cup-Winners' Cup and the League Cup in a spell-binding burst of success between 1968 and 1970. Noel didn't enjoy the same success as a manager. However, there was no doubting that he would get involved in management. In fact, the only surprise was that it was not with United, where he had ended his playing career.'

Over the years, many observers of the game have speculated

as to why Cantwell never took the reigns at Old Trafford, and while in many respects Busby and Cantwell were very similar – both were men of integrity and natural leaders, they liked and respected each other, they were obsessed with football, and they liked to analyse and study the game – they were also very different. They both had their own ideas on how the game should be played. The bottom line for both was exciting and attacking football, but Busby believed in natural instincts, adventure and richly talented players, while Noel was more philosophical and from a more theoretical school, believing passionately in the benefits of careful coaching.

This difference of opinion was apparent from their early days at Old Trafford. Soon after his arrival at Old Trafford, Cantwell, who would have been familiar with Carey's languid style from his days with Ireland and would have expected a more tactical and strategy-based management system in England, told friends that he was taken aback by Busby's pre-match talks, which apparently involved little more than wishing the players all the best and telling them to enjoy themselves. This also formed the basis of Johnny Carey's style of management, especially with Ireland, and this laid-back attitude must have been difficult to accept by a thinker of the game. Used to the tutelage of Ted Fenton and his café meetings with his West Ham teammates, Cantwell would have been looking forward to receiving complicated tactical insights from Busby. These insights were not forthcoming, however, and Cantwell was appalled to discover Busby believed that if he had to tell his footballers how to play, he wouldn't have signed them in the first place. Indeed, later in life Noel went on to describe the Matt Busby approach as being 'so simple it was frightening'. However, while Johnny

Carey held little power within the Irish set-up, Busby held all of the power at United and to challenge his way would have been detrimental to Cantwell's United career.

Shortly after retiring from international football, Cantwell was approached by the FAI to become the manager of the Ireland team. He agreed and indicated to the FAI that Sir Matt Busby would release him as required. Prior to his appointment, both Charlie Hurley and Cantwell had already looked after team affairs for a double match with Czechoslovakia; however, with the team requiring stability and a manager, Cantwell, who had also managed the Ireland Under-23 team for a match against France, was the FAI's first choice and was appointed Ireland manager. Despite his appointment to the Ireland side, Cantwell was also being sought to manage clubs in England.

In fact, a move into club management was imminent, but instead of assuming United's reins, Cantwell took over from Jimmy Hill at newly promoted Coventry City, guiding them clear of relegation during their first term in Division One. This proved to be disastrous for the Republic of Ireland team, however, as he had to resign from his role as Ireland manager due to his commitments with Coventry and was only in charge for one game, a 2–2 draw with Poland.

Over the next four years, he impressed at Coventry, leading the Sky Blues to sixth place in 1970, ensuring qualification for the Inter-Cities Fairs Cup. That first European campaign saw them perform admirably before they bowed out at the hands of the mighty Bayern Munich.

There were more relegation battles for Cantwell and his Coventry team, but despite the pressures he was intent on building for the long term, launching a successful youth policy.

Unfortunately, Cantwell would not be around to see his plans come to the fore, because he was sacked in March 1972 – as the chairman rather eloquently put it at the time, 'results have not come up to expectation' and 'we want jam today, not tomorrow'.

Of this first experience of being fired, Cantwell later reflected, 'The sack came as quite a shock. I had no idea what to do for a living. For seven months I was kicking my heels.'

After his stint at Highfield Road, the then home of Coventry, Cantwell took a job in the USA with the New England Tea Men. However, the move did not last long, and after seven months he was back in the UK.

Surprisingly, despite his name in the game, the only other English club he managed was Peterborough United, in two separate spells. During his first stint as manager at London Road, he took over a team that was struggling at the foot of the Fourth Division and managed to turn their fortunes around and lead them to promotion some eighteen months later, in 1974. At the time of his appointment, Peterborough were not only struggling at the bottom of the table, but their gate receipts had also dropped, and it was a brave move.

Cantwell began the task at hand by giving twelve players a free transfer, leaving him with a playing staff of only ten. Then, foregoing a summer holiday, he went about buying new players with a budget of just over £30,000. As with any club struggling at the bottom, Cantwell needed experienced performers, men he knew would be suited to life in the Fourth Division. He was now his own man again, and the only way was up, but he wanted to do it with the team playing the stylish football he believed in.

Peterborough won the title in his first full season in charge and in doing so entertained the fans with flowing football. The supporters had taken their Irish manager to heart and had nicknamed him 'the Messiah'.

With his reputation restored, Cantwell was back in demand and the lure of another club proved too much, so in 1977 he left Peterborough for a second stint in America, again coaching the New England Tea Men. At the time, he was reported to be one of the highest-paid managers outside the English First Division. In a five-year spell in the USA, Cantwell managed the franchises of New England and Jacksonville, winning the Eastern Division Championship of the North American Soccer League (NASL) in 1978 with the New England Tea Men. The Tea Men franchise then moved from New England to Jacksonville, and Cantwell moved with them, managing them for one year in 1981.

Dennis Wit was a part of the Tea Men squad under Cantwell in 1978, and he remembers the team well: 'We actually won our division that season and were the only team to beat the New York Cosmos, who were the team of the time, twice during the season. There were no real superstars on the side. Gerry Daly, an Ireland international, was in the team, and there was Mick Flanagan, who had been at Charlton. He was a big success for the Tea Men and was voted the most valuable player in 1978.

'I was one of only three Americans in the team. You see, in those days the NASL teams were pretty much made up of foreign players from England, Ireland and Scotland. The NASL, in an effort to increase the popularity of the sport in the USA and get Americans to play, made a rule that stated each franchise had to have three home-grown players in the first team. In general, one of the positions that would be filled by an American was that of goalkeeper – the USA has always had a tradition of producing good goalkeepers.

'I got involved with the Tea Men through my relationship with the assistant coach Dennis Viollet. I was a Baltimore lad, and he had played and captained the Baltimore Bays. I later played for Baltimore before moving on to San Diego and then the Tampa Bay Rowdies, who were a popular team at the time, with Rodney Marsh in their line-up. When the New England Tea Men franchise started up, I got traded there. The Tea Men name came about due to Lipton Tea owning the club.'

Arthur Smith was the personnel director of the Tea Men and was in a three-man partnership with Cantwell and Viollet. Arthur recalls the fateful day he set off on an adventure that would change his life: 'I had known Noel a long time. I was a childhood friend of John Barnwell, the former chief executive of the League Managers Association, and he had been assistant to Noel at Peterborough, so we all knew each other well. Phil Woosnam, a former teammate of Noel at West Ham who was then the commissioner of the NASL, had got in touch with Noel and asked him if he would be interested in coming to the USA to coach. Noel told him he would think about it. He would have been a big coup for the NASL. He rang me and asked me if I was doing anything and would I like to come down to his house for some dinner. I went down, and he asked me if I would go to America with him because he needed some help. I initially said no, but then had a think about it, and as I had such good time working for Noel I said I would.

'Dennis Viollet had been in America for a number of years with the Baltimore Bays. He was currently out of work, though, so we asked him to get involved as assistant manager. Dennis knew the American college players, and I knew players from England and Europe. I had previously been chairman at Halifax Town, so I had good contacts in football.

'In the end we only had six weeks to put a team together in time for the start of the season. We wanted players with ability and character, and we got them. We had an arrangement with Charlton and got Laurie Abraham and Mick Flanagan, who would become the League's most valuable player, and we also signed Peter Simpson, who had played for almost fifteen years with Arsenal. Even though we had a short space of time to get organised, we ended up winning the Eastern Division.

'The players all had great respect for Noel. They all knew what he had done in football, so we were very fortunate in that sense. After games, however, Noel was more like one of the boys and had a great rapport with them. He was a footballing purist and wanted the game played on the ground. I would often be in the dugout beside him and would shout, "Take him down!" and Noel would turn and look at me and give out to me.

'The training and coaching were very different from the English set-up. Noel had a canny knack of knowing if a player was dehydrated or carrying a knock, often before the player himself. If someone needed a break, he would see it and would say to me, "Make sure and have some water at the ready." He could see the little things that affected players.

'One of Noel's funnier attributes was that when he spoke, he would often get his facts mixed up. One time he was over talking to Chris Turner about the next game and how the opposition had this attacking midfielder who he would be marking, a Yugoslavian. I think his name was Mitic. Noel was telling Chris in great detail how this midfielder was physical and good in the air, and although he had two good feet, he always went to the left. He was emphasising to Chris this point when all of a sudden he said, "Not that any of this matters. He injured his leg last week and isn't playing."

'Another time he was naming the team and he called out twelve players. We had a young American keeper as understudy to Kevin Keelan. His name was Kirk Pearson, and his nickname was "the Kitten", as Kevin was "the Cat". Well, Kirk started laughing, and Noel asked him what was so funny. Kirk told him he had named twelve players, and Noel just turned and said, "And you're still not one of them." He had a quick wit about him.

'That said, he was very competitive and did not like to lose. He would get angry, but he never singled anyone out. Noel was a natural sportsman, and you can add golf to the list of sports he excelled at. He loved it around Jacksonville with all the golf courses. He was a terrific fellow. It's very hard to say a bad word about him. He was also very modest. His favourite saying was, "It's not a rehearsal, it's your one shot", and that was the way he lived his life. He was generous not just in terms of money but with his time and knowledge.

'He had a lovely charm about him. One time we were headed to New York for the Soccer Bowl, which was the equivalent of the FA Cup in America, and Noel and I flew to New York to meet Dennis, who had to drive from Boston with his wife Helen. Alan Ball was playing for the Whitecaps, and his father, Alan Ball senior, had come over. I had actually been Alan Ball senior's chairman at Halifax, so we all knew each other well. We had a cracking night catching up, and in the morning Dennis and Helen wanted to head back to see their kids. Dennis had agreed to drive us back, but we were to meet for breakfast first.

I eventually got up but left Noel in bed. I only had a cup of tea, as I did not want to delay them any further, but there was still no sign of Noel. An hour passed and still nothing. He eventually turned up, by which stage Helen was exasperated. She wanted to go, but Noel said we might as well have some lunch. So, we had our lunch, and then Dennis went and got the car. We got 100 yards before being stopped at a light. Noel and I were in the back, and Noel says to me, "Should we go back and stay the night with Bally?" I said we'd better head home. The light turned green, we moved another 100 yards and hit another traffic light. Noel said the same thing again. Finally, by the third set of lights, he said to Dennis, "Stop the car. We're staying." We left our bags and everything. But the way he went about it, it was so hard to be annoyed with him. He was a great friend, and I miss him dearly, even now.'

Kevin Keelan was Noel's first signing for the New England Tea Men and he has a huge amount of respect for his old manager and friend: 'Noel was an old friend of John Bond's, and he came to Norwich to talk to me. I had been at Norwich for seventeen years at that stage, and I was due a testimonial. John told me that Noel wanted to sign me for the Tea Men, so I met with Noel and had a chat with him about the League and what he wanted from the team and from me. By the end of it I had committed myself to them for three years, but I also decided to stay on with Norwich. I played in the NASL for three years, during which time I commuted from the USA to England. I played football for twelve months a year. They were hard times but good times.

'One time, I finished the season with New England, got on a plane on the Thursday and arrived in England to play for

Norwich against Everton on the Saturday. We won the game 3–1, but at the end of it I was on my knees.

'Before I went to the Tea Men, I had a call from George Best, who wanted me to come out to the LA Aztecs, but I decided I was better off where I was at the time. Then Noel came in and made me an offer. I remember we played the Aztecs when I got over there, and after the game we were in a bar having a chat when a young lad came over to me and said that Mr Cantwell wanted to talk to me in the back bar. I headed in there and there was Noel and Besty having a good chat. George was saying how he had tried to sign me, while Noel was saying how good I was. It made for good listening, but I think that if I had gone to the Aztecs, I wouldn't have got the extra few years out of my career.

'There was a lot of travelling in the NASL. It was not like with Norwich, where the furthest you went was the north-east of England. In the States we played in Detroit, LA, Portland and San José. We'd be on road trips for a week at a time. It was tough, but it was great fun. I saw places I'd never seen before. The League was an exciting thing to be a part of. There were some top players from England and elsewhere playing at that time.

'He was a great man, though. He enjoyed a good rapport with the players, and the training was exactly the same as it was in England, so it was of a good standard. He worked great with Dennis Viollet. They really bounced off each other and had a good relationship. Like all managers, however, you didn't want to go near him if the team lost. He hated to lose. That said, you could have a chat with him about the game over a beer, and he would tell you exactly where it had gone wrong.'

After some good times in America, it was tragedy that eventually brought Cantwell back to England when his only son died in a car crash at the tender age of twenty-two. While he never got over that loss, he managed to regain some semblance of normality when he returned once more to manage Peterborough in 1986, his second spell as a manager there. Cantwell remained in this role until he became general manager on 12 July 1988.

After he quit football, he settled into life in Peterborough and ran the New Inn pub for a number of years before he finally retired in 1999. He came back into football during the England reign of Sven-Göran Eriksson, who invited Noel to go scouting for him and to report on some of England's up-and-coming players. Sadly, Noel Cantwell died on 8 September 2005, after a battle against cancer, at the age of seventy-three.

NOEL CANTWELL'S CLUB MANAGERIAL HONOURS RECORD:

Fourth Division Championship: Peterborough United 1974

NOEL CANTWELL'S IRELAND RECORD:

Total number of games in charge: 3
Total number of wins: 1 (ratio 33.33%)
Total number of draws: 1 (ratio 33.33%)
Total number of losses: 1 (ratio 33.33%)
Biggest win: 2–0 *v.* Czechoslovakia

Biggest defeat: 2–1 *v.* Czechoslovakia

Longest run without defeat: 2 games

NOEL CANTWELL'S RESULTS AS IRELAND MANAGER:

Date	Home/Away	Opponent	Score	Result	Type of Fixture
21/05/1967	Home	Czechoslovakia	0–2	L	Competitive*
22/11/1967	Away	Czechoslovakia	2–1	W	Competitive*
15/05/1968	Home	Poland	2–2	D	Friendly

* Joint manager with Charlie Hurley

3

CHARLIE HURLEY

Charlie Hurley was nicknamed 'the King' and for good reason. A colossus of a man, he is regarded as one of the giants of English and Irish football, and to this day he is revered by Sunderland, the club to whom he gave the majority of his career. Hurley was a natural leader who led by example and demanded that others give the same commitment that he himself gave on the pitch. Such was the impact that he made on Tyne and Wear with Sunderland that he was named their player of the century. In his day he was a good, old-fashioned centre-half who played with his heart and soul and became a legend for whatever team he turned out for, whether that was Millwall, Sunderland, Bolton or the country of his birth, Ireland. Hurley is remembered as a player who never shirked the challenge.

At a time when change in Irish football was imminent, Noel Cantwell and Charlie Hurley were the last men to fall under the influence of the FAI committees. The history books do not really include them as managers, but from Johnny Carey's last game in charge in February 1967, to the appointment of Mick Meagan in 1969, there was a period when Noel Cantwell and Charlie Hurley were co-managers of the national team for two games, with the FAI eventually opting to give the sole responsibility to Cantwell. When he stepped down from his duties as national team manager due to his commitments with Coventry, Hurley stepped into the breach from 18 November 1967, when the FAI committee officially named him as the man to look after the team on match days. He was technically the player-coach during that time, and he took control of the team for a total of six matches, eventually calling time on both his Ireland playing career and his Ireland coaching career at the same time, in June 1969.

EARLY CAREER, MILLWALL AND THE KING

Hurley was born in Cork in 1936 but emigrated with his father and mother to England when he was still a young child. Growing up in Essex, he made his name with his local school team, Blacksmiths Lane, with whom he was captain and played outside-right. Then, having finished school, he was playing for Rainham, his local youth team, when he was spotted by a Millwall scout. As is so often the case, the scout on the day, Bill Voisey, had actually gone to the match to check out a player from the opposition, but the game finished with Charlie signing amateur forms with the London club.

Charlie made his debut for the Millwall reserves against Fulham and after the game was asked to join the grounds staff at Millwall to earn an apprenticeship. He decided to decline the offer and instead completed a tool-making apprenticeship, but the club were not to be deterred in their determination to have

Hurley on the playing staff and, at the age of seventeen, his professional career did get going when he signed for Millwall, breaking into the team that same year, 1953. The irony of his breakthrough, though, was that it came at the expense of another Irishman, Gerry Bowler, who had represented Northern Ireland on three occasions.

At that time Millwall were a Third Division team, and the season before Hurley's debut they had finished runners-up in the League. In those days the runners-up spot did not guarantee you promotion, so Millwall had to rebuild and entered a period of change, one that benefited the young Cork man, who became a permanent fixture in the side.

After four years with Millwall, and over 100 appearances, Sunderland, whose manager Alan Brown had been tipped off to his potential by a former Millwall manager, came calling for the then twenty-one-year-old. A fee of £18,000 was agreed with Millwall, and a prince was about to grow up and become a king.

Sunderland at that time were undergoing a new chapter in their history. In 1957 the club had been relegated from Division One for the first time and had also been fined and their board suspended for making payments to players above the maximum agreed amount. Those events rocked English football to its core and pushed the club into a period of turmoil. Their relegation meant that after sixty-eight years in England's top flight they were in Division Two, hardly the place for a young, ambitious centre-half who was already beginning to make a name for himself.

Although we now know that his time with Sunderland was the making of Hurley, his first two appearances were the stuff of nightmares. A 7–0 defeat to Blackpool that included an own goal, followed by a 6–0 defeat to Burnley, would have seen many older, more experienced men crumble. But to be fair to both the player and manager who signed him, they stuck with it.

Hurley suffered his fair share of heartbreak with Sunderland, as defeat on the last day of the season twice cost them the chance of promotion to the top flight, and it was not until 1964 that Sunderland would reclaim their place in the top tier of English football, ending a six-year absence. The previous season the club had come within one game of promotion to the First Division, requiring only a draw in their final game against promotion rivals Chelsea, who had another game left to play, to secure promotion. However, they were defeated, and Chelsea went on to win their last match and take their place in the First Division. However, there were no mistakes in 1964 when Charlie skippered the side and they finished runners-up behind Charlton Athletic, thereby winning the second promotion spot.

That promotion-winning season was also extremely pleasing for Hurley on a personal front, as he was runner-up in the Football Writers' Player of the Year award, just missing out to Bobby Moore. Hurley's stature in the game was growing, and his strength at the back for Sunderland was one of the key factors in the club's return to the top division.

Norman Howe, a close friend of Hurleys, is the vice-president of the Sunderland Former Players Association. He remembers the promotion-winning team of 1964 as one of the greatest in Sunderland's history: 'They played at Roker Park in those days, and it was a fortress. They went eighteen months without losing there at one stage. The players were highly regarded up in Sunderland, but they and Charlie never let it go to their heads.

'I remember they would often have their lunch in the local hotel before a game and then cross the public park to Roker Park. The fans would stroll with them. Then, once the players got there, it would be a case of, "See ya now. We're off to get changed." It's all very different nowadays, of course. There was so much interaction in those days.

'Charlie is a very good friend of mine, and I can tell you one of the most striking things about him is that he is very modest. He never looked for glory. I remember one time we were out in Sunderland for a meal and a drink, and people were clamouring to see him. He did all the signing the fans wanted, but then instead of staying with the young fans he went over to these three old men and sat down with them and chatted away and had a drink with them. Later he said to me, "See them? They are yesterday's men. They have worked all their lives and supported the club. It was nice to go over and chat to them and cheer them up." That's the way he is.

'Charlie always attracted attention wherever he went in Sunderland. Even now when he comes up to Sunderland it's the same. About three years ago he came up and we went for a game of golf. Word got around that Charlie was about. By the time we reached the clubhouse there was a queue of people looking to shake his hand, get some photos and ask for his autograph. Some of them were teenagers who would never have even seen him play.

'He has a great sense of humour, too, and loves a good joke. One time we were in the pub together and this gentleman came and joined us. He shook Charlie's hand and asked who I was. Charlie replied that I was his brother Chris. The bloke said it was lovely to meet me, and we got to chatting. He asked me if

I had ever played football. I thought I would get my own back, so I said to him, "Charlie, why don't you tell my story?"

'Without missing a beat, Charlie broke into this story about how we had grown up in London and money had been very tight. "Chris was actually a better footballer than me," he said, "but money was tight, and we could only afford one set of boots and kit, so Chris stood to one side and let me be the footballer." Well, the gentleman shook my hand and wouldn't let it go. He told me how much he admired me for what I had done. It was all very much in jest, and we couldn't keep it going for too long, but we had a good laugh with that one.'

Charlie Hurley, it seems, was a character on and off the pitch. In the late 1960s, alongside goalkeeper Jimmy Montgomery, Len Ashurst, Martin Harvey and Jim McNab, he formed one of the most notable and most settled back fives in Sunderland's history. Hurley was a rock-solid central defender, who, despite being renowned for his heading ability, did not get his first goal for Sunderland until 1960, scoring in a 1–1 draw with Sheffield United. In all he scored forty-three goals for the club.

Charlie would play anywhere his team wanted him. In fact, in one match, against Manchester United in November 1966, he made an appearance in goal after England keeper Jimmy Montgomery had to leave the game because of an injury sustained in the first half.

Charlie's last goal for Sunderland, a header, came against Arsenal in April 1968, while his last appearance in a red-and-white shirt came at Burnley in April 1969. One of his finest moments for the club was in the FA Cup fifth-round victory at Norwich in February 1961, when he led Second Division Sunderland to victory, scoring the only goal of the match. The team then went on to succumb to the double-winning, Danny Blanchflower-inspired Tottenham Hotspur in the next round.

Len Ashurst recalls what it was like to play with the King: 'I first signed for Sunderland in 1958, a year after Charlie. He was already established in the side and was vice captain. Alan Brown wanted to shore up a back line that was conceding a lot of goals. Even though he had Charlie back there, the fact was that there were players at the club who were not as enthusiastic about Sunderland as Alan and Charlie, and Alan Brown soon got rid of them. The likes of Jim McNab and I were brought into the first team at that point.

'One of the first things you noticed about Charlie was that he was a man of principle. He never let his standards drop, and he expected the same from those around him. I can tell you, if you ever did let your standards drop, Charlie would be sure and let you know that he was not impressed. He won players over with his attitude, though. They could see he was a leader, and he really encouraged the younger players around him. He led by example. His Roman Catholic background definitely helped him to shape his principles. He was devout in his religion and used to attend church on a Sunday. Along with Alan, he definitely held the team together in the early days when some much needed change was happening at the club.

'Despite being a big man, I never saw Charlie raise a fist or punch anyone in all my time playing alongside him. He was a commanding figure, but not physical in any way. He was a gentle giant of a man, although he could knock you out with one of his looks.

'When Stan Anderson left the club for Newcastle in 1963, Charlie became the captain. It was a role made for him, and he loved the honour and prestige of being captain. Charlie was close to Alan, and he had his ear. He would head up to the office on a Monday morning and talk to him about players and games, although Alan was an old-school manager, so I am not sure if he ever took any notice. That didn't stop Charlie, though.

'In those days you would get a couple of tickets for home games that you could give out to the family if they came up. You only got one or two, but if you ever wanted more, Charlie was your man. As captain he got a few extra, and he would keep them in his top pocket. Well, you'd ask him for how ever many you wanted, and whether it was one or two or even three – no matter how many – Charlie always managed to pull that exact number of tickets out of his top pocket.

'One vivid memory I have of Charlie is when he got his Ford Zephyr. The car was a creamy white, and I remember he pulled up to the training ground to show it off to the players. He was very proud of that car, and the players were all suitably impressed. As he was driving away, I had this feeling that he really was the king in his own white Zephyr carriage. It suited him. He was a great man, and he was a great friend. He deserved all his success.

'It was a good dressing-room in those days at Sunderland, and when you have a good dressing-room you end up making friends for life. The team that won promotion in 1964 was very close, and we are all still in contact with each other regularly. The club was set up for great things, but then Alan Brown fell out with the club and he left, and we didn't quite get where we should have got to.'

Alan Brown left the club in 1968 to take over at Sheffield Wednesday, and a year later Hurley himself moved on to pastures new, joining Bolton Wanderers on a free transfer, where he stayed until he retired in 1971. In a twelve-year period until he left the club in 1969, Hurley made over 400 appearances for Sunderland, although he managed to miss his debut for Bolton in a pre-season match against Bury, as he was moving into his new home at the time. Bolton were a Second Division side at that time, and in Hurley's final season as a professional footballer they finished twenty-second in the division and were relegated to Division Three. In all he played over forty games for Bolton. He retired from playing top-level football at the age of thirty-five.

IRELAND TIME

Charlie Hurley was first selected to play for Ireland in 1955. However, a knee injury prevented him from making his debut and it would be a full fifteen months before he got back to full fitness. He eventually made his debut for Ireland in May 1957 in a match that will forever be remembered, one that ensured Hurley would always be a hero for the national side. At the tender age of twenty, the then Millwall defender found himself thrust into the side that was playing in a World Cup qualifier against England, Ireland having lost 5–1 in London less than two weeks before.

In a historic match against an England team that contained Stanley Matthews, Billy Wright, Duncan Edwards and Tommy Taylor, Ireland took the lead in the third minute through Alf Ringstead. Some of the biggest names of the day had to wait until the ninetieth minute to salvage a draw, when Bristol City legend John Atyeo scored for the visitors. In all Charlie made forty appearances for Ireland, scoring two goals, with both coming in the same game, a 4–1 victory over Norway in Oslo in May 1964. Charlie played as a striker that day. His final match in a green shirt was a 2–1 defeat to Hungary in June 1969.

MANAGEMENT

Despite his stature in the game, Hurley's time in management was relatively uneventful and short-lived. A five-year spell with Reading was his only foray into club management in English football. At the time that he took over at Reading they were in the bottom tier of English football, the Fourth Division, and it was not until 1976 that Hurley guided the club to Division Three. Unfortunately, he could not keep them there and after one season they were relegated again, so Hurley left the club.

Steve Hetzke was a defender at Reading and later Sunderland, and he remembers Hurley from his time in the lower divisions with Reading: 'The club needed a change of direction, and for Charlie it was his first job in management since his retirement as a player. He initially started off in a player-manager role. I think he wanted to be one of the lads, but he learned very quickly and soon realised he couldn't do it.

'The surprising thing about his appointment was that he brought no one in with him. He had no one experienced that he could bounce ideas off or be his yes man. He needed a mentor, someone experienced in football to help his development as a manager, and I think long term that may have been his downfall. He found it hard at the start, but as time went on he got more and more into it. When he first took the role he adopted an open office, where everyone was welcome to talk to him, but as time went on he learned quickly and took the stance that if you wanted to talk to him, you better have a good reason. It was all part of his development as a manager.

'I remember his first pre-season in charge. All we did was running for the first few weeks. It was the turncoat syndrome: as a player you hate running, and then as a manager it's one of the first things you enforce. It was quite funny, though, as we asked him why all the running, and he said it was to get us fit. When we then asked him, "Do you like it?" he replied, "No, that's why I'm at the back."'

The change from being a player to a manager can be very hard. You go from being one of the lads to being the man in charge. You have to change your approach to the players. Hetzke recalls Robin Friday, who was a real character in the Reading team in those days and would have been a handful for even the most experienced of managers, not to mention a rookie: 'Robin was a rock star in the lower divisions in those days, and he is regarded as a legend of the game by Reading and Cardiff fans. He was a colourful character, well known in and around Reading. To be honest, I am not sure how Charlie handled him at all. I remember one time we were heading to an away game, and we were all on the bus waiting, but there was no sign of Robin. So we contacted his house, and his wife said he was on his way. Well, we went to pick him up when suddenly around the corner came Robin, dressed in a blue velvet suit, with cherry-red shoes, a T-shirt and a multicoloured scarf that was hanging down to his feet. It was clear that he had never made it home. Charlie looked at him almost in disbelief. I mean, if you could have taken a picture, you would have captured Charlie with his mouth wide open. To make matters worse, Robin, as calm as you like, just said, "Morning, gaffer" and went to the back of the bus to go to sleep. There was no apology, nothing. Charlie didn't say a word, but it was all over his face, which was red with anger. The fact that Charlie did not react to the situation as a more experienced manager would have done, shows that he probably wasn't used to seeing this type of behaviour as a player at his level and was unsure how to respond.

'I think as a coach Charlie would not have been considered a tactician, but his biggest attribute as a manager was that he treated us, and looked upon us, as men. It's a small thing, but I was a young player in those days, and a lot of managers treated players like children. But Charlie, he would lay it out for us, saying, "This is your job. Go out and do it." He was passionate and this alone could motivate you. Going out onto the pitch, you had a job to do and you did it.

'He was not afraid to tell you, though, if you did that job wrong. There was one game where the opposition winger pushed the ball past me, and I thought it was going for a corner, so I didn't fully chase it back. Even though the ball went out – the linesman missed it – their winger got a cross in and they scored. Naturally, Charlie gave out to me at half-time, asking me, "Why didn't you chase back after the ball?" I replied that I thought it had gone out. His only response to that was, "Well, then, where did it go?" The answer was it had ended up in the net and had cost us a goal. Charlie was so angry with me that he actually dropped me for the next game, which was against Torquay. As it turned out their centre-forward gave my replacement a torrid time and scored two, and at half-time he took off the other player and brought me back on. To me it showed his humility. He was angry with me from the previous game and wanted me to know it, but at the same time he wanted to do what was best for the team.

'As a centre-half like Charlie himself, he was great to learn from. You couldn't fail to learn from him. In those days we'd watch black-and-white videos of players, and everyone had seen King Charlie playing at Sunderland. Later on in my career I actually played at Sunderland, and when I got up there I saw exactly what he meant to the club and the respect in which he was held. It was amazing, really. We probably didn't fully understand down in Reading, but up there you really got a feel for it.

'Once, five of us were called into the office for a chat, and Charlie was talking to the strikers about how they needed to get stuck in more and to stop being so airy-fairy, to use his own language. As Charlie was talking, there was a wasp flying around the room. Even though we were listening, the wasp was a bit distracting, and it eventually landed on the phone. Suddenly, Charlie swatted the wasp, and he turned and said to the strikers, "That's exactly what I mean. I want you to have killer instincts." It summed the situation up nicely for all of us involved and it just seemed to perfectly emphasise the point he was trying to get across.

'Charlie was a hard and fair man. As I said before, he would have benefited from having an established right-hand man with him, but he was also lucky that the Reading changing-room was full of strong characters in those days. When he resigned the players didn't want him to go. We all went down to his office to discuss it with him. It showed the respect we had for him. It's something you rarely hear of now in football.'

Before his time with Reading, Hurley had a taste of

management with Ireland, but he was still a player himself and had limited impact on the squad that was picked. His main role was to motivate and organise the team. He would often turn up to a game to find that different players, players he had not seen play or had not even met before, had been called into the team at the last minute. Players were brought in and put anywhere. There was little of the organisation that was to come in future years, as Eoin Hand recalls: 'I remember I made my debut under Hurley. I came on as a sub for Mick Leech, who was a centre-forward, and Charlie Hurley said to me, "Go on there now." I said to him, "I have never played there in my life," but he just replied, "Ay, sure, go on there." His team talks focused on the pride of pulling on the jersey, and there was little preparation or knowledge about our opponents. The structure was not in place to support the men who were the figureheads of the team.'

Mick Leech, a Shamrock Rovers legend, had a similar experience: 'Charlie Hurley was the man who gave me my debut. That said, I didn't actually meet him for the first time until twelve noon on the day of the match, although as a fan and supporter of the national team before I played for Ireland, I was very familiar with Charlie Hurley. That game was against Czechoslovakia, and we lost 2–1 in Dalymount. As it turned out, a future Ireland manager in Eoin Hand came on to replace me during that game. He was a centre-half and I was a centre forward, so it was a strange move.

'The Ireland set-up in those days was very different to how it is today. It was almost farcical, really. The players based in England would come over on the mail boat from Holyhead, having caught a train to Liverpool beforehand, depending on where they were based. They would get in at about six or seven in the morning, take a taxi to their home and go to bed for a few hours, before getting up at midday to meet up with the team in the Gresham Hotel before the game. The League of Ireland players would meet up at the same time and place, but obviously without the travel. The team in those days was selected by an FAI committee and was decided on a Wednesday or Thursday. The hope was that nobody got injured over the weekend, but a standby list of League of Ireland players was available as back up.

'The team was picked, so the role of the manager was just to give the team talk and tell us we were going to play 4–4–2, or whatever formation they'd decided on. There was no training sessions beforehand, and there was no preparation. It was a different world. There was no bench made up of substitutes, and certainly any substitutes that did come on were purely due to injury. Tactical substitutions did not really exist then.

'It was 1972 before we saw the UEFA rules that we have today, at which point players were released by their clubs after the Saturday game and played with Ireland midweek, giving the manager two days of build-up to work and prepare with the players. UEFA knew they had to create a level playing field, and that if they wanted to take the game forward, they had to introduce the rules, but it changed the emphasis and preparation for games.'

Turlough O'Connor was in awe when he was called into the squad: 'I made my debut under Charlie Hurley. At that time I was with Fulham. I never got a call-up when I was playing League of Ireland football, and then when I actually was called up I had been out for three weeks with a small injury, so I was not one of the form players, you could say. Vic Buckingham was Fulham manager at the time, and I remember the FAI contacted him and told him I had been called into the squad.

Charlie had very little influence on who was picked, but it was still a massive honour for me.

'I was a young lad, only twenty-one, and had played for Athlone and Bohemians. While growing up, I watched players such as Mick Meagan, Alan Kelly and Terry Conroy. These were the guys we all read about in the papers, and they were all heroes to me, so to pull on the Ireland shirt and to be suddenly surrounded by them was a massive privilege.

'I was not 100 per cent fit, so Vic said he would leave the decision up to me. I decided I could not turn the opportunity down, so I flew over from London. Charlie was player-manager at the time, and I remember he started himself in the game. There was not a lot of input from Charlie beforehand, but he would tell us what position he wanted us to play in, getting the shape of the team right. He would tell us to put our hearts into it and that we were playing for our country. Those were difficult times for Ireland, but we still had some great players.

'I remember we played against Czechoslovakia, as they were known at the time. They only needed a draw to qualify for the 1968 European Championship. They went a goal ahead before Ray Treacy scored to equalise. Then, with four minutes to go, I netted the winner. It was a great feeling to score on your debut for your country. Afterwards we were sitting with Charlie, and he said to us, "A lot of you lads are only starting out in the game, but I don't care how long you are in football, you will never be involved in a better win for Ireland." It was another thirteen years before Ireland actually won another competitive away match [3–2 against Cyprus in March 1980], so it puts everything into context as to how hard it was at that time.

'We had John Dempsey, who was with Chelsea, Mick

Meagan and Eamon Dunphy, who was a good passer of the ball and a fine player. We also had Ray Treacy up front, so we did have some really good players in the team in those days.

'But it was great to play and put on an Ireland shirt. I was very proud. I flew back to London after the game and discovered I had developed a groin problem, which ended up being operated on a week later and meant I was out of action for a while, but it was worth it.'

The time for change was coming, and although there were some impressive performances under Hurley, the highlight being the win over Czechoslovakia, the suggestion was that he did not do enough to make the role his own. He could always hold his head high, though. Even in defeat Ireland were always in the game and not being his own man in terms of choosing the team was a definite handicap.

It is interesting to note that before the appointment of Mick Meagan, an article appeared in the *Irish Independent* in May 1969 that suggested that it was perhaps time to move Ireland forward and appoint Hurley as team manager, allowing him to pick the squad. The article went on to mention that Hurley had discovered on the eve of a game with Denmark that a player had been called into the team without his knowledge and had to be included in the side. This lack of input and control made conditions hard for him, and he could never develop the side or his own career as a manager under such a regime.

MODERN-DAY HERO

Following his retirement from the game Charlie Hurley was

part of the after-dinner circuit of ex-players. In October 2006, on his seventieth birthday, Sunderland renamed the Chairman's Suite the Charlie Hurley Suite in honour of their king.

CHARLIE HURLEY'S CLUB MANAGERIAL HONOURS RECORD:

No management honours

CHARLIE HURLEY'S IRELAND RECORD:

Total number of games in charge: 8
Total number of wins: 1 (ratio 12.50%)
Total number of draws: 2 (ratio 25.00%)
Total number of losses: 5 (ratio 62.50%)
Biggest win: 2–1 *v.* Czechoslovakia
Biggest defeat: 2–0 *v.* Czechoslovakia and Hungary
Longest run without defeat: 2 games

CHARLIE HURLEY'S RESULTS AS IRELAND MANAGER:

Date	Home/ Away	Opponent	Score	Result	Type of Fixture
21/05/1967	Home	Czechoslovakia	0–2	L	Competitive*
22/11/1967	Away	Czechoslovakia	2–1	W	Competitive*
30/10/1968	Away	Poland	0–1	L	Friendly

10/11/1968	Home	Austria	2–2	D	Friendly
04/12/1968	Home	Denmark	1–1	D	Competitive**
04/05/1969	Home	Czechoslovakia	1–2	L	Competitive
27/05/1969	Away	Denmark	0–2	L	Competitive
08/06/1969	Home	Hungary	1–2	L	Competitive

* Joint manager with Noel Cantwell

** The match against Denmark in December 1968 was abandoned after fifty-one minutes due to fog

4

MICK MEAGAN

If you are ever at a quiz and the following question comes up, 'Who was the first manager of the Republic of Ireland senior soccer team with control over the team?' jot down the name Mick Meagan. Not only will you impress those around you, but you will also get a point. For although the big names of Johnny Carey, Charlie Hurley and Noel Cantwell all sat in the dugout from 1951 to 1969, Meagan was the first man actually to manage the team, taking charge from September 1969 to October 1971. However, it was not all sweetness and light for Meagan, as his reign was marred by a lack of victories, and despite being a history-maker, the Ireland team under his management failed to live up to its potential.

His reign as Ireland boss was a plethora of firsts besides his appointment as manager in sole charge of the team. Meagan oversaw the first ever dismissal of an Ireland player when John Dempsey was sent off in an international against Hungary. His period in office then saw Steve Heighway become Ireland's youngest-ever international when Heighway played against

Poland at Dalymount Park, and less than a year later the record was broken again when Meagan handed the then seventeen-year-old Jimmy Holmes a cap as a substitute in a game against Austria.

So, while his results might not have been top mark, the changes that Ireland craved were slowly coming to the fore, and Meagan was the catalyst for that change. A quiet and laid-back man, he was popular with the players and seemed to be an excellent choice for manager.

EARLY YEARS

Born in Dublin, Mick started his career in football as a left-winger, signing for Everton in 1952; once on Merseyside he was soon converted to left-back, but he had to wait until the 1957–58 season to make his League debut. Although not guaranteed a first-team place, he stayed with the club until 1964 when he was transferred to Huddersfield Town in a part exchange deal for Ray Wilson.

One of his longest runs in the team coincided with the return to Everton's trophy-winning ways. The 1962–63 season saw Meagan play thirty-two times at left-back as the club won the League title for the first time since the Second World War. This was to be his last season with Everton, and after his spell with Huddersfield Town he joined Halifax Town, whom he helped to promotion from the Fourth Division.

Meagan's international debut came in May 1961 when he was chosen to play at left-back during a World Cup qualifier against Scotland at Hampden Park. Although Ireland lost 4–1, Meagan impressed enough to be selected to play in the return game the following week at Dalymount Park. By the end of his international career, Meagan had played for Ireland seventeen times.

After leaving Halifax Town in 1969, Mick returned to Ireland to become player-manager for Drogheda United, whom he led to their first FAI Cup final and he stayed there until 1974, when he moved to Shamrock Rovers. As well as playing for the Milltown-based team, he was also player-manager from 1974 to 1976, along with Theo Dunne. Although his return to the club was not the success many had hoped for, there are two games that stand out. The first one was when Rovers defeated Japan 3–2 in front of 60,000 spectators when touring that country, while the second saw history being made when Meagan played on the same team as his son Mark in the FAI Cup.

Mark Meagan grew up with a League winner for a father and always knew he wanted to follow in his dad's footsteps. He played League of Ireland football for Shamrock Rovers, Waterford United, Athlone Town and Kilkenny City, winning a League title with Athlone under Turlough O'Connor. But it was the club his father was managing at the time, Shamrock Rovers, that he signed for as a sixteen-year-old, making his way in the game for the first time: 'I remember it well, actually. Mick and the team were over in Japan with Rovers, and Dinny Lowry was in charge of the second team. They invited me down to train with them. It was difficult and wonderful at the same time. Mick was a perfectionist on the pitch and a huge influence on me and my career. I think as a manager he still wanted to be one of the boys and found it hard to distance himself from the players. Mick just wanted to play football and leave the team selection to other people.

'The game before we played together and made FAI history, I had played a stinker and was quite rightly substituted. Mick had not played in that game, and I was not expecting to be picked for the replay, but, luckily enough, I got in. We had drawn with St Patrick's Athletic 1–1 in Richmond, but we lost the replay 4–1. I played midfield that day. It was a great feeling to share the pitch with Mick, although it would have been nicer to have won.'

HISTORY IS MADE

In 1969 Mick Meagan became the first manager of the Republic of Ireland to be able to pick his own team. The top players, including Johnny Giles, had become frustrated with the FAI's approach and had battled for a team manager with real power to be appointed. The FAI eventually gave the players their wish, bringing in Meagan, although a compromise was made: the selectors would continue to select the panel from which Meagan would then choose a starting XI. The committee's influence was still a major factor in the make-up of the team, as was the voice of the crowd, which had the power to sway the selectors' choices.

Alfie Hale was one of the players who put the pressure on the FAI that would eventually lead to change: 'I actually sat on the committee that put the strategy in place to change the structure of the way things were being managed. I was back in League of Ireland football then, and I remember Frank O'Neill and Johnny Giles were on the committee too. We had the full backing of the players. The likes of England had a full-time manager, although Wales and Scotland only had part-time managers like us, but they had more say. I suppose one of the reasons it hadn't happened sooner was down to money. I don't think the FAI had a lot in those days.

'So the players got together and put their opinions to the FAI on how the team should be run. Johnny Giles had become a big player in England, and his opinion carried weight. All the players wanted Mick Meagan as manager. He was definitely the popular choice, although I am not too sure that Mick himself wanted the job.'

Meagan was determined to be his own man and even seemed to have defied the committee, who had ordered him to leave himself out of the team, by picking himself. However, Meagan states this was not the case: 'A lot of the team played in England in those days, and you always had lads who cried off, so the selectors asked me if I would play, and of course I said yes. After that game the players had a meeting with the selectors, and they agreed to take it a step further and the role of manager changed to allow him to pick the team, although the selectors retained control over the squad selection.'

Meagan himself admits that his interest in the role was not only about being part of history, it was also a means to stay at the top level of the game: 'I was attracted to the Ireland job mainly because I had just come back from England and was embarking on a new career. I had left Halifax and had come back to Ireland with Drogheda. For me the Ireland job was a way to remain in the big time and feel part of the big league. I had been appointed as player-manager with Drogheda at the time and Charlie Walsh, who was director at the club and on the FAI committee, approached me and asked me if I would like to be the manager of Ireland. I had no problem saying yes. It would have been very hard to say no, really.

'There was very little pressure in managing Ireland. It was not like it is nowadays. There were about four or five games a year including friendlies. Of course we all wanted to win, but it was very difficult to qualify for World Cups and European Championships. The likes of Yugoslavia, Czechoslovakia and Russia had a massive pool of players to call on, unlike today when they are separated into smaller countries again.

'My hands were often tied. The selectors were dedicated to the Irish cause, and they helped where they could, but the FAI did not have a lot of money in those days. None the less, one of the main changes I made when I came in as manager was to stop the players from staying in city-centre hotels, moving them out to Montrose instead. You see, at the time I was helping Tony O'Neill with University College Dublin, and Drogheda often used their Belfield training ground, so by moving our base out there the players had nice facilities and a nice hotel. It was something small, but it helped the players.

'The results weren't good, though. I think we only managed three draws during my time in charge. Despite doing my coaching badges while I was an Everton player, I can't ever say I enjoyed coaching or managing. For me it was always about being a player. I loved being involved with the players. Some people coach and some play. I loved playing. I would get a knock and would think, "I can run this off. It's only a small tweak." But there eventually comes a time when you have to stop playing.

'Even now I think back to matches I played in and wonder why I didn't do this and why I didn't do that, but at the end of the day the players and I gave it our all, no matter what team we had out. I think the League of Ireland players were the fall guys for Ireland in those days. Whenever an English-based player pulled out of the squad, the local players had to fill in the gaps, and they always had to be prepared. They were playing against some of the greatest sides in the world, and they were onto a loser before they got onto the pitch.

'After my career with Ireland I played with Rovers for a bit. They had a young team and wanted me to bring some experience to them. I couldn't say no. Even if a junior team came and asked me to play I couldn't say no. I loved playing football. The biggest disappointment for any footballer is finding out that their legs are no longer good enough.'

Turlough O'Connor played in Meagan's first game and remembers the build-up to the big decision made by the FAI: 'I was actually in Mick's first squad. He was passionate about Ireland and about the game. He wanted the players to stand up and take responsibility on the pitch. Mick spent a lot of time preparing things and organising the team, though there was not too much emphasis on the tactical side of it. Instead there was a freedom to express ourselves.

'That said, Mick was more responsible for the way things were done, especially compared to the previous coaches. Compared to past managers who would have worked with the First XI that were selected by the committees, Mick had the extended freedom to name his own team.

'He was an excellent manager, though. He was a man-to-man coach. He was a great guy to have a chat with and put an arm around your shoulder.'

For Tony Byrne, playing for Ireland under Mick was not

only an honour, it was also the first time he had played soccer on Irish shores. Despite growing up in Rathdowney in County Laois, Tony and his family had emigrated to England when the future Ireland defender was only twelve. Up to that point he had only ever played hurling: 'Joe Haverty had recommended me to Ireland and the FAI when I was at Millwall, but I never got a call-up. Then I moved on to Southampton and had a good season in 1969 and got selected to play against Denmark. I did not actually have much interaction with Mick in the build-up to the match. He appeared to be very laid-back, but he was good at motivating the lads. He just told me to go and play, and that was what I did. There was nothing more to it. I think as time progressed, the tactical side of things changed. Liam [Tuohy] was that bit further on from Mick, while Johnny [Giles] was different again, paying so much attention to the details. Each time there was a new man things were different and moved forward.'

Paddy Mulligan was another player who made his debut during what was a real period of transformation for football in Ireland, and he recalls the change that was happening: 'I did not get my first cap until 1969, by which time Mick Meagan had just taken over, although he was not in charge the day I made my debut. Mick was the first man to pick the team and actually manage it. Under the committee there was a feeling that if you played in England, whether it was for York or Manchester United, you got into the squad. The League of Ireland players had to work that bit harder to make the team. By that time the team spirit was quite low. There was a lot of frustration at the way the team was being run.

'We played Czechoslovakia and lost 2–0, but we were played

off the park that day and definitely didn't deserve anything from the game. Mick came in and immediately set about getting some confidence into the guys. He was a smashing fella, and he got us to understand our roles and brought some organisation and camaraderie to the team.

'We played a Scotland team filled with players such as Billy Bremner, Peter Lorimer and Colin Stein and got a 1–1 draw, which was a great result. It is a simple thing, but Mick picked the players who could play and were in form. Mick knew when to have fun with the players and helped instil a confidence in them.'

Jimmy Holmes was one of the youngsters that Meagan blooded during his time in charge: 'At the time I made my debut I was actually playing in the reserves for Coventry. Noel Cantwell was in charge of the club. Mick came over and had a look at me in a game against Wrexham, and I must have impressed because I was called into the squad and made my debut against Austria. I came on as a right-back. I was a left-back, though, so when I got on I went over to the left-back Tony Dunne, who was a hero of mine, and said to him, "The manager wants you to go to right-back." I apologised to him afterwards. We were 3–1 down when I came on with twenty-five minutes to go and ended up losing 4–1.

'When I first arrived, I went to the hotel to meet the team. We were staying in the Montrose. I got there before the others, and I asked the girl at reception if any of the players were in. She saw my bag, but assumed I was a fan, because she then asked me if I wanted an autograph. She obviously didn't know who I was.

'It turned out I was rooming with Don Givens. I was then

introduced to the likes of Terry Conroy, Steve Heighway and Paddy Mulligan, all heroes to me. They were taking the mickey out of me, but it was all in good fun. When I went up to my room that night I got a call from a reporter at the *Irish Press*. He was asking me about all the players and how I was getting on with them all. Well, I told him that they were all brilliant, and I was looking forward to the game. The next morning at breakfast the lads were quoting all the nice things I had said. It turned out that the reporter was Ray Treacy.

'That introduction helped me to relax and feel part of the squad, though. Mick was a good talker. He was intelligent and knew the game, although there was very little time to coach the players. You came over on the Saturday and then played on the Sunday. Mick had to make decisions based on the opinions of the players' club managers and more experienced players within the team. It was an exciting time, though, with Mick being the first real manager of the team. It was good to be part of it, and I learned quite quickly.'

Despite the positive impact Mick was having on the team and the new professionalism of Irish football, results were still not in line with the public's expectations, as Ireland failed to win any of their qualifiers for the 1970 World Cup. A draw with Denmark at home was the only point earned by the team in that campaign. A 3–0 away defeat at the hands of Czechoslovakia was followed by a 4–0 hammering away to a Puskás-led Hungary, the great man himself scoring the killer third goal. The campaign saw Ireland score only three goals, yet they conceded fourteen. These were dark times indeed for the new man in charge and for Irish football in general.

Things failed to improve during the qualifying campaign

for the 1972 European Championship, with the team only securing a single point from a possible twelve available, a 1–1 draw with Sweden in the first group match at Dalymount Park, although they lost the return match 1–0 in Stockholm. Two defeats to Italy followed, including a determined and narrow loss in Dublin in which a Jimmy Conroy goal saw Ireland equalise only to concede a killer second goal midway through the second half. Following this things went downhill, with Ireland suffering two very heavy defeats at the hands of Austria. In Dublin the team could only muster a lone reply to the four goals scored by the Austrians, the solitary Ireland goal coming from a Carroll penalty in the second half. In the away match the Austrian team scored six goals without reply.

That European Championship campaign saw Ireland again score only three goals, yet they conceded seventeen. The 6–0 defeat by Austria proved to be a step too much for the FAI, and Mick Meagan's time as manager of the team came to an end. But while the results might not have been as good as people had hoped for or expected, the building blocks were certainly being put in place for the future. And to Tony O'Connell, despite the poor results at that time, Mick was quite simply a fantastic manager: 'He had been a tremendous full-back and that experience in England helped him. The players respected him, and the fact that he had won a League title with Everton only added to that respect.'

Despite the obvious failings of the new project, the FAI persisted with the new approach they had adopted. And in later years Ireland would reap the rewards of the decision to appoint Mick Meagan back in 1969.

MICK MEAGAN'S CLUB MANAGERIAL HONOURS RECORD:

No management honours

MICK MEAGAN'S IRELAND RECORD:

Total number of games in charge: 12
Total number of wins: 0 (ratio 0.00%)
Total number of draws: 3 (ratio 25.00%)
Total number of losses: 9 (ratio 75.00%)
Biggest win: none
Biggest defeat: 6–0 *v.* Austria
Longest run without defeat: 1 game

MICK MEAGAN'S RESULTS AS IRELAND MANAGER:

Date	Home/ Away	Opponent	Score	Result	Type of Fixture
21/09/1969	Home	Scotland	1–1	D	Friendly
07/10/1969	Away	Czechoslovakia	0–3	L	Competitive
15/10/1969	Home	Denmark	1–1	D	Competitive
05/11/1969	Away	Hungary	0–4	L	Competitive
06/05/1970	Home	Poland	1–2	L	Friendly
09/05/1970	Away	West Germany	1–2	L	Friendly
23/09/1970	Home	Poland	0–2	L	Friendly

14/10/1970	Home	Sweden	1–1	D	Competitive
28/10/1970	Away	Sweden	0–1	L	Competitive
08/12/1970	Rome	Italy	0–3	L	Competitive
10/05/1971	Home	Italy	1–2	L	Competitive
30/05/1971	Home	Austria	1–4	L	Competitive

5

LIAM TUOHY

Liam Tuohy is a man who lives and breathes football, a man who was willing to give his all for his country whether as a player, coach or manager. For Liam, personal gain was often set aside for the love of the game and not many have given as much to the Irish game. In a career that saw Liam play in England with Newcastle, and become a Shamrock Rovers legend and manager, an Ireland international and ultimately manager of the national side, Liam gave everything he had to Irish football and deserves his ranking as a legend of the game. In the years after opting out of the Ireland hot seat, his love for the game never diminished, whether it was working with the Under-19 squads in the 1980s or teaching the latest crop of youngsters to come out of Home Farm.

The change that was sweeping through the national team in the late 1960s and early 1970s was taken even further when Liam became the first manager to have complete control over team selection. A man who had played in England for one of the top teams, he had the respect of the English-based players;

a man who had won trophies as a player and manager with Shamrock Rovers, he had the respect of the Irish-based players. It seemed the FAI had found the right man to lead the team in the new era.

EARLY YEARS

Liam Tuohy was born in the East Wall district of Dublin, the second youngest in a family of six boys. He was raised by his mother as his father Gerry died when he was young. As a youngster hurling was his first love, but he soon tired of being asked to play in goals and switched his attention to the bigger round ball, playing football for St Marys.

On leaving school Tuohy drifted a bit, working as a wheel builder at Royal Enfield bikes, and over the next couple of years he did pretty much everything, from delivering groceries to assembling prams, until he signed for Shamrock Rovers at the age of eighteen in 1951. His time at Shamrock Rovers saw him come under the tutelage of the late, great Paddy Coad.

After a season with the Under-21s and another with the second team he made his first-team debut in 1953. 'Coad's Colts', as they were known in those days, were blazing a trail through Irish football at that time, winning the League of Ireland in 1954, 1957 and 1959. They also won the FAI Cup twice in the 1950s: in 1955 and 1956.

In 1954, as a member of the team that had won the League title, Tuohy was starting to attract some attention from England, with both West Bromwich Albion and Aston Villa interested in securing his services. Tuohy, however, opted to remain in

Dublin with Shamrock Rovers. His development continued under Coad, and he subsequently became an important fixture in the successful Rovers team.

It was while he was at Rovers that Tuohy experienced Continental football for the first time when both he and the club made their debut in European competition in 1959. Liam managed to score the first of four goals for Rovers at this level when he scored their second in a 3–2 away defeat against Nice in the European Cup.

When he had a third League of Ireland under his belt Tuohy started to consider his future. Approaching twenty-seven he was at his peak as a footballer, and he fancied another challenge before the end of his career. He was now working for Guinness at the St James' Gate Brewery and with wife Sheila was the proud father of three children.

After nine part-time years it was time for a change, and that change came in the shape of Newcastle United. The switch to full-time football was always going to be difficult for Tuohy, but in three years with Newcastle he made a total of forty-two appearances and scored nine goals.

IRELAND CAREER

Liam earned the first of his eight caps for Ireland in 1955, whilst still on the books of Shamrock Rovers, starting up front in a 4–1 defeat to Yugoslavia. However it was not until four years later, in 1959, when he was a Newcastle player that he earned his second cap, starting in a 2–0 win over Czechoslovakia. He made a more lasting impression this time, as just twenty-one minutes into the game Liam became the first man to score in the European Nations Cup (now known as the UEFA European Championship). His history-making goal saw him keep his place for the return game, but this time Liam made less of an impact and was part of a side that lost 4–0. The lack of consistency in the selection process of the teams adopted by the committee meant that it was almost three years before Liam would feature again for Ireland. That game, a 3–2 friendly defeat at home to Austria saw Liam grab his second international goal in four appearances.

The next Ireland game saw Liam return to competitive international football as he started and scored in a 4–2 victory over Iceland, also netting another goal in the return game, a 1–1 draw. Almost seven years after making his debut for his country, Liam now had six caps and four goals to his name, impressive statistics despite the gaps between appearances.

Having left Newcastle to move back to Ireland with Shamrock Rovers, Liam won his seventh cap for Ireland in a 0–0 draw with Austria in 1965. Eleven years after making his debut, he won his last cap in a 2–0 defeat to Belgium.

MANAGEMENT CAREER

It was when Liam returned to Shamrock Rovers in 1963 that he began the journey that would eventually lead to the Ireland manager's job. He took the reigns at Milltown as a player-coach and helped the club win a League of Ireland/FAI Cup double in his first season. Despite winning the League and Cup double, the manager Seán Thomas had decided to leave the club and the club's directors handed Liam the chance to take on the management of the team, although he would remain a player on the club's books as well. Liam's job was made easier by the fact that he inherited a very talented squad with players of the calibre of Frank O'Neill and Johnny Fullam who were full Ireland internationals when Liam took over, while youngsters Mick Leech and Paddy Mulligan were soon to become household names in League of Ireland football and as internationalists.

Liam was in his early thirties when he took the player-manager role, and his time with Rovers would last a trophy-laden five years, during which time he led the club to a run of five consecutive FAI Cup Final wins. Despite this success he failed to win the League title during his time in charge.

With his record as a Cup specialist enhanced domestically, Liam got the chance to increase his stock as a player and manager against European opposition. Valencia, Real Zaragoza, Schalke 04, Cardiff, Nice and German powerhouse Bayern Munich were all opponents faced by Rovers during Liam's time in charge, and the man himself led by example, scoring in draws with Valencia (2–2) and Real Zaragoza (1–1). However, the game against Bayern Munich proved to be a highlight for his Rovers team, when they came close to beating the German superstars: the first leg in Dublin finished 1–1, although with the Germans having the advantage of the away goal, hopes of winning were low. However, despite Bayern racing into an early 2–0 lead in the second leg, Rovers fought back and levelled the tie, with Liam himself scoring the second goal. Sadly heartbreak eventually ensued for Rovers as they conceded a goal close to the end of the match to finish 3–2.

In 1969 Liam's time with Shamrock Rovers came to an end

and he left the club to become the manager of Dundalk. During a three-year spell, Liam led the Louth side to the Leinster Senior Cup in 1971 and the Shield in 1972 with a 5–0 win over local rivals Drogheda. The low point of his reign came not long into the job, when Liverpool came to town for a Fairs Cup game. With less than a minute on the clock before half-time, Liverpool scored and proceeded to add a further four more goals to their tally to lead 5–0. That score line was doubled by the end of the ninety minutes as Liverpool ran up one of their biggest ever wins.

It was while Liam was manager of Dundalk that he earned the chance to manage the Ireland side and he worked in both roles together before leaving his post with Dundalk. However, the lure of club football was hard to resist and he found himself once again back in familiar territory when in June 1972 he returned to Rovers for a second spell as manager. This was a short-lived reign that ended eighteen months later when Liam resigned in December 1973.

It was during his second spell as manager of Shamrock Rovers in 1972 that Liam met future Ireland manager Brian Kerr, who remembers: 'I first came across Liam when he was running the schoolboy team for Crumlin United and was involved in youth-team football. I had played Under-17 and Under-18 football with Shelbourne and knew Gerry Moran, who was Liam's chief scout. I was invited to run the youth team for Shamrock Rovers under Liam. So there I was, this twenty-year-old, and suddenly I was in the inner circle with a former Ireland player, manager and legend of the game. I had become more aware of him later in his career, particularly with Shamrock Rovers.

'The inner circle consisted of Hughie Fleming and the late Paddy Ambrose. It was amazing and a huge honour and privilege for me to be involved with Liam and the youth team at Rovers. Liam, Paddy and Hughie would talk about potential signings, and because of my knowledge of the junior league they would involve me and ask my opinion. It was a fantastic vote of confidence for me, being so young and in the company of a former Ireland manager.

'Liam is a football man, and he loves the game. I remember when the Kilcoynes took over at Shamrock Rovers, one of the first things they did was to get rid of the groundsman at Milltown. So when the youth team were playing a game we would have to mark out the pitch ourselves. I'd often come down of a Sunday morning and Liam would have the pitch already marked out for us.

'His knowledge of the game was amazing and the simplicity in the way he played the game, but I think in the end he was frustrated with the goings on behind the scenes, and he resigned out of frustration.'

Having earned his crust as a manager in the League of Ireland, the chance to manage his country came about in 1971 following the departure of Mick Meagan. At that time Ireland had not won in eighteen games, stretching back five years, so expectations for the team were low. His magic wand did not appear to work straight away, as Liam's first game in charge, a European Championship qualifier against Austria, saw a weakened Ireland team lose 6–0. Paddy Mulligan of Chelsea was the only English-based player in the first team that day.

Six months later Liam would have the chance to right the wrongs of that defeat. In June 1972, Ireland were invited to travel to Brazil for the Independence Cup (a tournament intended to celebrate 150 years of Brazilian independence). That tournament saw Ireland grouped with Iran, Ecuador, Chile and Portugal. The first two games were against Iran and Ecuador, and a full strength Ireland side managed to secure morale-boosting victories. Despite defeats in the remaining games in the tournament, Ireland came away with their heads held high and had managed to restore some pride ahead of the 1974 World Cup qualifiers.

Jimmy Holmes, Eoin Hand, Mick Leech and Paddy Mulligan had all travelled over to South America. Eoin Hand remembers his own call-up: 'I had gone for a walk with Niamh, my daughter, who was two at the time. When we came back there was Liam at the gate talking to my wife. He asked me if I was available for the tour. I remember Giles and Heighway had pulled out. I accepted and then had to make arrangements so I could travel.

'Nowadays when you travel abroad for an international tournament you usually stay outside the town in a quiet area. However, over in Brazil we stayed in a hotel in the middle of town where there were nightclubs and distractions. I'm not saying we were distracted, though, by any means. There were no TVs in the rooms, so we entertained ourselves with games of cards. But it was the first time I as a player had seen the full-time set-up and the benefit of training every day, and it showed, as we got some laudable results.'

Mick Leech thought the trip was an amazing experience: 'I can remember chatting to two of the professional players in the squad and saying, "Wouldn't it be great if we won the group and headed down to Rio?" And they were like, "Jaysus no, Mick." They couldn't wait to get home to their families, but for me it was different. I was not married at the time, but I can see it from their point of view now. It was a long season in England and then to have to travel over to the other side of the world was hard, but I wouldn't have changed a thing.'

Ireland had some impressive results on the trip, despite missing a lot of key players. Eoin Hand saw it as an opportunity to showcase the talent of the Ireland team: 'I remember I scored the winner against Ecuador in a 3–2 win, but then managed to get myself sent off in the match against Chile, which we lost 2–1. The referee had denied us a penalty, and I was so annoyed I turned on him. I probably said too much, as he sent me off. After the game I remember Liam was lecturing me on not getting involved with referees and that I should concentrate on getting on with the game.'

The aim of Liam's reign was to restore some pride to the Ireland team and while the Independence Cup in Brazil saw Ireland learn how to win again, the bread and butter of his job was to fight for qualification for the major European and World Cup tournaments. The qualification for the 1974 World Cup saw Ireland up against France and the USSR. Two defeats to the USSR ensured that Ireland's wait to qualify for a tournament would continue, although a win over France was a move in the right direction.

For Paddy Mulligan the tournament in Brazil was the perfect preparation for the 1974 World Cup qualifiers: 'It is a testament to the players and management that we spent three weeks in Brazil and there was not a bad word said by anyone. I had travelled abroad with teams while in England, and the spirit was not the same. We really gelled on that trip, and while we knew when to have fun, we never took it too far.

'I remember Mick Leech – who along with me was named in the team of the tournament, which was a fantastic achievement for us – turning a whiter shade of pale with the heat in one match and Liam having to take him off. But Mick had a fine tournament, and I was always surprised he never made the move to England. We had no Johnny Giles in that tournament, as he was injured, and it would have been interesting to see how we would have done had he been fit.

'The Brazil tournament was a great way to build up to the 1974 World Cup qualifiers, and it benefited us a lot. We were unbeaten against France, winning 2–1 in Dublin thanks to a Ray Treacy winning goal and then drawing in Paris thanks to a Mick Martin goal. We also narrowly lost 1–0 to the USSR in Moscow [Ireland was missing Terry Conroy, Steve Heighway and Johnny Giles for that game], but they beat us 2–1 at home. We were unlucky not to qualify, really. But we managed some great results under Liam, especially beating France at Dalymount Park.

'We played the standard 4–4–2 under Liam, which was the main formation of the time. We were very organised, though, and played with Terry Conroy and Steve Heighway on the wings, while Ray Treacy and Don Givens played through the middle. It was a good side. But despite taking the team so close, Liam sadly decided to resign due to other commitments.'

It was before the final game in the group against France, that Liam announced this would be his final game in charge. That 1–1 draw was one of the finest away results by the Ireland team that saw them gain their first away point in twelve years.

Sometimes, of course, being a football manager means that you spend less time preparing players and kicking a ball around than involving yourself in situations that are of a more political nature, and in 1973 Liam Tuohy found himself in such a situation when he took charge of the Shamrock Rovers XI that played Brazil. However, the title Shamrock Rovers XI is very misleading as the Rovers XI who played Brazil contained not one Shamrock player and instead was made up of players from both the Republic of Ireland and Northern Ireland. The 1970s were a tough time politically, with the well-documented Troubles casting a shadow over the entire country. Both football associations had long since distanced themselves from each other, with the IFA strongly opposed to the Brazil match, seeing it as setting a precedent that might encourage moves for the IFA to merge with the FAI. Liam revealed in later interviews that not only were the IFA against the match, but that the FAI also had some reservations about the fixture.

To appease the growing concerns of the IFA, the team was not referred to as an All-Ireland XI but was called a Shamrock Rovers selection. However, charity was the winner on the night, with UNICEF the benefactor, and a goodwill gesture of solidarity and hope prevailed.

The game was the brainchild of Louis Kilcoyne, who while on tour with Rovers in South America managed to persuade João Havelange of the Brazilian FA to fit in a game against a Shamrock Rovers XI on the Brazil team's summer tour of Europe. Louis enlisted the help of his brother-in-law Johnny Giles to get a team together. Derek Dougan, the Northern Ireland skipper who was head of the Professional Footballers Association (PFA), decided to play, along with other Northern Ireland stars of the time, including Pat Jennings, David Craig, Allan Hunter, Martin O'Neill, Liam O'Kane and Bryan Hamilton.

For the Brazilians, the game marked the end of a nine-match

tour of Europe, and they had so far won five, drawn once and lost twice. Their line-up on the day included two of the biggest names in Brazilian football in Rivelino and Jairzinho. In front of 34,000 fans, Ireland fought back from 4–1 to lose 4–3, with Pat Jennings doing his reputation no harm when he saved a penalty. Tuohy, like his players, later revealed the pride that he took from the Irish performance at Lansdowne Road that night. He recalled in an interview in *The Irish Times* in 2004: 'The game itself was great. They played their usual dazzling brand of football. There was more to them than that. They had great balance in the side and they all worked very hard.'

As well as managing Ireland, Tuohy had managed Shamrock Rovers and Dundalk, so he had worked with some of the players at club level and knew their strengths and weaknesses. Eoin Hand was one of those players, having played under Tuohy at Dundalk, so he knew the Ireland boss well: "I found him to be very astute, and he made the best of the resources he had at his disposal. He was involved with the players and was a very hands-on manager. He really knew what he expected from the team. Tactically he was prepared, although, that said, he did not always have the full team he might have wanted.

'One of our lowest moments was probably the 6–0 defeat to Austria in the qualification for the 1972 European Championship. We only had one professional on the pitch that day – Paddy Mulligan. None of the stars travelled with us. Clubs would not release their players, as the game was at the same time as League matches. It was a crazy situation, really, and hard on Liam. There were none of the long stints that Giovanni Trapattoni enjoys with the players these days. The training camps help the players to gel together, but we did not have that.'

Liam Tuohy brought Mick Leech to Shamrock Rovers: 'Liam was a great manager. He had this great ability to be a friend and a manager. His talent was split more on the motivational side of management than the tactical, not that he wasn't tactical. He was a great character. When he signed me for Rovers I was taking over his position, and he stepped down and let me play in the team and encouraged me. He was able to make the tough decisions with players but still managed to keep the team happy. He had a good eye for talent. Damian Richardson, Mick Lawler and I were all signed by Liam and all played at international level.'

Tuohy was Paddy Mulligan's manager for six years at Shamrock Rovers: 'I was very familiar with him when he became the Ireland manager and knew him well. He was a players' man and had a great way with the lads. I remember Ray Treacy calling me when Liam came in and asking me what Tuohy was like. And I said to him that in six seasons at Rovers he'd been brilliant and I couldn't fault him. Unlike the Noel Cantwells, Charlie Hurleys and Mick Meagans of this world, Liam did not have the same level of success in England and instead built his reputation with Shamrock Rovers, where he won the League in 1964 as player-coach and then led the club to five successive FAI Cups from 1965 to 1969. But Liam, like Mick Meagan, was big on his sides being organised, and during his time he took Ireland forward again. He was close to the players and would mix well with them, taking part in the singsong after the games.'

In all Liam was manager for eleven games and he helped usher in another stage in the development of the Irish manager.

LIFE AFTER IRELAND

When his stint with Ireland finished, Tuohy became involved with Dublin University (Trinity College), winning the Collingwood Cup, an intervarsity tournament, in 1979. He managed the Dublin University team for six years. Liam then returned to national football. Such was his love of football, and such was the character of the man, that he took an unpaid position as manager of the Republic of Ireland Under-19 team. While working with them, Liam also returned to League of Ireland management, taking the reins at Shelbourne. Liam's work with the youth team brought instant success and he led the country's youth to three European Championships and a youth World Cup. The 1984 European Championship saw Ireland reach the semi-finals, losing to the USSR and eventually finishing fourth. Two years later Liam resigned his role with the youth set-up when the arrival of Jack Charlton saw changes to the coaching staff. One of the biggest appointments of Liam's time with the Irish youth set-up was that of Brian Kerr to the coaching team, a move that proved to be one of the most inspirational and beneficial appointments in Irish football.

Kerr recalls: 'I got involved again with Liam at Shelbourne in 1982, but it was short-lived. I think he was promised a golden hoard when he took over, and it never transpired. He then took over the Irish youth team, and again he got me involved – me and Noel O'Reilly. It was completely voluntary. None of us got paid, and the better we did the more work we had to do, but it was a fantastic time. We played in three European youth finals and made the youth World Cup in Russia. He had a lot of trust in us, and he gave us the freedom to do what we wanted in terms of coaching. He would often get involved in the training games. It was amazing, watching him play, seeing the way he thought. His mind was so fast, and his finishing was still brilliant. He always had a knack of scoring. I was a St Pat's supporter, and Liam often scored against us.

'He is a unique character, and he has some memory for football. His preparation and judgement were key attributes. For me, he was a great confidence builder. It was the most enjoyable period of my coaching life, those days with Liam.

'In those days there was no Under-21, Under-23 or even B squads. It was Under-15, then youth and then the senior side, so Liam was involved in the development of many players. The likes of John Sheridan, Eamonn and Brian Dolan, and Denis Irwin all came through the youth set-up. He liked to have a Kelly in goal, too. He had Alan and Gary, Alan senior's sons, and also a keeper by the name of Paul Kelly.

'[When he resigned] he was a huge loss to the game, although people in the football know would often tap into his knowledge. He never got involved with the FAI again. They could have benefited from his knowledge, but he was never invited to speak at a coaching seminar. It was ridiculous, really. Liam loved the game, and he was not about ego or money, as he had proved throughout his career. I think it bothers me more than it does Liam.'

Eamonn Dolan is the academy manager at Reading and was part of the youth set-up for Ireland under Tuohy: 'I was seventeen when I was called into the youth team squad under Liam, and at the time my inclusion generated some controversy in England. I was born in England to Irish parents, and at the time I was doing well with West Ham, so I had got a call up to both the Ireland and England youth squads. I was never in any doubt that I wanted to play for Ireland, but at the time Bobby Robson was under pressure with England and my declaring for Ireland was used as proof of his incompetence, which was not the case, as it had very little to do with him. Before, if you did not make the grade with England and had Irish blood, people assumed playing international football for Ireland was the silver medal. However, now the press was putting the spin on it that England was the silver medal.

'Liam was great to me, and he handled the whole affair really well, with his own mix of humour, appreciation and dignity. Liam was a very straightforward and simple manager. He was a great motivator, and everyone loved playing under him. He was the perfect mix as a manager. He reminds me in many ways of Steve Coppell.

'Ironically enough, I actually played in a youth game against England when we became the first Ireland team to beat them in a competitive fixture. They had Tony Adams at the back, and we had Niall Quinn and Denis Irwin in the team, so that level was a good stepping stone for players for later years. That victory helped remove any air of invincibility that England had. That game was before the World Youth Championships in the USSR, and it really helped build momentum before the finals.

'The first thing we all noticed when we arrived in Moscow for the tournament was how downtrodden and bleak the city was. When we got into the hotel we were heading up to our rooms and amazingly there was a man at a desk on every floor. In those days everyone had a job in the USSR. It was a real eye-opener. Liam really had to keep us focused over there, and it was difficult for the coaching staff to get us to keep our eye on the ball, with so many distractions around.

'The food and water in the USSR were very poor, and Liam and the staff decided that they would bring all our own supplies with us. We used to have to sort out our food in the rooms.

'After Moscow we headed for Tbilisi, which is in Georgia, and it was such a contrast. Tbilisi was hot and beautiful, and the people were smiling, which although a small thing was not something we'd seen in Moscow. Wherever we went people followed us, and when the coach was taking us to training crowds would line the streets and watch us. They were very friendly.

'Liam was very good at the psychological aspect of things. Whereas in Moscow it was very much a siege mentality, when we got to Georgia, Liam had us embrace the town and it got the people behind us. I remember there was a square outside the hotel and all the squad and staff got together and decided we'd play a game that the locals had never seen, so we started a game of cricket. The funny thing was that we had no bats, no stumps and no ball. We just pretended. It was amazing. All the players bought into the game, and the lads were catching imaginary balls and making appeals. We all got caught up in it. By the end of the game, a large crowd had built up around us, and everyone was watching us and really enjoying it. It was a special thing.

'But that was the spirit that Liam created for us. He had great staff around him, with Brian Kerr and Noel O'Reilly, one of the greatest coaches Ireland ever had. The respect we had for them all was really evident. The experience that Brian got with the youth team helped him to become a great coach, and it was vindication for all his hard work when Brian got the top job. The best football people are really intelligent and really understand the game. This intelligence gives people confidence and helps people trust them, and that was what made Liam. He was one of those people.'

LIAM TUOHY'S CLUB MANAGERIAL HONOURS RECORD:

One League of Ireland Championship: 1964
Six FAI Cups: 1964, 1965, 1966, 1967, 1968 and 1969
Five League of Ireland Shields: 1964, 1965, 1966, 1968 and
1972

LIAM TUOHY'S IRELAND RECORD:

Total number of games in charge: 10
Total number of wins: 3 (ratio 30.00%)
Total number of draws: 1 (ratio 10.00%)
Total number of losses: 6 (ratio 60.00%)
Biggest win: 3–2 *v.* Iran
Biggest defeat: 0–6 *v.* Austria
Longest run without defeat: 2 games

LIAM TUOHY'S RESULTS AS IRELAND MANAGER:

Date	Home/ Away	Opponent	Score	Result	Type of Fixture
10/10/1971	Away	Austria	0–6	L	Competitive
18/06/1972	Away	Iran	2–1	W	Friendly

19/06/1972	Away	Ecuador	3–2	W	Friendly
21/06/1972	Away	Chile	1–2	L	Friendly
25/06/1972	Away	Portugal	1–2	L	Friendly
18/10/1972	Home	Soviet Union	1–2	L	Competitive
15/11/1972	Home	France	2–1	W	Competitive
13/05/1973	Away	Soviet Union	0–1	L	Competitive
16/05/1973	Away	Poland	0–2	L	Friendly
19/05/1973	Away	France	1–1	D	Competitive

6

SEÁN THOMAS

Seán Thomas, the man who led Shamrock Rovers and Bohemians on a trail of success in the 1960s, is a bit of an unknown entity. He did not have a football-playing background but had the interest and foresight to go to England and get his coaching badges. He is a football innovator who saw the potential in this country and impressed enough to be linked with coaching roles in England, manage in the USA and ultimately take charge of his country.

It is very hard to judge a man after only one game, but it would be equally unfair to leave Thomas out of this book, as he is still a big part of Irish soccer history. To fans of Shamrock Rovers and Bohemians he is a legend, and he managed some of Ireland's top talent. He was later honoured for his role in Irish football, receiving a Professional Footballers' Association of Ireland merit award in 1992.

Very little is known about Thomas' life before he became a manager. Tony O'Connell, who played under Thomas at Shamrock Rovers, recalls, 'I remember him at Rovers. He was one of the first men in Ireland to go and get their coaching badges in England. Nobody in Ireland had them at that time. He came in and moved things around, changing the system from the W–M formation that was used at every club in the country to the 4–4–2 system that we see now.

'Seán was a very good motivator, and he knew the game. He obviously must have loved it to go and get his badges. I think he worked as a carpenter before that, but he had always wanted to be involved in football. Getting the qualification in England gave him an edge over other Irish managers.

'He was very confident, and he could get his point across. That said, the times were ripe for a change. You see, the training in those days was a couple of laps around the field and a kick of the ball. It was very different to nowadays.'

Thomas' achievement at domestic level, where he enjoyed great success, earned him the right to manage his country, and in 1973 he took charge for a friendly against Norway in Oslo, ending his reign unbeaten with a 1–1 draw. The team included Preston's Alan Kelly, QPR's Don Givens, Jimmy Holmes of Coventry, Manchester United duo Gerry Daly and Mick Martin, and Paddy Mulligan. It was a strong team on paper, although to be fair to Thomas and the players it was an end-of-season game with little to play for, and on top of that, according to Tony Byrne, the grass that day was 'six inches long, making it almost impossible to play any ball'.

Ultimately, Thomas was merely a stopgap between Liam Tuohy and the appointment of Johnny Giles as player-manager. It was always going to be hard for a man who had never played at the top level of the game or managed in England to command the respect of players who were earning their crust in the English leagues. As former Ireland defender Paddy Mulligan puts it, 'It is very hard and almost unjust to judge Seán on his time with Ireland. He was only in charge for one game before he was forced to resign, I think over work commitments, and his only game in charge was a draw with Norway. I played under him for six months at Rovers, where he managed from 1960 to 1964, and during that time he won everything going – the FAI Cup, the League and the League of Ireland shield. He built a great team with some great players, including Pat Courtney, Frank O'Neill and Paddy Ambrose – all fantastic players.'

Before Thomas made his name at Rovers and Bohemians, he began his coaching career at Sligo, but he only lasted a few months, his time there including a first-round exit from the Dublin City Cup and a record 9–0 home defeat at the hands of a very strong Drumcondra side. He also had a short spell in charge of Home Farm. However, it is his time at Shamrock Rovers that made his reputation. He had big shoes to fill when he took over from Paddy Coad in 1960. Under Coad's guidance Rovers had enjoyed a successful period in their history, winning three League titles.

With Coad deciding to return to his home county of Waterford, Thomas was given the task of rebuilding the team, and under his tenure the Hoops bounced back in 1963, winning the League and Cup double in impressive style. Liam Tuohy had returned after a spell at Newcastle, and he was joined in the side by players such as Frank O'Neill, John Keogh, Pat Courtney, Johnny Fullam, Bobby Gilbert, Mick Leech and goalkeeper Mick Smyth, all of whom would become stars at Rovers. In four years under Thomas, Rovers, one of Ireland's most successful clubs, won the League, two FAI Cups and two League Cups as well as one Dublin City Cup.

As well as catching the eye in the League of Ireland, Thomas also came to the attention of the media and the FAI when in 1963 a League of Ireland selection played against their English counterparts. There was not too much between the countries in those days. Alf Ramsey was in charge of an English side which contained Bobby Moore, Ian Callaghan, Roger Hunt and Martin Peters, all of whom went on to be part of the team that won the World Cup just three years later in 1966. The League of Ireland XI beat them 2–1. Tony O'Connell recalls, 'Eddie Bailham was a prolific goal scorer but couldn't head the ball. He scored from outside the box. Seán had said to him, "You hang at the edge of the box, and when they head the ball out from a corner it will come to you." And it did. Ronnie Whelan senior scored the first goal that day. It was a great result for the League and for Seán.'

That double-winning season should have been the start of a golden era for Rovers and Thomas. However, not long after winning the double, Thomas decided to quit Rovers. He then took over at Bohemians, and in doing so became the club's first-ever manager. As seems to have been the standard for the period, Bohemians did not have a manager and relied on coaches, with a selection committee tasked with actually picking the side. But Thomas wanted to be a full-time manager. He was very ambitious and confident in his abilities, and the Bohemians role was, in some regards, made for him.

Managing Bohemians was a chance for Thomas to return to his roots, to where he had grown up. He had been a junior member of the club as a youngster, so the opportunity to bring success to his local team was a motivating factor in his decision to join the club. The season before Thomas had taken charge, the club had finished bottom of the table, but after only one season under the new manager, the potential of the former Rovers manager and the previously untapped potential of the players were shining through. The club managed an impressive third-place finish, ending up just five points behind winners Drumcondra. That Bohemians were still an amateur side and the rest of the teams in the League were professional, puts this achievement into context. Thomas was rewarded for his efforts with the Irish Soccer Writers' Personality of the Year award in 1965.

The following season, Bohemians again finished third in the League and this time managed to add some silverware to the trophy cabinet, winning both the Leinster Senior Cup and the President's Cup. The strong performances of his young players had not gone unnoticed and eight of the team left at the end of the season for the professional ranks. The most high profile of these moves was Turlough O'Connor and Jimmy Conway, who both signed for Fulham.

With his stock on the rise Thomas signed a three-year contract with Bohemians in 1966 and that season he led the club to the runner-up spot in the League. That summer he then made the brave decision to leave the League of Ireland for the chance to manage in America with the Boston Shamrocks. However, the move was not the success envisaged and it wasn't long before he was back in Ireland. At this point Thomas almost made the move to England to be manager of Fulham. Vic Buckingham approached him to join the coaching staff at Fulham, but the move fell through as Thomas was still in the process of resolving his contract with the Boston Shamrocks. Instead he returned to Dalymount Park, where the season without him had been a disaster for the club and they had finished bottom of the League.

As with the national side, changes were afoot at Bohemians and a historic EGM of club members in February 1969 saw the club change their constitution to allow salaries to be paid to players. One of the first salaried signings was Tony O'Connell: 'I remember he signed me, Dinny Lowry and Johnny Fullam. My transfer was actually a first in the League of Ireland as I had bought out my contract with Dundalk to secure the move to Bohemians. No one had ever done that before [Tony was also the first semi-professional player on Bohemians' books]. The move itself made more sense for me as I had a company in Dublin then. That first season we won the Cup under Seán.'

The arrival of some of the top talent in the League had the desired effect, as in 1970 Bohemians won their first major trophy for thirty-four years, beating Sligo Rovers 2–1 in the FAI Cup Final at the third attempt, after the first game and the replay both ended 0–0. The next three seasons saw Bohemians remain consistent in their performances, without ever really pushing forward, resulting in two third place finishes and a fourth place finish. However, under Thomas' guidance the young squad were flourishing. Such was his talent that he even spotted a young player who would later become a top Hollywood actor. Liam Neeson was playing university football when Thomas noticed him and he was invited for a trial at the club. He even came on as a substitute in a game against Shamrock Rovers, but the world of football was to miss out as Neeson failed to impress enough to earn a contract and instead turned to a different sort of entertainment, albeit on a bigger stage.

In July 1973 Thomas resigned as manager of Bohemians after a disagreement with the club's owners. He wouldn't be out of the game for long, however, and when Mick Meagan and

Theo Dunne resigned from Shamrock Rovers, Thomas returned to the club where had enjoyed so much success. He won the League Cup in 1976 having re-signed Johnny Fullam and Mick Leech, as well as John Conway from Bohemians.

That League Cup-winning season of 1976–1977 saw Rovers finish the League in a disappointing eleventh position. That summer saw Thomas replaced in the Rovers hot seat by Johnny Giles, who was also the Ireland manager at that time. Thomas then wound down his career in management with spells in charge of Athlone Town, Bray Wanderers and the Wicklow junior side before he left the game for good. Although out of the game, he was not forgotten and in 1992 his achievements in the League of Ireland were acknowledged when he was awarded a Professional Footballers Association of Ireland merit award.

SEÁN THOMAS' CLUB MANAGERIAL HONOURS RECORD:

League of Ireland: Shamrock Rovers – 1963–64

FAI Cup: Shamrock Rovers – 1962, 1964 and Bohemians – 1970

FAI League Cup: Shamrock Rovers – 1976

League of Ireland Shield: Shamrock Rovers – 1962–63, 1963–64

Top Four Cup: Bohemians – 1972

Dublin City Cup: Shamrock Rovers – 1963–64

SEÁN THOMAS' IRELAND RECORD:

Total number of games in charge: 1

Total number of wins: 0 (ratio 0.00%)

Total number of draws: 1 (ratio 100.00%)

Total number of losses: 0 (ratio 0.00%)

Biggest win: no victories

Biggest defeat: no defeats

Longest run without defeat: 1 game

SEÁN THOMAS' RESULTS AS IRELAND MANAGER:

Date	Home/ Away	Opponent	Score	Result	Type of Fixture
06/06/1973	Away	Norway	1–1	D	Friendly

7

JOHNNY GILES

Johnny Giles is an Irish footballing version of Carlsberg: he is probably one of Ireland's greatest ever footballers, probably one of Ireland's greatest-ever player-managers and now probably one of Ireland's greatest-ever football pundits. If there was ever a man who understood how the game is to be played, it is Johnny Giles. A player of the highest order, he is respected for his achievements with Ireland and for the part he played in an all-conquering Leeds United team of the 1960s under Don Revie.

Almost four decades on from his days on the pitch, Johnny is still as famous as ever, having become renowned in Ireland for his punditry work. He has formed a dream team on TV with Eamon Dunphy and Bill O'Herlihy, and his intelligent and insightful commentary makes him a firm favourite with viewers. Many people will be too young to recall his impact on the pitch, but to fans who are old enough Johnny Giles will always be remembered as being part of the great Leeds team of the 1960s and 1970s in which he formed a central-midfield partnership with Billy Bremner and won both domestic and European trophies. Giles was a fantastic player with Leeds and Ireland, and he is one of the undoubted stars of Irish football.

EARLY DAYS

Johnny Giles was born to Dicky and Kate Giles in 1940 and was raised in the inner-city area of north Dublin, growing up in 7A Ormond Square. It's testament to the impact that he had in the world of football that in July 2006 a plaque was unveiled outside the old family home in homage to him and his inner-city roots.

Football was in Johnny's blood from an early age. His father was a footballer, who, as well as playing for Bohemians, also managed Drumcondra. Johnny's own football journey began with famed youth clubs Stella Maris and Home Farm, but it wasn't long before his talent was spotted and in 1956 he signed for Manchester United. Johnny was still learning his trade as a footballer in England when the 1958 Munich air disaster occurred. The disaster, which sadly saw eight members of the United team die, led to Giles making his debut for the Reds in 1959, a lot earlier than he would have expected, at the tender age of eighteen. His debut turned out to be a 5–1 defeat at the hands of Tottenham Hotspur, but Johnny quickly put the poor start behind him and became a permanent fixture in the side. He earned his first winner's medal in England, when he was part of the United side which won the 1963 FA Cup, playing alongside another Irishman, Noel Cantwell. That summer, however, Johnny made the difficult decision to leave Old

Trafford and moved to join Leeds United who at that time were in the Second Division. The Leeds United manager Don Revie was assembling a side strong enough to win promotion and with Giles in the team the title was secured and with it promotion to the big time.

On their first season back in the First Division, Leeds made an instant impression and they only just missed out on winning the League, finishing as runners-up to Johnny's old club, United. That season saw also saw Johnny miss out on another FA Cup medal when Leeds lost to Liverpool.

The following season, 1967–1968, saw Johnny help Leeds to continue their upward march as they beat Arsenal 1–0 to win the League Cup and also experience European glory as they beat Ferencváros of Hungary in the Fairs Cup final.

By this stage Giles was coming into his peak as a player and, with twenty-six Irish caps under his belt, had progressed to become a key player for both club and country. Revie built his team around Giles and his midfield partner Billy Bremner, although it was often hard to distinguish whose role was what, with Giles equally adept at winning the ball in the tackle as well as creating chances for the team. The same could be said of Bremner and it was this adaptability in the middle that was the key to Leeds' success. The following season Johnny finally got his hands on a League Championship winner's medal as Leeds won the division title, losing only two games in the process.

The 1969–1970 season saw Johnny make his debut in the European Cup and he was an integral part of a three-pronged trophy assault as Leeds went for the League, FA Cup and European Cup. They ended up with nothing, however, finishing the season as runners-up in both the League and the FA Cup to Chelsea. Celtic emerged victorious from the European Cup battle of Britain, beating Leeds in the semi-final. Over the following two seasons, Giles' medal collection increased as he added yet another Fairs Cup winning medal (1971) and an FA Cup winner's medal (1972). In 1973 Leeds once again experienced the agony of finishing runners-up, only missing out on the title with a last day defeat by Wolves. Once again the club and Giles had finished a promising campaign empty-handed.

The 1973–74 season saw the inspirational Jack Charlton leave the club. This left Johnny as the most senior member of the side, and despite the loss of the World Cup winning centre-half, a twenty-nine-game unbeaten run ensured that Leeds did not feel his loss too much, and Giles finished the season with his second League Championship medal.

FULL INTERNATIONAL

Johnny Giles is one of the greatest-ever players to don a green shirt and it is a shame that, like many great Irish footballers before and after him, he never achieved his ambition of playing in a major international final. Every generation has players that deserve more from their international careers, and just as Ryan Giggs has never made it to an international tournament, neither did Giles. While his international career for the Republic of Ireland had some notable highs, it never scaled the heights of his club career.

His international career started in November 1959, when after just two first-team appearances for Manchester United a then nineteen-year-old Giles made the starting line-up for a match against a Swedish team that had lost the World Cup final to Brazil a year earlier. Four days before the game against Ireland, the Swedes had beaten England. They took the confidence this gave them into the Irish match and quickly established a 2–0 lead at Dalymount Park after only twelve minutes. However, Johnny helped reduce the deficit after sixteen minutes with his first international goal and then went on to help the Ireland team to a 3–2 victory.

In total Giles made fifty-nine appearances in an Ireland shirt, scoring five goals. His international career lasted almost twenty years, and for six of those he was player-manager of the team. He was without doubt one of the most influential players of his era.

THE MANAGER'S JOB

Johnny Giles' impact on the Ireland team as a player was renowned, and it was no surprise that the FAI approached him to become the player-manager of the Republic of Ireland team. Giles was the Ireland manager from 1973 to 1980 and set about instilling in the team the tactical know-how and professionalism that he had learned under Matt Busby and Don Revie, two of the greatest managers the game had ever seen. 'I learned more under Johnny Giles than I did from any Christian Brothers school,' says Alan Campbell, who played under Giles at Shamrock Rovers. 'It was not just football with Johnny. It was the way he approached life. He was very educational, more of a teacher than a coach, and you would listen to what he had to say.'

Paddy Mulligan thinks Giles was appointed because the team needed a big name to take them to another level and move things forward: 'I think after Liam and Seán Thomas, Johnny was the big name that the team and the FAI needed. He took the role on and set about taking Ireland up another step on the international ladder. He was so professional and a legend of the game. For example, rather than speaking to the players about qualifying for tournaments, he wanted us to look to the next level and think about getting out of the group when at a tournament. He was very forward-thinking and ambitious. More than anyone he wanted Ireland to do well, and there were some great players coming through at that time, especially Liam Brady, as well as some wonderful players already in the team. We managed to beat the USSR in one of Johnny's first matches in charge. They were a powerhouse at the time, but Don Givens scored three that day and we beat them 3–0. Actually, Liam Brady made his debut that day.

'Similar to the Charlton era, which would follow Giles' some six years later, Johnny set about instilling belief in the players and getting them to play his way. Johnny promoted a passing game, one that began with the keepers and involved patient build-up and maintaining control of the ball. The simple philosophy was that the opposition can't score if they don't have the ball.

'Johnny was meticulous in his planning. I remember we played a Poland team that had qualified for the 1974 World Cup in West Germany and had just beaten England on the Wednesday before, but we beat them 1–0. He had us organised. The dressing-room was very calm, and we all knew what we had to do to win. He would analyse the game for us, and he definitely brought us forward. I suppose, a bit like Liam, he was unlucky in not getting us to a tournament, but we were robbed, especially in Bulgaria, where we lost 2–1 but had a perfectly good goal disallowed.

'It was the same story in Paris, where we lost 2–0 to a fantastic French team that was one of the most talented at the 1978 World Cup, but it could have been a very different story, because we had a goal disallowed before they scored. I think it was Gerry Daly who was deemed offside, but he was nowhere near offside. It was very frustrating, but we had no standing in international football at that time. At the end of the day it was the away results that let us down.'

Jimmy Holmes recalls that Giles was a terrific motivator of players: 'He had a small squad, but he got us to give 100 per cent every time. Injuries had a real impact on our squad, but no matter what team we had out we always played well. Unfortunately, we just never seemed to get there. The highlight for me was the game against Brazil that we played at the Maracanã [Rio de Janeiro] in 1974. It felt like there were about 150,000 people in the stadium that day. It was an amazing part of our South American tour, and we only lost the game 2–1.

'They had Jairzinho, Rivelino and Pelé in their line-up. I was playing left-back and was up against Jairzinho. In the first minute he skimmed past me and got a lovely cross in that almost led to a goal. I turned to Paddy Mulligan and said, "He is even quicker than on TV. I am going to need your help." Paddy shouted back, "Sorry, I can't help you. I have to mark Pelé."'

A bad-luck theme runs through the history of the Ireland team right up to the 1980s. The football might have been improving, the organisation getting better, the professionalism gathering pace, but the one thing that Ireland could not change, it seemed, was the bad luck that continually hampered their progress. When a team is not getting the rub of the green they feel they deserve, then the simplest decision is analysed and broken down, and over time it becomes a focal point for any perceived failures. However, the team was definitely on the up under Giles, and while the country failed to qualify for any major finals, the common perception was that Giles was ahead of his time. He wanted to change not only the way Ireland played but also the whole set-up of the team.

Gerry Peyton thought Giles was in a league of his own: 'Looking back, I would have been in my early twenties then, Giles was definitely ahead of his time. He wanted to keep the ball on the ground, starting with the goalkeepers. He wanted us to throw the ball short to a defender or midfielder and build from there. John was player-manager at that time, and he would come deep from midfield to get the ball and then try and play it around. If I'm honest, I'm not sure people were ready for the football he wanted to play.

'The pitch was against us, too. Lansdowne Road was also a rugby pitch, as it is today, and the grass was always too long and the ball would bounce unpredictably. If you compare Dalymount and Lansdowne Road to say the current Arsenal pitch, the latter is like a bowling green. In fact, all of the top clubs today have pitches like bowling greens. Ireland did not have that.

'John had high standards, as he had played under Don Revie at Leeds. Jack Charlton, Terry Yorath and Billy Bremner all became managers, while Gordon McQueen and Eddie Gray were coaches. These guys had all learned from Revie.

'The Leeds team of that generation were a tough unit, but they played attractive football and were winners. John tried to take that with him to Ireland. He wanted to play the beautiful game, and we had the players to do it. There was Liam Brady, Frank Stapleton, David O'Leary, Mick Martin, Jimmy Holmes and Steve Heighway – all good players.

'I think if he had stayed on a bit longer and waited for the improvement in pitches, he would have got the best out of the squad. Liam Brady used to talk to him a lot. He moulded Liam into one of the best midfielders in the world. Liam was very keen to hear what John had to say. After all, he was a legend of the game, not just to Liam, but to us all.

'John gave me my debut in 1977 against Spain as a second-half substitute for Mick Kearns. I will never forget the reception I got. It was fantastic. I was born in Birmingham, but my father and mother were Irish, from Mayo and Galway. I had actually been selected to play for England, but Johnny gave me a call after hearing my parents were Irish and asked me if I wanted to play for Ireland. I had a talk about it with my mum and dad and decided to go for it, and I never looked back. I played thirty-three times for Ireland in sixteen years and managed to keep thirteen clean sheets in that time.

'I really enjoyed my time in the Ireland set-up, and I know my parents were very proud of me. I have a young son now, and he can play for England or Ireland. If the time comes, I will sit with him and help him make the best decision for him.

'I think the fact that I chose Ireland over England helped me get a good reception from the fans. I had been selected for England at a time when they had Peter Shilton, Ray Clemence, Phil Parkes – the most expensive keeper of the day – Jimmy

Rimmer, Joe Corrigan and a young Paul Bradshaw at Wolves, so it was quite an honour to be considered for England. But once Johnny Giles called that was it. He was so charismatic you wanted to please him. Not only was he a big name, he had a great knowledge of the game, and, of course, he had a good record with West Bromwich Albion, which he got promoted.'

Dave Langan started his Ireland career when Johnny was in charge: 'He actually gave me my debut in a testimonial match against Leeds. The match was for Paul Madeley, who was a Leeds legend. Johnny then told me I would be in the squad for a home match against Turkey. I was a young player then at Derby, and Johnny was player-manager. He pulled me aside the day before the game and had a little chat with me, telling me what he expected of me. Johnny never missed a trick. He had a knowledge of the game I have never seen before or since. He really balanced being a player and the manager of the team.

'We would train the morning before a game and then have lunch. Afterwards Johnny would give his team talk, focusing on us and what he expected from us. He included everybody and asked them for their thoughts. He was never too worried about the opposition. He was one of the lads, but at the same time he would tell you off if he had to. He could switch into manager mode quite easily, but you always knew he was right. He knew the game inside out, and everyone in the squad had so much respect for him.

'The team spirit under Johnny was great. As I said, he involved everyone, and he was very approachable. Even if you were in the squad and on the bench, he made sure you felt like you were part of the team. I remember one time we were training out at our base near the airport and Johnny arranged for Pelé, who was in the country with UNICEF, to come out and meet us. Pelé shook every one of our hands. It was fantastic.'

Jimmy Holmes, who is Ireland's youngest-ever debutant, played thirty times for the national side before an injury during a challenge for the ball in an international game ended his career: 'I remember the game. It was against Bulgaria in Sofia in 1979. It was very unfortunate. It was a 50–50 ball, but, you know, when it's your country you don't pull out of them. That was it for me.

'In all I played for Ireland for eight years, and it was an amazing experience. Giles was the best manager I played under. He was a perfectionist and really looked after his body. And it showed, as he kept playing with Ireland until he was thirty-nine, which was some achievement.

'The FAI did not have a lot of money, but they did the best they could. We sometimes used to get frustrated travelling with the press and fans, but there was always good banter. I remember Johnny would say to us that if a hotel was not great – and there were some dodgy hotels – we should show our professionalism on the pitch. Johnny brought a more professional approach and attitude to our game. He was a great man for pulling you aside and having a pep talk with you. Some players need that approach.'

John Wilkes senior, who would later coach under Giles at Shamrock Rovers, reckons that Ireland were maybe not ready to move forward as fast as they had in such a short space of time: 'I think that when Johnny came in, Ireland was still in the doldrums internationally. The FAI had set about revamping the set-up and change was taking place. In those days if you were at an Ireland match the fans would cheer when the goalkeeper kicked the ball out long to the centre-forward. However, Johnny wanted to play football a different way, and the supporters might not have been ready for it. They were not used to seeing the keeper roll the ball to the defender and build from the back. It was about possession and passing, but Johnny got a lot of stick for it, as it was perceived as negative football. [Irish football was used to a kick and rush game where the idea was to get the ball to the front men as fast as possible, but Johnny's system was to keep possession, with the idea that if you had the ball then the other team could not score.] The perception was that Johnny's system was to kill games off, hold onto the ball and play for draws, but the truth is his teams never played for 0–0 draws. He wanted to win, but win playing in a certain way. I still think it was unfortunate he left when he did. I think if he had been there for 1982 when we lost out on goal difference he would have made a difference, but in the end his private life was being affected by the public criticisms.'

While he was manager of Ireland, Giles also managed West Bromwich Albion and Shamrock Rovers. His time at Albion was very successful, with the club being promoted to the First Division in 1976 and then not only staying afloat, but finishing an impressive seventh in his first season managing in England's top division.

John Wilkes senior was a youth-team coach with Shamrock Rovers and was part of the new-look backroom team under Giles: 'I first encountered Johnny through my work with youth-team football at Cherry Orchard. I had run a successful youth team there, and a lot of players from the 1975 team had been signed by Shamrock Rovers, so I had a reputation and was known in youth football. I had been recommended to Johnny, and we spoke about what he was trying to achieve and set up.

He had taken the reins at Shamrock Rovers under the Kilcoynes [the club's owners] and wanted to re-establish the youth set-up. Johnny took the job at a large financial loss, especially compared to what he could have earned in England. The idea of his appointment was right, but I don't think the investment was there to back it up. Johnny believed in the project, and his heart was definitely in it. He wanted to get the youth scheme up and running, with players who would play football a certain way. He wanted to play a passing game, but the pitches in Ireland in those days were not suitable for that kind of approach. Johnny had come from a full-time background in England, and his preparation and training were way ahead of what we had here. In those days part-time footballers only trained twice a week – Johnny changed that, though. Johnny brought a more professional and full-time approach to the training set-up: even though the players were part-time, the commitment was full-time. Players would come in at weekends for training, and on Sundays before a game we would have a light training session followed by lunch followed by the match. It was unheard of in those days.

'The likes of Johnny Fullam, Alan O'Neill, Alan Campbell, Pierce O'Leary and Jim Beglin all came through the system, and they understood what Johnny was trying to achieve and how he wanted to play. It was a different style of management for these players. Johnny liked to talk calmly and constructively. This was new to a lot of people. Also, his retention of information was unbelievable. He could remember aspects of a game and analyse it as if he had a monitor in front of him. It was an interesting and illuminating time, especially from the coaching side of things. Sadly, it all comes back to results. With the set-up that was in place Rovers were expected to win everything in sight. Results were hard to come by, and in the end he turned to the big names such as Ray Treacy, Eamon Dunphy and Eoin Hand to help the team fight and scrap for wins.

'When there was no sign of that dominance, I think people, including Johnny himself, became disillusioned, and in the end he left Rovers by mutual consent. You would think that it would have been good for the League to see a team set up professionally and have a good youth set-up, but there was a lot of opposition to what Rovers were trying to achieve. Barriers were put up to stop us. Professional apprentices were prevented from playing in the local Leagues. Then when a good player came through the system, they were sold to fund the project, the likes of Alan Campbell, Pierce O'Leary and Jim Beglin all being sold on. Personally, it was a great experience working with Johnny, and my time in the game afterwards at schoolboy level was pretty successful, much of which I attribute to what I learned from him. He was a superb person to work with.'

JOHNNY GILES THE FOOTBALL PUNDIT

Since retiring from the everyday hustle of football management, Giles has settled into a career as a pundit and forms part of the team for RTÉ's Champions League coverage and also their Premier League show. Giles also writes columns for *The Evening Herald*, a Dublin-based newspaper, as well as being involved in radio. His columns and punditry are renowned for their honesty and insightfulness. His relationship with the shows' other pundit, Eamon Dunphy, forms the basis for the success of both shows.

Here are some of the more entertaining Johnny Giles quotations from his role as football pundit:

On the big-match atmosphere:
'I'd rather play in front of a full-house than an empty crowd.'

Defending forwards who go down easily:
'It's like somebody walking down the street and there's a big block of wood. If you don't see it, you're going to walk into it and fall over.'

And on the declining standards in world football:
'The problem is that the kids nowadays have got personal stereos and higher education.'

Bill O'Herlihy: 'So you think they [Arsenal] can score, even in Spain?'
Johnny Giles: 'Well, I don't know what you mean by "even in Spain". I mean, the goals there are the same size and all that …'

On Lee Carsley:
Bill O'Herlihy: 'Carsley lacks a bit of skill in those situations. Let's call a spade a spade.'
Johnny Giles: 'Yes Bill, he's in there to dig.'

Johnny Giles achieved fantastic success as a player and as a manager, and then made a success of his career in TV. It is a testament to the man that he will always be remembered as one of Ireland's most successful gentlemen of football.

JOHNNY GILES' CLUB MANAGERIAL HONOURS RECORD:

FAI Cup – Shamrock Rovers 1978

JOHNNY GILES' IRELAND RECORD:

Total number of games in charge: 38
Total number of wins: 15 (ratio 39.47%)
Total number of draws: 9 (ratio 23.68%)
Total number of losses: 14 (ratio 36.84%)
Biggest win: 4–0 *v.* Turkey
Biggest defeat: 4–1 *v.* Czechoslovakia
Longest run without defeat: 8 games

JOHNNY GILES' RESULTS AS IRELAND MANAGER:

Date	Home/ Away	Opponent	Score	Result	Type of Fixture
21/10/1973	Home	Poland	1–0	W	Friendly
05/05/1974	Away	Brazil	1–2	L	Friendly
08/05/1974	Away	Uruguay	0–2	L	Friendly
12/05/1974	Away	Chile	2–1	W	Friendly
30/10/1974	Home	Soviet Union	3–0	W	Competitive
20/11/1974	Away	Turkey	1–1	D	Competitive
11/03/1975	Home	West Germany	1–0	W	Friendly

11/05/1975	Home	Switzerland	2–1	W	Competitive
18/05/1975	Away	Soviet Union	1–2	L	Competitive
21/05/1975	Away	Switzerland	0–1	L	Competitive
29/10/1975	Home	Turkey	4–0	W	Competitive
24/03/1976	Home	Norway	3–0	W	Friendly
26/05/1976	Away	Poland	2–0	W	Friendly
08/09/1976	Away	England	1–1	D	Friendly
13/10/1976	Away	Turkey	3–3	D	Friendly
17/11/1976	Away	France	0–2	L	Competitive
09/02/1977	Home	Spain	0–1	L	Friendly
30/03/1977	Home	France	1–0	W	Competitive
24/04/1977	Home	Poland	0–0	D	Friendly
01/06/1977	Away	Bulgaria	1–2	L	Competitive
12/10/1977	Home	Bulgaria	0–0	D	Competitive
05/04/1978	Home	Turkey	4–2	W	Friendly
12/04/1978	Away	Poland	3–0	W	Friendly
21/05/1978	Away	Norway	0–0	D	Friendly
24/05/1978	Away	Denmark	3–3	D	Competitive
20/09/1978	Home	Northern Ireland	0–0	D	Competitive
25/10/1978	Home	England	1–1	D	Competitive
02/05/1979	Home	Denmark	2–0	W	Competitive
19/05/1979	Away	Bulgaria	0–1	L	Competitive
22/05/1979	Home	West Germany	1–3	L	Friendly
29/05/1979	Home	Argentina	0–0	D	Friendly*
11/09/1979	Away	Wales	1–2	L	Friendly
26/09/1979	Away	Czechoslovakia	1–4	L	Friendly

17/10/1979	Home	Bulgaria	3–0	W	Competitive
29/10/1979	Home	United States	3–2	W	Friendly
21/11/1979	Away	Northern Ireland	0–1	L	Competitive
06/02/1980	Away	England	0–2	L	Competitive
26/03/1980	Away	Cyprus	3–2	W	Competitive

* UNICEF benefit game

8

ALAN KELLY SENIOR

Alan Kelly senior will long be remembered as one of the true legends of Irish football. A fantastic goalkeeper who played at the highest level in England, Kelly was a hero to fans wherever he played. Whether it was with Drumcondra in Dublin, Preston North End in England, the Republic of Ireland or, later in his career as a coach with DC United in America, Kelly always demonstrated devotion and loyalty to a game he clearly loved.

Over the years Ireland has produced some fantastic goalkeepers. From Gerry Peyton and Packie Bonner right through to Shay Given, it seems to be in the genes of Irish football to produce goalkeepers of world-class ability. However, to many people Alan Kelly is the father of Irish keepers.

While footballing siblings are not uncommon, and there are a number of sons who have followed their fathers into football, it is very rare to come across a footballing dynasty and rarer still to find a goalkeeping dynasty. However, that is what Alan Kelly senior and his sons achieved. Alan senior and his youngest son Alan were full Ireland internationals while eldest son Gary was an Under-21 and B international; these achievements, coupled with his own net-minding talents, ensured that Alan senior would long be remembered in footballing circles.

Kelly is also the only Ireland manager to have a 100 per cent record, winning his only game in charge in 1980. Other commitments prevented him from taking the job on full-time, and just as with Seán Thomas in the 1970s, we will never know how successful he could have been.

EARLY LIFE AND PRESTON NORTH END

Born in Dublin in July 1936, Alan Kelly began his career with Bray Wanderers before making the short move to Dublin to join Drumcondra. A two-year stint with the north Dublin side saw him impress enough to make the move to England with Preston North End. Preston would become Kelly's life – he spent fifteen years there as a goalkeeper before moving into coaching and later management with the club. In all he made 513 appearances for Preston, with 447 in League games which to this day remains a club record. However, it could have been much more had a shoulder injury, suffered in a game against Bristol City in 1973, not curtailed his career at the age of thirty-seven, considered young by today's goalkeeping standards.

Kelly made his Preston North End debut on 28 January 1961 in an FA Cup tie against Swansea Town, and he became first-choice goalkeeper the following season. John O'Neill, who first played with Kelly at Drumcondra and was then part of the transfer deal that took both players to Preston North End, reflects on his time with Kelly: 'I first got to know Alan when we were both at Drumcondra. We played in the first team together. I was a defender and, as everyone knows, Alan was a goalkeeper. We actually went to Preston North End at the same time. The transfer came about at the end of the 1958 season, Drumcondra having won the League that year.

'At the end of the season I went to the club to collect my wages. I spoke to the chairman, and he said to me, "How do you fancy playing in England?" I said that I would like to. The chairman then told me that Spurs and Preston North End were interested. Spurs wanted me on my own, while Preston wanted both me and Alan Kelly. I decided to go to Preston with Alan, as I figured it would be easier to settle in with someone I knew.

'The done thing in those days was that the chairman would go and talk to your father, so he spoke to my mine and to Alan's, and the transfer was approved by them. A fee was then agreed with the clubs, and we were told we would get paid a set amount – I can't actually remember how much – and if we made twenty first-team appearances it would get reviewed, and then again if we played fifty games.

'For the first twelve months at Preston we actually lodged together, sharing a room. It's funny, but before that, even though we played together at Drumcondra, we didn't know each other that well. I was twenty-two and Alan was twenty-one, so there was not much between us, but I lived in Crumlin and Alan lived in Bray, so we trained and played together and then went our separate ways. Even stranger is the fact that we were both apprentices with the same plastering firm, but we never actually worked a job together.

'When we signed, Cliff Briton was the manager, and I thought he was a good boss, but, sadly, after three years of his being in charge, the club was relegated and he was sacked. Unfortunately, my own career with Preston North End did not last too long, and in the end I only played about fifty games before I moved on. Later I received an offer from Australia to go over there to work and play.

'Alan had a hard job when he first arrived at Preston, as Fred Else was the keeper, and he was a club legend and had played for the England B team. In those days the set-up for matches was a bit different. At that time clubs would only take one goalkeeper to away games, so Alan would often be left behind to play with the reserves. But he was very dedicated. He never took a drink, he never smoked and he never stayed out late. He was very professional and determined. And he worked hard at training and eventually grabbed his chance when Fred went to Blackburn.

'We lived closed to the ground, and in those days you would train between ten and twelve in the morning and between two and four in the afternoon. We always had to get the bus to training, as I was always bloody late getting up. Outside of football we would play snooker and golf and go to dances together. He was a lovely man, and I can't say a bad word about him. Alan was a very private man, almost shy. He seldom had a lot to say, but he was never rude, and, you know, I never heard him curse.'

Alan remains a huge part of Preston North End's history. He made a club record 513 appearances, and one of the highlights of his time there was the 1964 FA Cup final defeat by West Ham United. Preston twice led in the game, but a Ronnie Boyce goal in the ninetieth minute denied Kelly a winner's medal.

Alan was named Preston's first Player of the Year in 1967–68 and finally got his hands on a medal in English football when he won a Third Division Championship medal in 1970–71 to add to the League winner's medal and FAI Cup medals he won with Drumcondra.

IRELAND CAREER AND MANAGEMENT

Alan Kelly was already an international goalkeeper by the time he made his Preston North End debut in 1961. In a seventeen-year career, he won the first of forty-seven caps in a friendly against West Germany in 1956 at the tender age of twenty. Having successfully defended against all German attempts on goal in that match, Kelly kept his place on the team for a World Cup qualifying game against England at Wembley. Unfortunately England thrashed Ireland 5–1.

It epitomises the managing policy of the FAI and their committee in that period that after this defeat Kelly was left out of the side for a five-year period, and a string of other goalkeepers were used in Irish games including Tommy Godwin, Jimmy O'Neill and Noel Dwyer. This inconsistency in the selection process did not help the development of the team or individual players, and this lack of direction was proof, if it was needed, that a full-time manager was the only way for the Irish team to successfully develop.

In 1961 Preston were demoted from the First Division and Jimmy Milne was appointed as the new manager of the team. Under Milne's regime Kelly became the first choice goalkeeper. This consistency at club level saw him finally reach his potential and saw him regain his place on the Irish won his third cap in a 3–2 defeat by Austria at Dalymount Park in April 1962 but, despite the loss, managed to keep his place for the next nine games, during which time Ireland reached the European Championship quarter-finals. Despite this he was left out of the squad to play the qualifiers for the 1966 World Cup finals in England.

Towards the end of the 1960s Kelly regained his place on the team and in October 1972 became the first goalkeeper to captain Ireland. Unfortunately that game finished in a 2–1 defeat to the Soviet Union.

Following his forced retirement from football due to a shoulder injury, Kelly joined North End's coaching staff and was eventually promoted to assistant manager under Nobby Stiles in 1977. In 1980 he briefly managed the Republic of Ireland side, presiding over the team for one match, against Switzerland. The game was a one-sided affair, with Ireland dominating the Swiss. Don Givens and Gerry Daly scored the goals that gave Kelly a 2–0 win.

His assistant manager on the day, Eoin Hand, recalls, 'When Alan Kelly became manager he got in touch with me. We were good friends from playing together for Ireland and had always got on well. He asked me if I would be his assistant. Alan had actually been Johnny Giles' assistant [Kelly stood in for Johnny on two occasions, and did not taste defeat in those matches either, as Ireland won both], so all the players knew him well, and he had their respect. However, Alan was still involved with Preston North End, and the club put a bit of pressure on him, I think. He also had a sports business in Preston, and in the end he decided not to take the role full-time and to return to Preston.'

Gerry Peyton, who played under Alan in his only game as Ireland manager, remembers, 'We beat Switzerland that day. We were missing a lot of big names, but, as it turned out, we won, and Alan Kelly is still the only manager to have a 100 per cent record to this day. As a goalkeeper coach and assistant manager he was very well liked. He introduced some good exercises for the keepers, and he was a legend of the Irish game. For me, he is the best goalkeeper ever to have pulled on an Ireland shirt. There was an awful lot of respect for him within the team.

'As a goalkeeper coach now myself, I understand more than most that there is a lot of psychology involved in preparing keepers for games. The right word at the right time can really help a keeper, and Alan was very good at that. He would never put you under too much pressure. Another thing about goalkeepers is timing, knowing when to train hard and when to push players. Alan always had good knowledge of our opponents and what we would face.'

Despite returning to North End as a coach, Kelly did not have to wait too long before he got his chance to be a boss, and in 1983 he was appointed manager of the team. His first full season at the club saw them finish sixteenth in Division Three. Following a bad run of results over the Christmas period of the next season, he resigned in February 1985. Kelly's time at Preston North End had come to an end after almost twenty-seven years of service, but with Alan junior soon to take his position between the posts at Deepdale, the Kelly legacy at the club would continue.

Life away from Preston began with a brief coaching spell with Everton before Kelly made the biggest decision of his career and decided to go to the USA. He spent the remainder of his life there, beginning his state-side adventure in Washington DC before later moving to Maryland.

In America he continued to coach, spending five seasons with Washington's DC United, where he helped produce talented goalkeepers such as Mark Simpson, Tom Presthus and Scott Garlick, who all recall Kelly fondly. For Mark Simpson, himself now a coach at DC United, you get a sense that Alan Kelly senior was more than a coach. He was a man who was respected and a good guy to have around. His time spent in America, much like his time spent at Bray and Preston, seems to have left a lasting impression on the people he interacted with, and you get a real sense of who he was from them: 'Alan was so straightforward and as far away from being a complicated man as I ever met,' says Simpson. 'To me he was not just a coach but also a friend. Some of my fondest moments in his company were outside of football. I was thirty years old when I met him, and even though there was a thirty-year age gap between us, we got on really well. Alan would never BS you, and I appreciated that.

'He was always telling stories – they used to come thick and fast. The funny thing was he used to tell a story and then a month later he would come in and tell the same story again, although it would be just as funny the second time round. If you said anything to him, he would just tell you to go away and continue talking.

'We used to catch up every now and again at the DC reunions. I met him in 2007 and again in 2008. Sadly he won't be with us this year, and we will miss him. When we caught up it was like we had never been apart.

'Alan was very humble, and it almost felt like he did not want people to know about his achievements. I think he is the only Ireland goalkeeper inducted into the Hall of Fame, and he had a stand named after him at Preston. He was a legend of the game. During training we used to tease him about it. But in a nice way. We would call him "the Legend".

'Joking aside, Alan was a massive influence on my career. Not only while I was playing but also since I have become a coach. The game itself might have changed, and still be changing, but the basic concepts of positioning and mental strength remain the same. As a goalkeeping coach he was old school. He would push me, Tom [Presthus] and Scott [Garlick] hard. He was a good motivator and always on your side. His philosophy was for us to do the basic things well, not to drop our heads and to have good starting positions. He helped raise my game and my understanding of it.

'Alan came to DC United in 1997. The season before we had won the Championship in the first season of Major League Soccer. For me personally it was a Cinderella story. Before I joined DC I had played futsal [indoor soccer] for eight years, which was prior to the advent of the MLS. It was played on converted hockey pitches. Futsal helped me dispel the myth about keepers and their footballing skills. In futsal the keeper is almost like a defender and has to be able to pick a pass, so when the MLS was starting I felt I had an edge over other keepers, and I decided to give it a go. I went on trial with 160 other players all hoping to get drafted for DC. I missed the boat the first time, as I was injured, and in the trial I played for seventy-five minutes but was not picked; I returned to lower league football. However, about ten days later I got my big chance, as the goalkeeper at DC was injured. I was thirty at the time, and this was my big chance. The first season I started on the bench, but I was patient and eventually got my chance.

'Even though we had won the Championship, there really wasn't much goalkeeping coaching. For one thing, there was no coach, and we only had two goalkeepers. We trained with the team and our training was mainly six-a-side on big pitches. When Alan joined the team nothing changed at first. He basically observed us and our training. The first major change he introduced was that we did not train with the team any more. We would do our warm-ups and then practise diving and catching crosses. Later on when we joined in the five- and six-a-side games Alan would be behind the goals, whispering advice into our ears.'

'Everything was geared to preparing us for games and building our concentration,' says Tom Presthus. 'The success of DC at that time meant that the main purpose of the goalkeeper in the team was not to keep us in games but to be alert enough to make one or two saves when called upon. One of Alan's key coaching skills was to help us concentrate for those moments.

'He had a number of sayings he would call upon during training. For example, "one save and one save only" and "kick the ball off your face", which basically meant that you were to use any part of your body to make a save, be it your hands, face or, if required, private parts.

'Alan had a good sense of humour. He was very witty and liked a laugh. I had not seen him for a while – it must have been nearly four years – but when we finally caught up it was like we had never been apart. I can't imagine anyone would have ever thought ill of him. He had a glass of White Zinfandel, and although it was hard to get old football stories out of him – he left that to others – he sat and talked for hours about things outside of football.

'He was very loyal to us goalkeepers. If you had a bad game, he would protect you in front of the managers and coaches, but behind closed doors he would tell you how it was and give you his opinions. He exposed your problem to you and would be tough on you, but in front of everyone else he supported you.

'We won the Championship again in 1997 and 1999, while we reached the finals in 1998. I think in the USA nobody really had any idea about his standing in the game. He probably did not get the respect he deserved, outside of the people he worked with. That said, Scott, Mark and I had the utmost respect for him and his achievements.'

Scott Garlick actually began his goalkeeping career in Ireland: 'It's funny, you know, but before I played in America with DC United, I played for Waterford United, so I was very familiar with Alan Kelly senior and also his son Alan junior, who was with Sheffield United at that time.

'When I actually met him, he was great. I mean, he was a legend of the game, and from the first day we hit it off. On a personal level, he was very good for my career. He lobbied for me and helped prepare me for my first start for DC. I suppose my game had evolved more than that of other American keepers from my time spent in Ireland. The football there was similar to in England. There were lots of crosses and the ball was constantly in and around the box, so in that respect I was a bit ahead of other keepers in the country.

'I remember my first game, though. I let in a bad goal, as I tried to dribble the ball out of the box and was caught out. As I looked over to Alan his expression said, "I want to kill you", but he was very supportive and later told me, "We all do it, so forget about it and learn from it."

'Even though he had high standards he brought a human element to coaching. A lot of coaches do not understand keepers, and sometimes goalkeeping coaches side with the manager of the team, but Alan always had our back. We worked for him, and he defended us.

'Alan was very old school. His training was influenced by the way he played the game. We would work on building strength and saving shots. And he had a good shot on him. He would fire the ball at us from all over the pitch. He kept it simple. We worked with medicine balls to build our strength, and he worked us like boxers. He'd jam the medicine balls into our stomachs to build us up.

'Alan was a very humble man. There were no airs or graces about him, especially given what he had achieved in the game. You could go and have a drink with, and he really did like a glass of white wine. We met a couple of times at DC Championship reunions, and I appreciate having had the chance to meet up with him again. He never got the credit for the part he played in those Championships, but he was a massive part of the success at DC. He helped create a dynasty there. We won the Championship with four different keepers playing, and anyone at a top club will tell you it is not easy to replace a keeper. Think of United after Schmeichel or Chelsea without Cech, and you see how important the role of goalkeeper coach is. He kept us competitive and ready for action.'

THE FAMILY

Both Alan Kelly's sons followed in their father's footsteps and became goalkeepers. His eldest son Gary began his career with

Newcastle United in 1984, under Jack Charlton. In five years he made just over fifty League appearances for the club before he had spells with Blackpool (month loan), Bury, West Ham (loan) and Oldham. Gary's career wound down with shorts spells at Northwich Victoria, Sheffield United and Leigh Genesis.

Younger son and namesake Alan junior started his career at Preston North End who were in the Fourth Division. After seven years he moved on to Sheffield United and remained there until 1999, when he transferred to Blackburn Rovers. He stayed with this team until his retirement in 2004. He also won thirty-four caps for the Republic of Ireland, and was a member of the 1994 and 2002 World Cup squads, although as a reserve he did not play in any of the games. Following in his father's footsteps, Alan is now involved with the Irish team and is currently their goalkeeping coach.

Sadly, Alan Kelly senior died in May 2009, but through his sons the Kelly name will live on in the footballing world. Kelly senior will never be forgotten and such was the impression that he made on his former clubs that both Bray and Preston honoured his achievements. At Bray he was named an honorary life president, while Preston ensured that his name will forever be etched in North End folklore when they named a stand at Deepdale the Alan Kelly Town End in his honour.

ALAN KELLY'S CLUB MANAGERIAL HONOURS RECORD:

1997 MLS Supporters' Shield winners
1997 MLS Cup Champions

1998 CONCACAF Champions Cup Champions
1998 InterAmerican Cup Champions
1999 MLS Supporters' Shield winners
1999 MLS Cup Champions

ALAN KELLY'S IRELAND RECORD:

Total number of games in charge: 1
Total number of wins: 1 (ratio 100.00%)
Total number of draws: 0 (ratio 0.00%)
Total number of losses: 0 (ratio 0.00%)
Biggest win: 2–0 *v.* Switzerland
Biggest defeat: none
Longest run of games without defeat: 1

ALAN KELLY'S RESULTS AS IRELAND MANAGER:

Date	Home/ Away	Opponent	Score	Result	Type of Fixture
26/03/1980	Home	Switzerland	2–0	W	Friendly

9

EOIN HAND

In football it is often possible to look back and identify a defining moment in the fortunes of a particular team or player. The career of Sir Alex Ferguson offers a prime example of this. Many people will recall that back in 1989 Manchester United had spent large sums of money on the likes of Gary Pallister and Paul Ince, and the team was expected to win the League. However, after a good start (they beat Arsenal 4–1) United's form took a dive, and the team went on a run that included a 5–1 defeat at the hands of their neighbours Manchester City. The media and fans alike were calling for Ferguson's head, but the board held firm, and later that season United won the FA Cup with a 1–0 replay win after the first game ended 3–3. History will tell you things turned out for the best. But it took a lucky win in the FA Cup to kick-start an era, and if things had not gone Ferguson's way, modern-day football would be very different.

Eoin was in charge of the Ireland team for five and a half years, from May 1980 to November 1985, and his reign ensured that he would be best remembered as the nearly man of Irish football. Eoin was the youngest man ever to manage the Republic of Ireland and with a bit more luck could have enjoyed the popularity, success and legacy that Jack Charlton did. Football – not to mention life in general – is filled with 'what if' moments, and that's what makes it the game it is. People love to read about failure just as much as they like to read about success.

Possibly the most enduring image of Hand's time in charge of Ireland was the picture beamed around the world of him with his head in his hands following a late goal conceded to Belgium. It told of the heartbreak of being so close to success. Sport needs nearly men, however, and Hand's tenure, despite its positives, ranks as one of the 'nearly' moments of Irish sport.

EARLY LIFE

The journey for Eoin Hand began in Dublin, where he was born in March 1946. He started his footballing career as a winger with Stella Maris, a noted Dublin feeder club famous for the footballers it has produced, including John Giles, Eamon Dunphy and Stephen Carr, before moving to centre half – it was in this position that Eoin started to make an impression. As a young seventeen-year-old, Hand caught the eye of Swindon Town and was signed up. However, the move was short-lived, with Eoin being released following Swindon's relegation to Division Three, and after only one season in England he returned to Ireland to rebuild his career in League of Ireland football. In the 1965–1966 seasons he played for Dundalk before moving to Shelbourne FC and then to Drumcondra, where he enjoyed his greatest success as a player. His performances for this club saw

Johnny Carey
relaxing with
his pipe in
1965.
*Courtesy of
Getty Images*

EUROPEAN NATIONS CUP

REPUBLIC OF

IRELAND

versus

TURKEY

DALYMOUNT PARK, DUBLIN

on

WEDNESDAY, 16th NOVEMBER, 1966

KICK-OFF 8 P.M.

OFFICIAL PROGRAMME 1/-   *Secretary.*

Programme from Ireland *v.*
Turkey 1966.
Author's own collection

Noel Cantwell with Dennis Viollet at the Boston Tea Men. *Courtesy of Dennis Wit, former Boston Tea Men player*

1979 New England Tea Men

1979 New England Tea Men team photo shoot – Noel Cantwell is in the middle. *Courtesy of Dennis Wit, former Boston Tea Men player*

CANTWELL IS TEAM MANAGER

THIRTY - FOUR - YEARS - OLD Cork-born dual soccer and cricket International Noel Cantwell (Manchester United) was unanimously appointed Republic of Ireland International Team Manager at last night's meeting of the F.A.I. Council in Dublin.

Cantwell, who has won 36 international soccer caps, had intimated to F.A.I. Secretary, Mr. Joe Wickham that Matt Busby had promised to release him on all occasions he was required.

Cantwell, has previously managed a Republic under-23 side against France at Dalymount, as well as sharing the managerial duties with Charlie Hurley (Sunderland) on a Continental tour two years ago.

The recommendations of the Emergency Committee following their meeting with the Referees' Society regarding adequate protection at League grounds produced a prolonged discussion.

The Emergency Committee made four recommendations which last night's Council meeting considered. The first, to the effect that all grounds be fenced in, was carried by nine votes to seven with ten abstentions.

PASSED

The second recommendation that safe dressing accommodation must

Left: Noel Cantwell is confirmed as Ireland team manager in 1968. *Courtesy of the Irish Independent archive*

Below left: Cantwell resigns as manager later that year. *Courtesy of the Irish Independent archive*

Below right: Programme from Ireland *v.* Austria, Nov. 1968. *Author's own collection*

Cantwell resigns

NOEL CANTWELL has resigned from the post of Republic of Ireland international soccer team manager because of the pressure of his commitments as manager of Coventry City.

Cantwell was appointed by the F.A.I. when he was a player with Manchester United, but his first official assignment did not come until he had taken over the managership of Coventry.

That was the Republic's European Nations Cup game against Czechoslovakia in Prague last May, and Cantwell had to opt out because of Coventry's predicament at the time.

Cantwell's only game as manager of the full Republic XI was last May, when the Republic drew 2-2 with Poland at Dalymount.

INTERNATIONAL MATCH

REPUBLIC OF

IRELAND

versus

AUSTRIA

SUNDAY,
10th NOVEMBER, 1968

DALYMOUNT PARK
DUBLIN

KICK-OFF 3.30 P.M.

OFFICIAL PROGRAMME

PRICE 1/-

Liam Rapple

Hon. Secretary.

Dacon (D.P.S.) Limited, 50 Lower Baggot Street, Dublin.

Charlie Hurley shaking hands with Denis Law before an FA Cup game in 1964.
Courtesy of Bob Thomas/Getty Images

Hurley is appointed player-coach of Ireland in November 1967. *Courtesy of the Irish Independent archive*

Hurley to be player-coach

IRISH SKIPPER Charlie Hurley will take on the post of player-coach to the Republic of Ireland team to play Czechoslovakia in the European Nations' Championship in Prague, on Wednesday (writes N. J. Dunne).

This was decided last night by the members of the International Selection Committee who discussed the question of a replacement for manager Noel Cantwell who is unable to make the trip because he has to take Coventry City to Blackpool for a week's special training.

F.A.I. secretary, Mr. J. I. Wickham, said last night: "We very much regret the fact that Cantwell will not be with the team but we understand his very heavy commitments with his club at the present time. Hurley has filled this post before and on our last tour of the Continent was jointly player-coach with Cantwell."

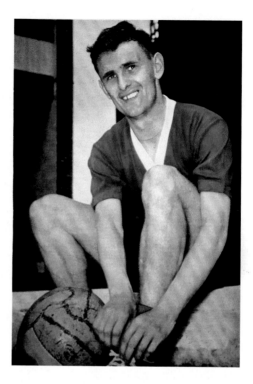

Mick Meagan in his playing days with Everton. *Courtesy of Sportsfile*

Passing on the knowledge – Liam Tuohy coaching kids in 1991.
Courtesy of Ray McManus/Sportsfile

Liam Tuohy with Johnny Fulham in 1982. *Courtesy of Ray McManus/ Sportsfile*

Seán Thomas.
Courtesy of the Irish Independent archive

Johnny Giles (*right*) shaking hands with Danish captain Per Rontved prior to the European Championship game in 1979 which resulted in a 2–0 Irish win. *Courtesy of Getty Images*

Master and Student – Johnny Giles with Liam Brady. *Courtesy of Getty Images*

A young Johnny Giles in 1975. *Picture from Switzerland v. Ireland away program 1975.*

Alan Kelly senior coaching at DC United. *Courtesy of DC United*

Programme from Alan Kelly senior's only game in charge – Ireland *v.* Switzerland.

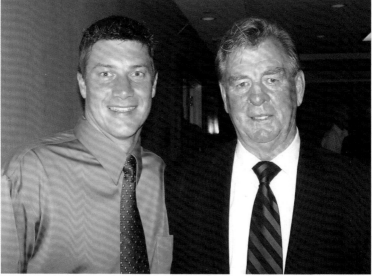

October 2007 – Alan Kelly senior with goalkeeper Mark Simpson at the DC United championship-winning team reunion dinner. *Courtesy of Mark Simpson*

Eoin Hand (*right*) remonstrates with Portuguese referee Raul Nazare after the World Cup qualifier against Belgium in 1981. *Courtesy of Ray McManus/Sportsfile*

Jack Charlton looking on during a European Championship qualifying game, Ireland *v.* Portugal, in November 1996. *Courtesy of David Maher/Sportsfile*

Charlton watching with intent in 1995. *Courtesy of David Maher/ Sportsfile*

Mick McCarthy consoling future manager Steve Staunton after defeat in the World Cup second round match against Spain in 2002. *Courtesy of David Maher/Sportsfile *EDI**

McCarthy at the end of the qualifier for the 2004 European Championships against Russia, with the final score in the background. *Courtesy of Brendan Moran/Sportsfile *EDI**

A young and upcoming manager – Brian Kerr in his early days. *Courtesy of St Patrick's Athletic*

Kerr talking tactics with Noel O'Reilly. *Courtesy of St Patrick's Athletic*

Celebrating a League win over Dundalk in 1996. *Courtesy of St Patrick's Athletic*

Plenty to think about post match – Don Givens at the Ireland *v.* Belgium UEFA Under-21 European Championship qualifier in 2006. *Courtesy of Ray Ryan/Sportsfile*

Steve Staunton applauding the fans in a rare moment of joy – a win over San Marino in November 2006. *Courtesy of Awaythelads.com*

Tactical decisions – Steve Staunton at the San Marino match in February 2007. *Courtesy of Awaythelads.com*

Giovanni Trapattoni getting animated during a game with Bulgaria in June 2009. *Courtesy of Awaythelads.com*

Giovanni Trapattoni, up close and personal. *Courtesy of Awaythelads.com*

him catch the eye of English sides once again and in October 1968 he was signed by Portsmouth FC for a transfer fee of £8,000. A more mature Hand soon settled into life in English football. A year after making the move to Portsmouth, Hand received his first call-up to the Irish squad and over the course of six years he would go on to win twenty caps.

As Hand recalls, 'I made my debut under Charlie Hurley. I had gone back to England and settled into the Portsmouth side and was playing good football. The call-up came from the FAI, and I made my way home for the game. I did not start but eventually came on as a sub for Mick Leech, who was actually a centre-forward. Charlie said to me, "Go up front." I replied, "I have never played there in my life," and he turned to me and said, "Aye, sure, go on there."

'I played for Ireland for six years and won nineteen caps, although I argue it's twenty, as I played in a game versus a West German B team. I think if that had been nowadays it would be about thirty or forty caps, given the amount of international games that countries now play. I never scored on home soil but managed two away goals, against Chile in Santiago and the USSR in Kiev.

'The highlight of my playing career for Ireland was a match against France in 1972 when we beat them 2–1. I played in midfield that night and set up a goal. It was a wet evening, and I remember I chased down a lost ball, won it and crossed it in for Ray Treacy to score. In that game I had a collision with the French goalkeeper, and the press were telling me that in the return game France had singled me out for some treatment. The word was that Raymond Domenech, who famously went on to become manager of France, was assigned to do a hatchet job on me. However, in the first five minutes I went in strong on him and did not see him again for the rest of the game.'

Hand stayed with Portsmouth until being released in 1976. He decided to move to South Africa, where he was offered a role as manager of Amazulu FC, a Durban-based club: 'My final game for Ireland was a 4–0 win over Turkey in which Don Givens scored four goals. Afterwards I had a chat with Johnny [Giles] and told him that I had committed to an offer in South Africa. I had fallen out with Ian St John at Portsmouth, as he'd said to me that it was highly likely that he would try out a youngster for the next campaign. It turned out that the youngster was David O'Leary.'

The spell in South Africa was to be shortlived, however, as the club failed to deliver on the promises made prior to his appointment. Hand returned to Ireland and was persuaded by Johnny Giles to return to playing at Shamrock Rovers. Rovers had a young squad and Giles needed the experience of Hand to help guide the team. Only nine games into his spell with Rovers, Hand made the move back to England, to Portsmouth. He left Portsmouth for the second time in 1979, having made almost 280 League game appearances for the club.

MANAGERIAL CAREER

Hand's previous experience in South Africa had not put him off management and after leaving Portsmouth he took the chance to become player-manager for Limerick FC. He made an immediate impression, with Limerick winning the League title in his first season. According to Johnny Matthews, 'Limerick was the making of him and set him up for the Ireland job. I was one of his first signings. Despite having doubts about the eighty-mile round trip for training, Eoin sold his vision to me, and I signed. Eoin was a good player and a good manager, probably one of the best I have played under, and I played under about thirty.

'That Limerick side was full of local players, which was the key to their success. We used to train together during the week, and the morning before a game we'd have another session and a meal. It helped create a real bond within the team. Despite being a young manager at the time Eoin was meticulous in his preparation. We used to travel overnight for games and even had a fitness coach, which was rare in League of Ireland football in those days.

'Eoin was very insightful and a good tactician. Gerry Duggan and I were the two wingers, but there was not the same rigidness that there is today. We had carte blanche to take on defenders and would swap wings on a regular basis. It was very much attacking football. I think nowadays coaches are all trained the same way and learn the same methods and use the same tactics. Eoin was different. He hated terrible soccer. If were we up against a six-foot centre-half, there was no point in hitting in high balls, so Eoin would switch things around. He'd move someone like Johnny Walsh, who was only five feet six inches, up front from midfield, and we would start playing the ball into his feet. Eoin was very adaptable and could change formations depending on the situation.

'Every week Eoin encouraged us to go out and play, and he kept us all on our toes. We had a small panel of about sixteen players, and each week you had to prove you were good enough to start. Eoin had no problem giving you a bollocking if you messed up, and you were never guaranteed to be in the side. Some weeks you would be on the left, other weeks on the right and at other times not in the team at all. It kept things fresh.

'Eoin was a players' man and could take a joke with the best of them. However, while he could be your best mate, reputations and friendships counted for nothing when it came to the team. His preparation was second to none.'

Those preparation skills, not to mention his success with Limerick, saw him catch the eye of the FAI, but if they needed further proof of his talent, a match against Real Madrid in the European Cup, Limerick's reward for winning the League, was a good start. That year Real Madrid reached the European Cup final and only conceded four goals during their run to the final. Two of those goals were scored by Limerick FC's Des Kennedy. The Lansdowne Road match ended in a 2–1 defeat; but for a couple of late goals and some unusual refereeing decisions, the result could have been very different. For Johnny Matthews, the Real Madrid games played a large part in Hand's appointment to the role of Ireland manager: 'Those were the games that brought him to the attention of the FAI. His preparation over the two legs made people sit up and take notice of him.

'It's interesting to note that the FAI claim League of Ireland football is making a lot of progress, but I think the reality is a lot different. Back then you only had one champion from each country qualifying for the European Cup, not like today when there are in effect four champions from some Leagues. Back then it was more luck of the draw, as the draw itself was open, and there were no qualifiers, as there are today. I suppose you could say getting drawn with Real Madrid was either lucky or unlucky, depending on your point of view, but for us it was amazing getting to pit our wits against superstars ten times better than us. However, we were not overawed. 'We gave them an awful fright in that first game, and it could have been a different story, as I had a goal disallowed. That said, the second leg was a different affair. We travelled to Madrid and were on the end of a 5–1 defeat.

'The experience of playing in the Bernabéu was one of the highlights of my career and one which will stay with me forever. I remember the day before the game we trained on the pitch and practised crosses. Eoin was studying the angles of the lights for the crosses, as the game was being played under floodlights. The next morning we trained again on the pitch, and it was rock hard, so we decided to wear soft studs. Well, once everyone had left the stadium the Spanish turned on the sprinkler system and soaked the pitch. That evening when we returned for the warm-up before the game we kept slipping on the pitch. Eoin sent one of the backroom boys back to the hotel in a taxi to get the screw in studs. Eoin had been naive and they had caught him out, but he did not let it hamper our build-up.

'Unfortunately, we lost the second leg, but we still managed to give mighty Real a fright, and who knows what might have happened if my goal in the first leg had not been disallowed. Afterwards a few of us got the opportunity to go out on the town with Laurie Cunningham [Real Madrid's first English player], and that in itself was an amazing experience. Cunningham was delighted to have some English-speaking friends to show around the town, and he definitely showed us the nightspots. He was like a god over there, with doors opening for him wherever he went. It was an insight into the life of a top footballer.

'I think League of Ireland football teams were more honest in their approach to games and were naive to the tricks of European sides. I remember being at Waterford United, and we were drawn against Omonia Nicosia. Alfie Hale gave us a perfect start, and we were 2–0 up after ten minutes. Then Omonia changed their goalkeeper, who had never played on grass, and he managed to keep them in the game before they pulled a goal back, though we still fancied our chances.

'When we got to Cyprus for the second leg we were in for a shock. The "pitch" was a dirt pitch and not only that, there was a power failure, so the game was moved from a 7 p.m. kick-off time to a 2 p.m. kick-off, so the match was played in searing heat. The dirt pitch was being watered, and we kept running behind the goals to where the water cannon was to cool down.'

Des Kennedy was also a member of the successful Limerick team of the late 1970s and 1980s, and famously scored against Real Madrid in the European Cup. He recalls Hand as being 'strict but fair. You did what he wanted you to do, but it helped that he would do it too. If he wanted you to run ten kilometres, he would do it as well. And he never demanded things that you could not achieve. I mean, I was a different player to say the likes of Gerry Duggan, who was fast, so he worked to those strengths.

'When he first took charge we used to train in the market field, but shortly afterwards he moved training out to the university. There were all-weather pitches and running tracks out there. It was much more professional. He had played in England, and it showed. He trained us like we were professionals. We trained Tuesdays, Wednesdays, Thursdays and Saturdays, with a light session of set-pieces on the Sunday before a game. He took us up another level and raised the bar.

'The Madrid game was the reward for winning the League, but the League was the greatest thrill, as it had been twenty years since we had last won a title. Eoin set everything up for us to win that title. He treated each game differently, although he liked us to play a certain way. But, again, it was down to the set-up and facilities. If we were playing Sligo or Dundalk, we would travel up the night before. These things help.

'If you gave it your all and did the business, Eoin appreciated it. The bus home would be great fun. Eoin loved a bit of fun and a singsong. We would often stop for a bite to eat after a game, and if we had done well, Eoin would say, "Have a pint on me, lads."'

Johnny Walsh was also a member of that famous Limerick team: 'He had played in England, and when he first came to Limerick as player-manager he was in his mid-thirties and still very fit. Limerick were only semi-professional. We weren't used to the full-time training. It was very different to what we were used to. There was a lot of focus on ball work and organisation.

'Eoin was a good man manager and treated everyone as individuals. When he took the Ireland job he was very good to me. He gave me my only cap. It was on a tour of America, and we played against Trinidad and Tobago. A lot of the players from England were unavailable for the tour, and I got called in. It was a wonderful experience. We played four games in total over there, and I was involved in two of them, although only one was a full international.'

Hand's reward for his success with Limerick was the biggest job in Irish soccer, the job of Ireland's national team manager. Initially he worked both jobs, but eventually he resigned from Limerick to focus on the Irish job. As Eoin himself states, 'I had been the assistant for Alan Kelly's only game in charge, and then the chance to manage Ireland came about because of my time with Limerick. Alan and I were good friends from playing together for Ireland. He had been Johnny Giles' assistant and had also just become the Preston North End manager. Preston put a bit of pressure on Alan, and he also had a sports business in Preston, so in the end he decided to return to England full-time.

'I was caretaker for one game, against Argentina. We put on a decent show and ended up only losing 1–0. Maradona played. I was then interviewed by a panel of twelve people for the job. Paddy Mulligan also went for it, but I ended up getting it. I was Ireland's youngest-ever manager.'

Hand was very young when he was put in charge. In fact, he was only thirty-four when he found himself thrust into the position of managing the golden crop of Ireland footballers, players such as Mark Lawrenson, Frank Stapleton, Kevin Moran, Kevin Sheedy and David O'Leary. These were big-name players, playing for the biggest sides in England at the time – Liverpool, Manchester United, Arsenal and Everton. If you compare the Ireland side now to then, John O'Shea is the only player who plays for a top-four side. There were, therefore, a lot of big personalities in the changing-room in those days, but although they were trained by top managers, they still needed to be managed on the international stage.

According to Kevin Sheedy and Gerry Peyton, who both played for Ireland at that time, Hand suffered a little from a lack of experience at international level and this led to some problems. 'Eoin had experienced success with Limerick FC,' says Sheedy, 'but he was not prepared for international football. The demands and expectations are different. There were big players in the team at that time, and Eoin did not have the necessary experience to know how to handle them properly. They would often dictate how we played. There were a lot of big personalities within that team. It was different when Jack came in. It was a case of his way or the high way. Eoin was a bit too easily influenced by others.

'I remember we played against Switzerland and won 2–0. I scored one of the goals. We then travelled to Russia for the next game, and I was not even in the squad, never mind the team. Eoin struggled a bit with the man-management side of things. He would chop and change his mind, but there was a lot of pressure on him.'

Peyton backs up Sheedy's point of view: 'Eoin was Alan's assistant for the game against Switzerland and was already known to the FAI, as he had done a great job with Limerick, so he got his chance. Being honest, I think Eoin is a good guy, and I like him as a man, but the role might have been a bit overwhelming for him. There were a lot of big personalities in that team. Liam Brady, David O'Leary, Frank Stapleton, Kevin Moran, Paul McGrath, Mark Lawrenson and Ronnie Whelan were all playing with top sides. Eoin might have been a little intimidated by the players.

'It was hard to know where we stood under him. I don't think he ever knew his best squad. For example, Packie and I rotated the support-keeper role under Seamus McDonagh, and the two of us rarely travelled together.

'That said, we were very unlucky not to get to a tournament under Eoin, and we came close to qualifying for the 1982 World Cup. We were a "hit the post team" under Eoin – nearly but not quite. Ireland had a very talented group of players at that time, but you need confidence, and qualifying for a tournament would have given us that confidence.'

Eoin's first qualifying tournament with Ireland was for the 1982 World Cup, where they finished level with France as runners-up behind Belgium, but goal difference cost them a place in Spain. In fact was it not for a perfectly legitimate goal being disallowed in the away game to Belgium, then Ireland would have been on the plane to Spain and their first place in a World Cup. If that decision had been reversed, Ireland could have embarked on a golden era long before Jack Charlton took over.

Hand remembers it all too well: 'I think the Belgium match wasted us. We had a perfectly good goal disallowed. It was a Brady and Stapleton routine from the Arsenal training ground, but for reasons unknown it was disallowed. Their goal was even more dubious. They got a corner, and we managed to clear it. The ball fell to Eric Gerets, and he wangled a free-kick out of Steve Heighway. The free-kick came in, and one of their players nearly came in on top of Seamus McDonagh, but Jan Ceulemans scored, and that result cost us. Belgium ended up topping the group.

'If we had managed a draw in that game, we would have been in the World Cup. After the game Jack Charlton came into the changing-room. He told us that we had been robbed and that the decisions had been crazy. If things had turned out differently in that match, Jack might not have become the manager.

'We knew we had a good team, though. We scored seventeen goals that campaign. Everyone was disappointed, but we played some really attractive football, and the players were allowed to express themselves. We used to get only two days to prepare for games. If we had qualified for Spain '82 we would have had a six-week build-up. Success breeds success, and if we had been able to prepare together like that, we could have done well.

'As a manager, however, I didn't think of myself. Naturally I was disappointed, but I was more disappointed for the players, the likes of Liam Brady, Frank Stapleton, Gerry Daly and Tony Galvin, all good players who deserved to play at major tournaments.

'As a reward for nearly qualifying we got a tour to Brazil. The Falklands War between Britain and Argentina was going on at the time, so we struggled to get a team together, the English clubs being very reluctant to release their Irish players. [The initial itinerary included a game with Argentina and they felt it was inappropriate for representatives of English clubs to be involved in such a game.] I remember voicing my concerns to the FAI, but I was politely told I was a manager not a politician. [The FAI eventually smoothed over the situation by cancelling the game with Argentina but the damage had been done.] Ron Atkinson was very angry about the tour, and a lot of fellas did not travel. As it was, we had a weak team, and we lost 7–0 to Brazil, who managed to reach the semi-finals in 1982.

'There was a bit of picking up to be done for the 1984 European Championship qualifiers, where we were drawn with Spain, Holland, Iceland and Malta. We managed to draw 3–3 at home with Spain but lost away, and we lost twice to Holland, although we beat both Iceland and Malta. That second campaign was tough – it was a case of second-season syndrome, but in a qualifying tournament sense. We were missing a couple of key players during that campaign and were never able to put out our strongest team.

'My final campaign was the qualifiers for the 1986 World Cup in Mexico. We were drawn with Denmark, the USSR, Switzerland and Norway. We lost our first game to Norway, who, although not the force they are today, were on the up. Again, we did not have our strongest team out – that always seemed to be the case. We had a great team but a small squad, and we felt every injury.

'We needed to beat the USSR away in Moscow. I knew that over in Moscow you ran the risk of "Moscow tummy". I wanted to bring over our own chef to avoid any such risks – most national sides always travel with their own chefs these days. Anyway, the FAI did not see the logic of it, so I brought along my wife to cook food for the team.

'We ended up finishing fourth in that campaign, and even though I knew I was not going to get offered another term in charge, I didn't want another campaign anyway. That third campaign had been tough. I had a young family, and they often suffered as a result of my commitments to the team. After six years in the job I knew what it was like to be a hero and then the opposite. At that time I was managing St Patrick's Athletic and also running a business in Dublin, so it was very demanding.

'The Ireland manager's job was part-time before Jack Charlton, but it was very much a full-time commitment. I tried to get as involved as I could. I would fly to England the Wednesday before a game and watch the match that had the most Irish players in it. Even though I was part-time, I worked full-time on the role. I would scout the opposition – I travelled to Moscow to see Russia play Denmark, and I watched France play – and I would try to exploit any weaknesses I saw. I'd head over to England quite regularly to see the players in action. It was very full on.

'In those days Manchester United versus Spurs was a good game for Irish players. As soon as the match was over I would be in the secretary's office ringing around to the other clubs to see if the players could get over to Ireland as soon as possible. I also wanted to know about any injuries as soon as possible. If you had left it to the FAI, you would only find out on the Monday or maybe the Tuesday who was not available. I tried my best to change things in other ways for the team – for example, travel arrangements and hotels. Ireland used to stay in the Green Isle Hotel and then train over in Crumlin. The pitch was not in a good state, and we had to travel over there. I changed it so that we stayed out by the airport in the International Hotel, as it was called then. We then trained over the road. And I would always interact with the travel agent about the flights and hotels for away games. I know that Johnny Giles, for example, was never involved in this side of things, but I felt it was one area that I could improve upon.

'We only had two days preparation, so there was not much time for tactics. We only had one winger at a time, so I played a 4–3–3 system. I tried to keep it as simple as possible, and I played a system to suit the players. Jack did the opposite. He had a system, and the players had to fit into it. It's hard to argue with his philosophy, as he got results, but I think the football we played was more attractive, if not quite cavalier. It's disappointing that we did not qualify for a major tournament.

'There were strong characters in my team, although not as many as there were in Jack's and Mick's teams, and if they were out, you really missed them. Since the retirement of Roy Keane, Ireland are missing that a bit, although Richard Dunne is a strong character in the team. These are men who do not need telling what to do. The likes of Kevin Moran, Andy Townsend, Paul McGrath, Mick McCarthy, Ronnie Whelan and Ray Houghton were all men who knew what was needed.

'My last game in charge was a 4–1 defeat to Denmark. They had a great team then, with Michael Laudrup one of their stars. I indulged myself that day, and my experiment answered a couple of questions I had. We played a 3–4–3 system but were rubbish and could not handle the system or the Danes. We scored first through Stapleton, but they hit back with four. I had Kevin Moran man-mark Laudrup, with Lawrenson as sweeper, but the players were not used to it. They all played 4–4–2 and 4–3–3 with their clubs. It confirmed what I knew, though, about the preparation needed. Competitive matches were about getting results, and you could not try out new things in these games, while you were often missing the big names for the friendlies. I remember playing against Israel and adopting a diamond formation. Again, we lost, as the players were not used to it. One day's preparation was not enough.

'If you look at my record, my win ratio at competitive level is quite good. Out of twenty-three competitive games I won nine, drew five and lost nine, while in seventeen friendly games my record is two wins, four draws and eleven defeats – big difference.'

After the close call of the 1982 qualifying tournament, expectations were high for the European qualifiers in 1984. However, Eoin and Ireland failed to deliver once again, finishing third in their qualifying group, four points off group winners Spain and runners-up Holland. Following this Eoin decided once again to combine a club job with the national job and became the manager of St Patrick's Athletic. A disappointing eleventh place finish in the League saw Eoin leave the club after only one season. Two successive third place finishes were followed by a fourth place for Ireland in the qualifying groups for the 1986 World Cup. That campaign saw Ireland suffer a humiliating defeat to Norway (who were not the international force that they became in the 1990s and 2000s) and the team appeared to be moving backwards. Hand finished the term of his contract and parted ways with the FAI. He was later replaced by Jack Charlton.

According to Johnny Matthews, 'the general feeling was that Eoin was definitely unlucky during his time as Ireland manager. He narrowly failed to qualify for the World Cup, missing out to a late goal and having a genuine goal disallowed. The FAI should have given him more time. He suffered from the fact that he had not played at the highest level and was not a big name.

'Hand was and still is the youngest-ever manager of Ireland, and he probably needed more experience or even a guiding hand in the set-up – a bit like Steve Staunton received – to help his development. A lot of kudos goes to Jack and the work he did, but the groundwork for that was laid by Eoin. He was the initial advocate of the FAI's grandparent rule – or "find an Irishman" rule, as I call it – that became popular under Jack Charlton.'

Dave Langan enjoyed his most productive spell in an Ireland jersey under the tenure of Eoin Hand and fondly recalls Hand as one of the nicest men he ever came across: 'He was very good for me and my career. He gave me the most caps of any manager I played under, and he was always giving me good press. Eoin was different from his predecessor Johnny Giles, in that whereas Johnny was never too worried about the opposition and concentrated more on the players and their formation, Eoin focused more on the opposition and their players.

'Eoin was not just a good manager, he was also a great singer and loved to be involved in the singsong after the game. He was a young manager at the time, but he and his assistant Terry

Conroy were a good team. I remember at one stage I was out injured for eighteen months, and Eoin would ring and ask me how my treatment was progressing and when I'd be able to return. It was great management, and made you feel wanted.

'I think he liked my work rate. Eoin liked his players, quite naturally, to give 100 per cent. I remember one match in particular. We were playing Argentina, and Eoin asked me to man-mark Diego Maradona. It was one of the highlights of my career and a great show of faith in my ability. I didn't get a roasting, either, although it was a friendly, so I am not sure if he was on top of his game. That said, I have never seen a player like him. His balance was amazing, and he'd just bounce off you.'

In 1988 Hand was appointed manager of Huddersfield Town and remained there until 1992. His career in management finished with a brief spell in charge of Shelbourne in 1994: 'Managing Ireland opened doors for me though, and helped raise my profile, especially in England. It was a great help, and managers knew who I was from dealing with me at international level. It was a great experience. When I took over I was thirty-four years old and when I left I was thirty-nine. I probably knew more at the end than I did at the start. It seems, though, that there is an unwritten law that you never get a second chance to manage your country.

'When I was Limerick manager I was full-time with part-time players. When I was Ireland manager I was part-time with full-time professionals. It was not until I managed Huddersfield that I was finally full-time with full-time players. A manager's job, whether it is supposed to be full-time or part-time, is an 8 a.m. to 10 p.m. job.

'After the Ireland job I headed to Saudi Arabia, where the

standard was not as good but the money was much better. It was a role whereby I had to develop skills rather than work with the finished article. When you were working with the top players you never had to worry about their skill level.'

At the age of sixty-three, Eoin Hand remains an integral part of football in Ireland. Commuting between his home in Kerry and Dublin, Hand is the FAI's player-support service manager, a role that involves helping young players. His assistant from his management days with Ireland, Terry Conroy, is also involved in the FAI player-welfare group. This represents part of the FAI's commitment to football and gives guidelines to parents and guardians to help them encourage young people to play football. It also aims to enable coaches to maximise players' enjoyment and potential. This is a massively important role in the future of Irish football, and it's a testimony to what Hand has to offer that he is involved.

EOIN HAND'S CLUB MANAGERIAL HONOURS RECORD:

League of Ireland: Limerick FC 1980
FAI Cup: Limerick 1982

EOIN HAND'S IRELAND RECORD:

Total number of games in charge: 40
Total number of wins: 11 (ratio 27.50%)
Total number of draws: 9 (ratio 22.50%)

Total number of losses: 20 (ratio 50.00%)

Biggest win: 8–0 *v.* Malta

Biggest defeat: 0–7 *v.* Brazil

Longest run without defeat: 5 games

EOIN HAND'S RESULTS AS IRELAND MANAGER:

Date	Home/ Away	Opponent	Score	Result	Type of Fixture
16/05/1980	Home	Argentina	0–1	L	Friendly
10/09/1980	Home	Holland	2–1	W	Competitive
15/10/1980	Home	Belgium	1–1	D	Competitive
28/10/1980	Away	France	0–2	L	Competitive
19/11/1980	Home	Cyprus	6–0	W	Competitive
24/02/1981	Home	Wales	1–3	L	Friendly
25/03/1981	Away	Belgium	0–1	L	Competitive
29/04/1981	Home	Czechoslovakia	3–1	W	Friendly
21/05/1981	Away	West Germany	0–3	L	Friendly
23/05/1981	Away	Poland	0–3	L	Friendly
09/09/1981	Away	Holland	2–2	D	Competitive
14/10/1981	Home	France	3–2	W	Competitive
28/04/1982	Away	Algeria	0–2	L	Friendly
22/05/1982	Away	Chile	0–1	L	Friendly
27/05/1982	Away	Brazil	0–7	L	Friendly
30/05/1982	Away	Trinidad	1–2	L	Friendly
22/09/1982	Away	Holland	1–2	L	Competitive
13/10/1982	Home	Iceland	2–0	W	Competitive

17/11/1982	Home	Spain	3–3	D	Competitive
30/03/1983	Away	Malta	1–0	W	Competitive
27/04/1983	Away	Spain	0–2	L	Competitive
21/09/1983	Away	Iceland	3–0	W	Competitive
12/10/1983	Home	Holland	2–3	L	Competitive
16/11/1983	Home	Malta	8–0	W	Competitive
04/04/1984	Away	Israel	0–3	L	Friendly
23/05/1984	Home	Poland	0–0	D	Friendly
03/06/1984	Away	China	1–0	W	Friendly
08/08/1984	Home	Mexico	0–0	D	Friendly
12/09/1984	Home	Soviet Union	1–0	W	Competitive
17/10/1984	Away	Norway	0–1	L	Competitive
14/11/1984	Away	Denmark	0–3	L	Competitive
05/02/1985	Home	Italy	1–2	L	Friendly
26/03/1985	Away	England	1–2	L	Friendly
01/05/1985	Home	Norway	0–0	D	Competitive
26/05/1985	Away	Spain	0–0	D	Friendly
27/05/1985	Away	Israel	0–0	D	Friendly
02/06/1985	Home	Switzerland	3–0	W	Competitive
11/09/1985	Away	Switzerland	0–0	D	Competitive
16/10/1985	Away	Soviet Union	0–2	L	Competitive
13/11/1985	Home	Denmark	1–4	L	Competitive

10

JACK CHARLTON

Good things come in pairs. Just like Bonnie and Clyde, Lennon and McCartney, Barbie and Ken, and Batman and Robin, the pairing of Jack Charlton with the Ireland soccer team was a match made in heaven. After the lack of success under Eoin Hand, and because of the perceived lack of a big-name Irish manager to lead the national side, the FAI took an unprecedented risk when they decided to appoint a man from outside Ireland. Their decision to hire an Englishman as the next Ireland manager was probably one of the bravest moves they ever made, and they certainly reaped the rewards.

While it is fair to say that Jack Charlton might not have been the first choice of the fans, he did not have to wait long to change people's minds, and he will forever be etched in Irish footballing folklore – and not too many Englishmen can claim that honour. The man transformed Irish football in the 1980s and secured Ireland's status as one of the most feared teams in Europe, with his own unique brand of football, albeit one that was often criticised. However, few can doubt the success that was achieved, not to mention the heroes he helped create for young footballers around the country. His success contributed to the increased popularity of soccer in Ireland, really challenging the supremacy that the Gaelic Athletic Association (GAA) enjoyed at that time.

In an amazing six-year period from 1988 to 1994, Charlton guided Ireland to sixth place in the FIFA world rankings, the highest Ireland have ever reached in these rankings, not to mention two World Cups and one European Championship. In total Charlton reigned supreme for ninety-four matches. During that time a legend was born.

EARLY LIFE

The future Ireland manager was born John Charlton in Ashington, Northumberland, on 8 May 1935 into a family that had a strong tradition in the game. And it was not just any family, but probably one of the most famous in English footballing history. 'You have to remember, football was part of me,' Jack says. 'I was brought up in a footballing family. My mother was a Milburn [Jack's cousin was Jackie Milburn, who played for Newcastle, while his uncles George and Jack both played for Leeds, as well as Bradford and Chesterfield respectively] and my brother Bob was a player [with Manchester United], so I was involved with football at a young age, and I understood it.'

It is hard to live in the shadow of any successful sibling, but when the sibling in question survives the Munich air disaster, becomes the top scorer for England and is a Manchester United legend you get an idea of how difficult it might have been for Jack Charlton to make a life as a footballer. And it is fair to say that while he was a success in his own right, the young Jack Charlton was initially overshadowed by his brother Bobby and, with the exception of Leeds United and Ireland fans, he will probably always remain in that shadow.

Bobby Charlton's career is imprinted on the minds of English football fans who are old enough to remember him play. Such was the impact that Jack's baby brother made, that his England goal-scoring record of forty-nine remains to this day, some thirty-nine years since his last appearance in an England shirt at the 1970 World Cup. That said, both brothers are legends of the game and World Cup winners.

And while he might have been younger, Bobby got his break earlier than his big brother when he was taken on by Manchester United while Jack was doing his national service.

Despite his status within the game, Big Jack had an unconventional route into football, a journey that is very different from that of most modern-day footballers. At the tender age of fifteen Jack began working down the local pit as a coal miner, but soon decided that a life in the pits was not for him and resigned to join the police cadets. During this time he continued to play amateur football when he could and soon caught the eye of Leeds United, who offered him a trial. This offer caused a huge dilemma for young Jack and the decision he made would shape the rest of his life, as the trial was to take place on the same day he had an interview for the police. Jack picked football. His trial was a success and in 1950 Leeds offered him apprentice terms. Two years later, at the age of seventeen, he signed professional terms with the club. The following year Big Jack made it into the senior side for the first time, and two years later he was a regular name on the team sheet.

The 1950s were a poor time for Leeds United, who were in the Second Division for much of the decade. However, the team finally won promotion to the First Division in 1957 and Jack's journey to the big time was complete. Leeds' first year back in the top flight started well, with the club sitting in second place after the first nine games of the season; however, disaster struck when the club's main stand was destroyed by fire. Everything from jerseys to the club records were burned. The club soldiered on, with a combination of insurance money and donations from the people of the Leeds contributing to the rebuilding of the stadium.

Despite their solid start the team faded as the season progressed, and during the following campaign, having sold their star player, John Charles, to Juventus, things went from bad to worse. The reign of manager Raich Carter came to an end, and he was replaced by Bill Lambton, who, despite only having a short spell in charge, had a massive impact on the future of Leeds and Jack Charlton, for it was he who signed Don Revie from Sunderland in 1958. Bill left the club to be replaced by Jack Taylor, who was in charge when Leeds suffered relegation back to the Second Division in 1960. After Taylor's departure, club chairman Harry Reynolds managed to persuade the board to take a risk on the untried and untested Revie and at the age of thirty-three Revie became player-manager of the club.

The appointment of Revie as player-manager nearly saw the end of Jack's time with Leeds, as both were large personalities in a struggling team and had had disagreements in the past as players. With Don now manager it seemed as though Jack didn't have a future with the club. Liverpool and Manchester United both showed an interest in Jack, but failed to match the asking price Leeds had put on his head. With no transfer forthcoming, the two men put aside their differences and Jack became a pivotal part of the Leeds United defence. Both Revie and his coach Les Crocker remained an influence on Charlton and would shape his career as a manager: 'When I was at Leeds I worked under Les Crocker, who was a coach. Les and Don both were good people to learn under. With Revie you could say to him, "I noticed something in the last game. Is this something we can have a look at and try?" and Don would always listen to you. Don managed to get the right players to play the right way, and we were very successful.'

With Jack on board Revie was building for the future by bringing through a host of players from the youth team. In 1962, after almost eight years in the first team, Charlton was joined at centre-back by Norman Hunter, a product of the youth policy, and a defensive wall was created. Some of the other youth team players who made it into the senior team around this time included Peter Lorimer and Billy Bremner. They came into the side, and Leeds won promotion back to the First Division in 1964.

Leeds' first season back in the top flight saw them surprise everybody outside the club when they almost won the League title. The race with Manchester United for the title went down to the wire and Leeds needed to beat Birmingham to seal a sensational debut season under Revie. However, they could only manage a draw (coming back from 3–0 down) and Manchester United were crowned champions. Leeds also narrowly missed out on the FA Cup that season, being beaten in the final by

Liverpool. The FA Cup final match saw Charlton add another string to his bow – operating as an emergency striker in the mould of the legendary John Charles, the big man set up Billy Bremner to score the only goal for Leeds. The following season Leeds were once again runners up in the League, this time behind Liverpool.

The 1966–1967 season was a personal milestone for Big Jack as despite Leeds failing to follow up their two previous title challenges (they finished fourth), Jack was named Footballer of the Year. The following season saw Leeds and Jack finally get their hands on a major trophy, as the club enjoyed a League Cup victory over Arsenal. That season Leeds also won their first European trophy in the shape of the Fairs Cup (now known as the Europa League). That double Cup-winning season saw Jack become the club record appearance holder when he broke Ernie Hart's record of 447 games.

The Cup wins gave Don Revie's team the confidence they needed and the following season, 1968–1969, saw the club finally win the League Championship they so desperately craved. Jack was in inspirational form for a team that lost just two games all season. The 1969–1970 season saw Leeds go for an unprecedented treble of trophies as they chased the League, FA Cup and European Cup but, in an anticlimactic year, they failed to win any. In what must have been a devastating outcome for Charlton, in the final of the FA Cup he inadvertently headed a long throw across his own area allowing Chelsea's David Webb to score the winning goal.

Jack bounced back from this the following season as he helped Leeds win another Fairs Cup. Yet again they finished runners-up in the League, losing the Championship to Arsenal.

The 1971 season itself was overshadowed by events off the field, as Jack became embroiled in controversy following an interview he gave with Fred Dinenage on Tyne Tees Television. During the interview Jack stated that he kept a little black book that had two names in it (he refused to name who was on the list) and when he got the chance to do them (i.e. tackle them hard) then he would do so. The interview spread to the national papers and Jack was charged by the FA for bringing the game into disrepute. Nowadays the comments appear innocuous enough, particularly since Jack did state in the interview that he would never do anything nasty to them.

This episode was soon confined to history and the following season, at the age of thirty-six, Jack finally won that elusive domestic Championship, when he helped Leeds to win the 1972 FA Cup. However the following season he suffered a hamstring injury that saw him miss the final games of the season and also saw him miss the FA Cup final (Leeds lost 1–0 to Second Division Sunderland in one of the greatest FA Cup final shocks ever). Time was catching up with him – he was almost thirty-eight – and his days at the top were coming to an end. That 1972–1973 season saw Jack retire from playing. His spell with Leeds covered twenty-one years and during that time he won every domestic honour available.

ENGLAND CAREER

Given his exploits with the Ireland team, it is easy to forget that Jack Charlton was also a successful international player for England. He was a World Cup winner with the country of his birth. As with his route in professional football, his debut for England followed on the heels of his baby brother. Footballers rarely make their debut for their country as they approach their thirtieth birthday, but Jack proved an exception to the rule. A year before the 1966 World Cup, Jack joined his brother in the England squad for a 2–2 draw against Scotland. Within the year, Jack was a regular in the team and scored his first goal in a pre-World Cup game against Denmark. His place in history was assured when Sir Alf Ramsay handed Jack the number 5 jersey for the World Cup squad. The 1966 World Cup remains the defining glory of English football, although the squad's opening game in the tournament revealed their nerves when they drew 0–0 with Uruguay. Following this, they composed themselves enough to progress to the knockout stages with victories against Mexico and France. England eliminated their modern-day footballing foes Argentina in the quarter-finals, taking them to a semi-final against Portugal where they won 2–1. That semi-final was a tight affair that saw Jack block a shot on the line with his arm to concede a penalty, but despite this England survived to reach their first World Cup final.

On 30 July 1966, England faced West Germany for the ultimate prize. In a game etched in footballing folklore, the West Germans took an early lead in the twelfth minute, but England equalised just six minutes later through Geoff Hurst (only his second goal in the tournament). With the game evenly poised the initiative switched to England in the seventy-eighth minute when Martin Peters volleyed England ahead. However, the West Germans continued to press for an equaliser and in the ninetieth minute they got their reward. Big Jack was adjudged to have fouled Uwe Seeler whilst trying to reach a header and from the resultant free kick Wolfgang Weber scored to level the match and bring it to extra time. Extra time saw England dominate, with Liverpool striker Hurst completing a hat trick with two more goals to give England a 4–2 win. At the end of the 120 minutes England were finally world champions. At thirty-one, Jack was the second oldest member of the team and he had a World Cup winner's medal, the biggest prize in football.

With the national team on the rise, two years later they qualified for their first European Championship. Despite being the third European Championship ever held, this was England's first appearance on Europe's biggest stage. The 1968 tournament saw England beat Spain home and away to qualify for the semi-finals. England were drawn to play Yugoslavia in Florence, but Yugoslavia won 1–0, eventually losing to Italy in the final. England beat the USSR 2–0 to claim an unsatisfactory third place. For Jack the tournament was a non-event, as he failed to play a part in any of the games, Brian Labone having taken his place at the back. At the age of thirty-three his England career was slowly grinding to a halt.

Two years after the European Championship, England travelled to Mexico to defend their World Cup crown and, despite being almost thirty-five years old, Jack retained his place in the squad. However, as in the 1968 European Championship, Jack was not the team's first choice defender, although he did play his thirty-fifth and final England game in the 1–0 group win over Czechoslovakia. West Germany avenged their 1966 defeat, knocking out England in the quarter finals and Jack decided following this, that his international career had run its course.

A PRELUDE TO THE IRELAND JOB – CHARLTON'S FIRST FORAY INTO MANAGEMENT

Once his time as a player had come to an end it was almost certain that Charlton would become a manager, given his status in the game and the leadership qualities he had displayed at Leeds. In 1973, at the age of thirty-eight, Charlton accepted an offer to take his first managerial job as the manager of Second Division Middlesbrough, a move that brought him back near his home town. However, his career as a coach and manager had actually begun during his time at Leeds: 'When I was at Leeds as a player I used to coach at local schools and universities. I started getting my coaching badges when I was twenty-six. I suppose even as a player I always knew I wanted to be a coach. Through Leeds I got involved with the local schools and coached a number of Under-18 teams. The fella who was doing it at that time preferred the organisational side of things and did not want to coach full-time, so I ended up getting involved. I did it for twelve years in all while I was still playing. During that time I was prepared to listen and was observant.'

These traits were evident during his first season in charge, when he led Middlesbrough back to the top flight. Such was the considerable margin between his side and the rest of the division that they managed to claim their place in the First Division in March with eight games remaining in the season, having amassed a then record sixty-five points, and Charlton was given the Manager of the Year award. To put this into context it is worth noting that before Charlton won the award, the honour had never been given to a manager outside of the First Division.

Stuart Boam had only been at Middlesbrough for one

season when Jack came in to replace the departing Stan Anderson: 'I will never forget it. He went through the team and told each and every one of the players how good they were. He came to me last and absolutely tore shreds off me. It was not a great start. He had still been playing for Leeds when he joined Middlesbrough, and I think he thought that he would play himself and that I was his competition. I had originally come from Mansfield, and after settling in I had formed a good defensive line with Willie Maddren. We had actually finished the previous season on an eight-game winning run before Stan left the club and Jack arrived.

'Despite his criticism of me, Jack stuck with me and Willie at the back, and before the start of the season he made me team captain. The first game of the new campaign was against Portsmouth, and he held a team meeting beforehand. The press were all wondering who the captain would be, as none had been named yet. Jim Platt and Graeme Souness were being mentioned, but in the team meeting he said I was the captain. It was a big surprise, I can tell you. Over the years we had our rows, and we started off rough, but in the end we got on well together.

'Being captain in those days was like being a shop steward. All the players would come to me and tell me their gripes, which were mainly about money, and then I would go to Jack and we would have a chat about it. He would listen to me, and then he would do what he thought anyway.

'Jack did not like to spend money. I think the only player he signed when he took over was Bobby Murdoch, and he got him on a free from Celtic. He was a great signing, too, a real gentlemen of the game. He used to keep all his medals in a box under his sink. It was strange, really. He had won everything with Celtic, and as a reward for his loyal service they allowed him to join Middlesbrough for nothing.

'But players aside, there was a lot of change that first season. We had a new chairman, a new manager and a new captain. We also had a lot of young players, such as Graeme Souness and David Hodgson, in the team.

'The thing with Jack was, and I saw this with Sheffield Wednesday and also with Ireland, he organised his teams to play a certain style of football, and he never changed his ways according to the opposition. It was always the same system, and it was drilled into the coaches. If other teams got the better of us, then so be it. But the system worked most of the time. If we lost on a Saturday, Jack would look at where we'd lost a goal and then have the coaches recreate the situation in training. We'd go over things and see where we'd gone wrong.

'He was good at motivating players too, and it was a real family atmosphere. There was no rotation of players and large squads in those days. We used only thirteen players that promotion-winning season. If a player was injured or suspended, Jack would have a reserve player come in, and he would know the system, as that was what was used in the reserves as well, so there was always consistency.

'Jack liked a big man up front with a runner beside him. He hated slow players. He liked the ball to be moved at pace. He put grafters in midfield and employed overlapping full-backs long before they were the in thing in football.'

Jim Platt was also a member of the Middlesbrough team of 1974 that won the Division Two title under Charlton: 'Jack was a great manager, one of the best I played under. He could come in at half-time and, rather than rant and rave, change things around and turn a defeat into a draw and a draw into a win. He could analyse a game and see where things were at. He was a very blunt character, although he always had the players' best interests at heart.

'He did a great job with Middlesbrough and then with Sheffield Wednesday and Ireland. I remember in his first season we won the title by a comfortable fifteen points. We set all kinds of records for number of wins and points. In those days it was only two points for a win. We actually started the season with a defeat at home to Fulham. We were murdering them, but they scored two late goals to beat us. Well, we had yet to see Jack angry, as pre-season had gone really well. He said, "Look, there are some games you can't win and you have to settle for a draw. Six draws compared to six defeats can be the difference between promotion and heartbreak at the end of the season." Those words really stood out for us throughout the season, and we only lost three more games.

'Tactically, Jack was very good. He inherited a good side when he took charge, but the signing of Bobby Murdoch was an inspired addition. However, I'm not sure that Jack would be able to hack the modern game, especially dealing with agents. He was as tight as old boots. I remember when we got promoted we all went to his office at different times to ask for a rise. In those days we would have been on about £200 a week, and we went to him with the intention of getting £250. As soon as he saw you at the door he would yell, "What the bloody hell do you want?" And sure enough you would panic and ask for £230 and end up walking out with £210 and be glad of it.

'One of the funny things about Jack was that he could not

remember names. He could remember the names of the first-team players, but if a new lad came in, there was no chance he would remember the fella's name.'

Craig Johnston was one such youngster in the youth team who crossed Jack Charlton. To many people Craig will always be remembered as a Liverpool legend, but his career could have taken a different turn after his introduction to Jack Charlton at Middlesbrough: 'Jack Charlton has been a crucial figure in my life. As a manager I have loved and hated him, sometimes at the same time, but I always respected him and who he was as a person. He was the manager of Middlesbrough when I came over to England first to try and make a life as a footballer.'

Craig was an aspiring footballer back in 1975 when, as a jet-lagged fifteen-year-old just landed in a far-from-sunny Teesside, having travelled on his own from Australia, he took part in a trial match: 'Our side were getting beat 3–0 at half-time, and Big Jack Charlton walked in and savaged everyone in the dressing-room. He finally finished up by pointing at me and saying, "Where are you from?" I gulped and said, "Australia." He then said that I was the worst footballer he had ever seen in his life and to hop off back to wherever it was I had just come from. Well, he didn't quite use the word "hop" – it was actually a lot stronger than that.

'I was shocked, ashamed and despondent. This was my introduction to football in England. At least I knew where I stood with the manager. The truth is, though, that he wasn't wrong. I really was that bad. I then made it my lifetime's ambition to prove him wrong. Some two and a half years later, after practising for eight hours a day and hiding from Charlton in the car park, a new manager called John Neil came in. I think John felt sorry for me, as he took me under his wing, and shortly afterwards I made my debut in the first team. At seventeen and a half I was the youngest player ever to play for Middlesbrough, and this time there was no half-time tongue lashing, as I actually played pretty well. You can imagine my surprise when the very next day in the newspapers the headline was taken from a Jack Charlton quote: "I always knew 'The Kangaroo' would make it." Thirteen years later I met Jack again at Jupiter's Casino in the Gold Coast in Queensland, Australia. We were both speaking at a gentlemen's function. We talked openly about the Middlesbrough days, and he explained that I had too much energy but no skills. He also told me that he knew I was hiding behind the cars every day he came in to work but thought I had a lot of heart to hang around and still want to learn the game. That day I finished off my speech by telling the audience and Jack that if an over-keen Australian kid approached him on the beach for a trial, then he should please give him a second look before dismissing him so colourfully. The crowd loved it.

'For me, Jack is a fascinating and remarkable character. He is essentially a man's man. I could imagine him being in the military. But you knew that whatever he said it was coming from the right place and that he had a great big heart. You always had the impression that he wouldn't ask you to do something he wouldn't do himself. And he doesn't so much talk as shout. A conversation with him is a very direct conversation. The dressing-room turned blue on many occasions if he wasn't getting through to a player. It was definitely old-fashioned stuff, but it worked. There is a thorny and gruff Jack Charlton, but at the same time there is a real noble quality about him. He is a prince among men.

'Many people these days are clones of what people think they should be. They are politically correct and extremely careful not to offend any sensitive souls. I think you can end up losing your own soul trying to be all things to everyone. Jack Charlton was not one of those people. He somehow respected everybody, but at the same time he called a spade a spade.

'I will always believe that the FA missed a trick not hiring the likes of Brian Clough and Jackie Charlton. Jack got the most out of his players with a direct and simple plan of how to win a football match. The Irish players loved him, and the Irish public loved him. They don't make them like that any more.'

Jack stayed for four seasons with Middlesbrough before leaving the club in 1977. After leaving Middlesbrough he applied for the England job but lost out to Ron Greenwood, before taking the reigns at Sheffield Wednesday, leading them to promotion from the Third Division in his second season in charge. The next three seasons saw Wednesday consolidate their position in Division Two without ever challenging for further promotion. In 1982 Jack decided to leave the post, having taken the Owls as far as he could (Jack himself had stated prior to the 1981–1982 season that if Wednesday did not get promoted he would resign his post and true to word he resigned when the objective was not achieved). He returned for a short stint to Middlesbrough, before fulfilling a childhood dream by becoming manager of Newcastle United, the club he had grown up supporting.

Given his history with Middlesbrough and his status as a purveyor of what some people described as negative football, it was a shock that he took the Newcastle job. The Magpies pride themselves on playing attacking football, so it was no surprise that dissent soon arose and less than a year after taking the job he resigned. A lesson can be extracted from the coming together of Jack Charlton and Newcastle. You only have to look at the case of Sam Allardyce, often criticised himself for the brand of football his team plays. Although he was successful in his time with Bolton, his attempt to turn a so-called big club such as Newcastle into a winning outfit proved unsuccessful, and he was never accepted by the fans. Newcastle want to win beautifully. The fans want to see four and five goals a game and have the ball passed into the net. Both clubs pride themselves on their forwards and not their defenders. At Newcastle, Big Jack, like Allardyce years later, did not give them what they wanted.

THE BIRTH OF AN IRELAND LEGEND

Newcastle's loss was Ireland's gain. After taking a brief break from the game, Charlton was approached to manage the Republic of Ireland. The story goes that Charlton had agreed to take the job before the money side of things was negotiated. 'What about money?' an FAI official asked.

'Ah, give me the same as the last manager,' Charlton replied.

When the FAI man informed him what Eoin Hand had earned, Charlton replied, 'Bloody hell. I'll want a bit more than that!'

The FAI had long been viewed as being behind their English counterparts. However, a lot of the players in the Ireland squad in the early 1980s were performing at a high level in England

and were becoming more accustomed to the professional approach being adopted by their club sides. The FAI could be accused of having too often taken the easy way out in terms of their management appointments, going for former heroes or men of the moment. By appointing Charlton a small statement was being made, not just to other European countries, but also to the players.

Jack recalls: 'The FAI first approached me to take over at Christmas of 1985. At the time I had taken a break from the game after my spell at Newcastle. It was the first break I'd taken from football since first starting out. I had been offered other jobs, but I wanted to rest. However, when the Ireland job came along it was a chance to manage at international level. I knew international football from my time with England, and I was also an FA-qualified coach, so it was a good opportunity.'

When Charlton took charge of Ireland, soccer in the country was at a low ebb. The Hand era, although unlucky, had once again failed to deliver a major tournament, and football trailed GAA and rugby in popularity. However, Charlton, with a little luck, some tactics never-before-seen at international level, strong team organisation, and the crafty and imaginative stretching of the eligibility rules, managed to change that.

The now famous granny rule became a big part of the Charlton era and, when he was barely in the door, he set about getting the most out of the resources available to him. He approached players with even the most tenuous of Irish links to hook up with the Republic of Ireland team: 'When I took the job I realised Ireland needed a couple of players who would help me play the game I wanted to play, so we got a few players. We did our homework and got all the paperwork filled in. The papers were completed, and the government then arranged for their Irish passports to be released.'

In his autobiography Tony Cascarino claimed that he did not qualify for Ireland, writing that he was a 'fake Irishman'. However, it was later confirmed that through adoption his mother had gained the right to Irish citizenship and he was therefore eligible. Jack dismisses the Tony Cascarino controversy: 'It's funny but a lot of people mention Tony Cascarino as being a perfect example of the grandparent rule. However, he actually made his debut before I was in charge, and he was a member of the squad before I took over. The likes of John Aldridge and Ray Houghton were brought in, but everything checked out for them.'

Bernie Slaven benefited from the grandparent rule, and he recalls his call-up to the squad very well: 'I remember I was banging in the goals for Middlesbrough under Bruce Rioch at the old Ayresome Park, and the Scotland manager Andy Roxburgh was reported to be looking at me, but no call had come. After one particular game I told the reporters, more in sarcasm than anything else, that even though I was brought up in Glasgow I had Irish grandparents. I didn't really think any more about it until I went to see a Newcastle game with my mate Stuart Ripley. We were going to collect our tickets at the ground when I saw Jack. I had never spoken to him, but he must have recognised me, as he said to me, "Aye, son, I hear Andy is looking at you. Hang on in there and you will get a cap against Wales." All I thought was that Jack must be on the drink and had mistaken me for someone else.

'I then met with Craig Brown [assistant to Roxburgh] after an epic Cup game against Everton, and Scotland were promising me a cap too, either at full or B level. Then, true to his word, Jack called Bruce and told him that he wanted to speak to me after training. So at 1 p.m. I took a call in the security office, and straight away Jack asked me what my qualification was. I told him how I was eligible to play for Ireland. He told me that he would have the FAI check it out, and if it worked out, I'd get a call-up. He only promised me one cap, mind, and said that if I wasn't up to scratch, that was that.

'Everything checked out, and as Jack had promised I was called into the squad for the Wales game. I had grown up in Glasgow and was a massive Celtic fan, but the way I saw it Scotland had never done anything for me, so to have the chance to pull on the Ireland jersey was the stuff of dreams.

'I remember the Wales game well. The build-up was strange for me, as I was in a room with the likes of Whelan, McGrath and Aldridge, all big names. We were sitting in the changing-room, and there were a load of balls that needed signing, so the rest of the squad started signing them. However, I didn't sign any. I mean, I was not a name in the team yet, but Jack must have seen this, so he made a point of saying to me, in front of everyone, "Are you going to sign a ball? You might not be back." It was his way of helping me feel at ease in the squad.

'The one thing Jack could do, and I have never met a manager that could do this so well since, he could have a drink and be one of the lads and then just like that he could switch into manager mode. It was an amazing ability to have.'

When Jack first took the job as Ireland manager the mood in the Ireland camp was very sombre. The team was at their lowest ebb after the final years of the Hand regime. As Kevin Sheedy, the scorer of Ireland's first-ever goal at a World Cup final tournament, recalls, 'After Eoin Hand, Ireland needed to take a new direction, and with Jack you had someone who did things his way. He was very straight with people, and all the players knew what was required. If a player was suspended or injured, then the player coming in knew what had to be done. As a coach now myself, if I could take away anything from that time, it would be his honesty, his straightforwardness – you knew what you were getting.

'Another thing about that team was that Jack brought players into the squad who were late entrants to international football. I myself had been there from the youth levels. I had played in the Under-21s and had then made the step up to the senior side. However, other players did not go down that route. Before Jack there had been some dark days in Irish football. I remember being 5–0 down to Denmark with thirty minutes to go in a game, so the change in fortune under Jack was great.'

The players seemed to respond to the approach of the new management team, and so it was that Big Jack and his motley crew of Irish players set off in search of qualification for their first-ever major competition. First up was a Euro '88 qualifying group that included Belgium, Scotland, Bulgaria and Luxembourg. Ireland started off the campaign by earning a creditable draw in Brussels, but they were also held to a draw by Scotland in Dublin. In February 1987, however, they enjoyed a fine 1–0 win in Glasgow. Gerry Peyton, who played under four Ireland managers in all, the last of whom was Big Jack, says, 'The first thing Jack did was set about getting some belief into the team. The Scotland game in Glasgow was one of the major turning points for us. Mark Lawrenson scored after a smart dribble. Following that win the belief and confidence started to come. The players started to believe in the system, and everyone was beginning to understand their role. History will tell you that it was a Scotland victory over a near impenetrable Bulgaria at home that got us there, but the group matches were very tight, and I suppose in a twist of irony Bulgaria became the Ireland of previous qualifying campaigns, as they hit the post in that game and came close on a number of occasions.'

Ireland qualified for the 1988 European Championship in Germany, and the team were drawn against England in a group of death that also contained the USSR and eventual winners Holland. In preparing for the finals, Ireland won all four of their friendly matches, against Israel, Romania, Yugoslavia and Poland. Peyton says, 'I think once we qualified for the European Championship in Germany, a noticeable change came over the squad. The victory over Scotland was a case in point. Confidence was flowing through the squad, and that's what Jack brought to the Irish team.

'In Germany, the media wrote us off and were claiming that we were only there to make up the numbers and would get thrashed. I remember the morning of the first game, against England. We were having breakfast and were all very nervous. Paul McGrath in particular looked very nervous. There would normally be a bit of banter and a joke, but that morning it was all very serious. Next thing Jack came into the dining area, and it was obvious he could sense that the lads were nervous. He went over to the first table and said, "You lot had better not do something stupid today and score a goal. I'm going fishing tomorrow." Those couple of lines really helped lift the tension and relaxed the boys.'

In their opening match of the Championships, the World

Cup winner found himself plotting England's downfall, and he delivered. Ireland met England at Stuttgart and heroically won the match 1–0, with the goal coming from Ray Houghton. It also proved to be a great day for Packie Bonner, who made a string of fine saves.

Gerry explains how the players felt after that famous game: 'The emotions after the England match were very strong. Packie had made a couple of fantastic saves, and, of course, Ray's goal had won it, but the team had really performed that day. I remember Liam Brady, who had missed out on the tournament due to injury, was visibly upset, and I think everyone saw the passion that the team had.'

For Charlton, however, it was just another match: 'When Ireland played against England at Euro '88 and Italia '90 I was not overcome with mixed emotions. I was employed by the FAI to manage Ireland no matter who we were playing. I wanted to get a result, and I always sent the team out to get one.'

Ireland met the Soviet Union in their next match, the game ending 1–1, with Ronnie Whelan scoring an incredible goal. Ireland needed only a draw to qualify for the semi-finals. However, they lost their final match, going down 1–0 to the future European champions Holland, but as Sheedy says, 'You have to remember that we were just six minutes away from the semi-finals, which was an amazing achievement.' This is backed up by Peyton, who adds, 'If it had not been for a fluke spin of the ball against Holland, we could have gone further still.' For his part Charlton was rewarded with the runners-up prize in the *World Soccer* Manager of the Year awards in 1988.

The key to Charlton's success was not only the brand of football he promoted, but also the relationship he enjoyed with his players: 'I like to think that you must treat players as friends. You need the players to understand what you want to do and what you are trying to achieve. With Ireland we had a way of playing. Each player had a part to play. You'll be familiar with the phrase "put them under pressure". Well, that was what we wanted to do. Players had to get back behind the ball and pressure the opposition from all parts of the pitch.'

Sheedy agrees: 'Jack treated all the players as grown-ups, and you could enjoy a pint of Guinness when the time was right, as long as you didn't abuse the privilege. It helped build a good team spirit. We would head off to the races together, and travelling with the Ireland team was the same as it was with Everton. Everyone got on, and the spirit was good.

'The thing about Jack, though, was that sometimes you couldn't tell if he was being clever or if that was just his way. I remember we were playing a game against Wales, and he had written the team on the back of a box of cigarettes, with all the names of the players wrong. I was wondering, "Is he being clever here and telling us it doesn't matter who these guys are, or is there something else going on?" In my opinion Jack was a very simple and wise man. He knew what he had, and he knew the system he wanted to play. It was a case of the players understanding and fitting in to that system. Lansdowne Road was a fortress during his time in charge, visiting teams found it very difficult to go there and get a result.'

Following on from their success in Germany, Ireland successfully qualified for Italia '90. The team prepared for the trip to Italy with a two-week training camp in Malta. Bernie Slaven was a late joiner to the squad ahead of the competition, and he remembers the experience, not all of it good: 'I was very lucky to play international football. I was twenty-nine when I made my debut against Wales, and thankfully I scored. Jack had said to me that if I played in two games, I might make the World Cup squad, so there was a big incentive there. I missed the next Ireland game, though, as Middlesbrough had a game against Ipswich and Colin Todd pulled me out of the squad. I had a stinker that night as my mind was on Ireland, thinking that I had blown my chance.

'Thankfully, Jack gave me another forty-five minutes before he named his squad, and I was lucky to get in. I think the fact that Jack was based in Newcastle might have helped me, as it was only forty-five minutes down the road from him, and he could easily come and see me play.

'I roomed with Gary Waddock, and in the build-up to the World Cup we played a game against Turkey. I only played forty minutes and Gary played the full ninety. We were back at the hotel later, and Gary was lying on the bed. He said to me, "I think I'm going home. You know, I just have a feeling."

'When we landed in Malta for the preparation camp I was talking to Niall Quinn, and I saw Jack having a word with Gary. I then saw Gary's head drop. Back at the hotel Gary told me that he was not part of the final squad and that he was going home. He was upset and rang his wife. Jack came in to see if Gary was all right and turned to me and said, "It could have been you." Although that showed that Jack could make hard decisions, there was another side to him too, a softer side almost, and he did offer to allow Gary to travel with the squad. After the game against Holland, Mick McCarthy got Ruud Gullit's jersey and had it signed and gave it to Gary.

'What people often don't realise is that while going to a

World Cup is an amazing experience, it can be hard too, especially if you don't play. You are away for a couple of weeks from family and friends, and at the end of the day you are training hard, probably harder than the others, as you want to make an impression, but you still don't get on the pitch. The players who did not get a game called ourselves the muppets. It was a joke at our own expense. From my own point of view, I guess I had played no role in getting Ireland there, so Jack was always going to stick with the guys who had led him there.

'Boredom is the hardest thing at a World Cup, whether you are Ireland, England, Germany or Brazil. You can't go out and sunbathe, as Jack did not want us doing that, even if we were not playing, so you have to stay in your room a lot. It can be hard. There is no room for letting your hair down.'

The performances in Italy were not so easy on the eye, but the results were impressive, and after draws with England, Egypt and Holland, Ireland eventually went out to the hosts Italy in the quarter-finals by a single goal.

The draw with England once again saw Charlton up against his country of birth. It must have been even harder for Jack to prepare the team for a World Cup match against England, but Kevin Sheedy recalls that Jack didn't need to say too much to the team: 'Personally, I think there was a lot of pressure on the players and Jack ahead of the game against England. Our main objective, though, was not to lose the first game. We could not afford that. In some respects it was not just an international World Cup match; it was a bit more than that. It was more like a local derby, an Everton versus Liverpool match or a Manchester City versus Manchester United game. The pressure was building, especially in the papers, and I suppose you could feel it, but we were pumped up for the game. As I said, it was like a derby, so everyone wanted to play. Going a goal down so early in the game [Gary Lineker opened the scoring after eight minutes] was hard, but we dug in, and then I scored after seventy-two minutes. It was a great experience.'

It was a tremendous achievement for a team with no previous World Cup experience. As Charlton explains, 'I remember when we came home from Italia '90 the airport was mobbed. It took us sixty minutes to get out of the airport, then another two and a half hours to get into O'Connell Street. There were kids climbing up poles. We were getting a bit worried about them. There were people throwing things up to the bus, and then when they were falling back down people were jumping out to catch them. We had to get the police to go in front of the bus to keep an eye on people.'

Gerry Peyton continues, 'When we came back from the European Championship in 1988 about 500,000 people welcomed us home. By the time we arrived home from Italy there were 1.5 million people there to welcome us. Jack's team had become a phenomenon. Everyone wanted to be a Packie Bonner, a Paul McGrath or a Ray Houghton, and Jack helped these guys become household names.'

Modern-day players such as Shay Given would have looked up to Packie and the others and wanted to emulate them. Successful countries breed successful players. Just as the England heroes of 1966 would have inspired a host of youngsters to take up the game and try to copy the saves of Banks or the shots of Hurst, likewise youngsters all over Ireland were now diving to their right to save penalties and heading the ball into the England net.

One of the most memorable experiences of Italia '90 was a meeting that Jack Charlton and his squad had with Pope John Paul II at the Vatican. Gerry Peyton says, 'This for me was definitely one of the highlights of my time with Ireland. Italia '90 was an amazing experience. The results themselves were fantastic, but the whole trip was organised to a tee. On a personal note, the audience with the pope will forever rank high in my life. I remember I was standing next to Packie, and we saw the pope talking to a number of players at the top of the group. He then made a beeline down to me and Packie. He shook Packie's hand, and then he reached over to me and told me about how responsible the position of goalkeeper was and that he himself had been a keeper in his day.'

Monsignor Boyle was a supporter who got closer to the team than he could ever have imagined when he made his way to Italy to support Ireland in pursuit of their World Cup dream. As it turned out he had a massive role to play in the team's audience with the pope: 'I was initially in Italy as a supporter watching the Ireland team. I just happened to be staying in the same hotel as the FAI officials on Sardinia. I was saying Mass in the hotel, and the FAI approached me and asked me if I would say Mass for the team, who were staying at another hotel, the following night, which was a Saturday. I agreed, but they couldn't make the Mass in the end. Instead, we did the Mass on the Sunday, which was the day before the England game.

'I went up to the team hotel. There was a lot of security around the hotel. People were nervous because of the England and Ireland meeting, but there was no need to be. There was no trouble. I said the Mass, and it was just me and the team for it.

'Jack Charlton then invited me to have lunch, and he asked

me, as long as I was around, would I mind saying Mass for the team for the rest of tournament. Naturally, I agreed. Once we had made it out of the group stages we were paired with Romania, with the match to be played in Genoa. Before the game Jack said to me, "If we win, we will go to Rome, and if that happens, a couple of members of the panel want to have an audience with the pope. Will you be able to arrange that for them?"

'I contacted the director of the Irish college in Rome, Monsignor Brady, who is now Cardinal Brady. I explained the situation to him; however, we had to keep it hushed, as the game had not been played yet.'

Ireland won the game and then had to make their way down to Rome, where they were to face Italy. Monsignor Boyle continues, 'Audiences with the pope are held on a Wednesday, and the players only arrived down on the Tuesday, so there was not a lot of time to make arrangements. However, they had their audience with the pope, and the Vatican was very pleased. Ireland were the only team that arranged for an audience with the pope during the tournament.'

Craig Johnston had retired from football when he met up with Jack again, at Italia '90: 'Ireland had just beaten Romania on penalties. I was in the crowd that day, and Jack saw me amidst the mayhem and chaos. He had the presence of mind to come over to me and to ask me how I was and what I was doing with a big film camera on my shoulder. I told him I was filming a documentary for UNICEF, and I really needed a lift back to the team hotel. Much to my surprise, he pulled me up out of the crowd and put me on the team bus. It was amazing, really.

'After Ireland lost to Italy in Rome the players were with their wives, having a singsong like only the Irish can have. The lads were all in good spirits, as they had dramatically over-delivered on their World Cup promise. They were all very proud of their achievements. It was going to be a long night at the end of a long but successful campaign.

'It dawned on me as I was sitting there watching and listening to the singsong what Jack had just achieved with his players. Sometimes it takes an outsider to tell a ragbag army of blokes how good they can all be. Sometimes it can't come from within the ranks. I thought it was a bit like Bill Shankly with Liverpool and how a Scot had somehow made the Scousers believe they were the best in the world and then they became the best club in the world. This was the same. Here was Jack Charlton, the big proud Englishman, and he had just helped Ireland to their best World Cup position ever. In their presence he was like the messiah.

'It was a fantastic evening. Everybody was having a good time. I remember Chris de Burgh took it upon himself to sing a song in tribute to the gaffer to the tune of "Hey Jude". He sang a whole parody, starting off with the words "Hey Jack". One by one all the players sang a song. Liam Brady was there, and he sang "Ruby Don't Take Your Love to Town", while Andy Townsend chipped in with "I'm Leaving on a Jet Plane" and Ronnie Whelan sang a traditional Irish song. It was a privilege to be there, and I escaped largely unnoticed until Ronnie Whelan made me get up and sing a rendition of 'I Still Call Australia Home'. Mick McCarthy, another big gruff Englishman, then picked me up and threw me into a fountain, camera and all. At the end of the night, or the start of the morning or whatever, it must have been about 5.30 a.m., all the lads were still singing, although their throats were now red raw. When Big Jack got up to move all the players in unison called for one last song from the gaffer. Without missing a beat the big man launched into a stirring rendition of "The Blaydon Races". It brought the house down.

'Jack then grabbed his wife's hand and led her off to bed. The lads weren't going to let him have the last word, though, and they turned into a schoolboy choir and started singing "We know where you're going, we know what you're doing!" If everybody thought that was the end of it, it wasn't. Just as the laughter had died down, the shutters of the master suite on the third floor balcony were flung open. Big Jack appeared before us all, semi-naked, with a towel covering his bits and pieces. He made a series of very lavish and generous hand gestures, which received a rapturous round of applause from his congregation. The night had finally ended, and it was now time to put a very funny and memorable night in Irish football history to bed.

'I had met Jack's son John Charlton years ago up in Newcastle. He was a very good footballer himself and a great lad. The Irish lads loved him, and he was helping his dad out as an extra pair of hands and eyes in the Ireland squad. One night John invited me to the team hotel. They were having a few beers and a bit of team bonding. There were a few silly games that footballers often play and one that I hadn't seen before. It involved someone sitting in the middle of the floor and a penny being pushed into his forehead. The natural suction of the slightly moistened penny keeps it on the forehead until the person whacks the back of his own head hard enough that it falls off.

'Jack, who had sunk a few pints of the old Guinness himself, was watching a few players do this and saw that it took them about three whacks before the penny fell off their foreheads. As a competitive man, he just had to have a go himself. After all, how hard could it be?

'Big Jack sat on the stool in the middle of the room. As the lads gathered round him you could hear a pin drop. Ronnie Whelan approached him, licked the coin and stuck it onto Jack's forehead. Jack then began to whack the back of his own head. Once, twice, three times. He looked down to see if the penny had fallen. No, it hadn't. He whacked again harder and harder. Six, seven, eight whacks. Nothing. Nine, ten. Even more feverish whacking followed. Eleven, twelve. He was whacking away as the crowd begged him to hit harder and harder.

'The Big Englishman man got up to fifteen very hard whacks of his own head when he finally twigged that the coin was not there. The look on his face was priceless. He had been done like a kipper. Ronnie had pressed the coin very hard, so it felt like it was actually stuck there, but it wasn't.

'That little prank shows just how much the lads respected him. Jack was one of the boys, and the fact that he actually got involved says something about his management style. It is very hard to think of another manager who would do that. Jack's personality was big enough that he was willing to put himself into the firing line and be laughed at, in the process endearing himself to the squad even more.'

PUT 'EM UNDER PRESSURE

The well-known Irish song 'Put 'Em Under Pressure' produced by Larry Mullen of U2 that topped the Irish charts during 1990 was based on the catchphrase that Jack had adopted during his reign with Ireland. As Jack himself puts it, 'I suppose people talk about the long-ball football we played, but when you look at the players we had in the team it was long ball with quality. We pressurised teams in their own half, and they were not used to it. They were used to having time on the ball.'

Jack understood perfectly what he wanted to achieve from day one in the Ireland job: 'It was around 1981, I think, and I was doing some TV work. Denmark were playing Italy, and they managed to beat them 3–1. They did it playing one man up front and hitting the ball up to him. The forward would then knock it back to the midfielder, and because Denmark had an extra man in midfield the Italians did not know whether to come, stay or drop back. This meant that Denmark were winning all the ball. The result surprised a lot of people, but I was not surprised.

'Before the Euro '88 qualifying campaign I went to Mexico to see the teams that Ireland had been drawn against, Belgium and Bulgaria, and I saw that they had real tidy passing games. Straight away I knew we had to adapt and change our game plan, as I felt we were not good enough to play at that level. So we set about introducing a new system.

'I remember Belgium had a fella called Ceulemans. He was an attacking player and about six feet two inches in height, and their full-backs would try and get the ball up to him at every chance. He would more often than not win the ball, so I knew we had to look into that. The key was to cut out the supply to their full-backs. I said to the players, "Once the ball gets to their full-backs charge them down." That meant they then had to move the ball, and it stopped them playing the way they wanted to.

'I was a defender as a player, and I understood the relationship between defender and goalkeeper. When I first came in I moved

Mark Lawrenson, who played as a defender for Liverpool, into centre midfield. I felt that by having a defender in there the link between centre-half and midfield would be enhanced. It worked, too, and then when Mark retired through injury I moved Paul McGrath in there. The reason for having a centre-back in midfield was because your centre-backs need to be the fittest men on the field. There is a lot of concentration involved in defending. For example, when a right-back or a left-back is caught out of position the centre-back has to cover them. When that happened we had Mark and Paul who knew how to defend and would be able to drop back into the centre of defence to cover them. All the players had a responsibility to cover positions when other players were caught out. If they could not do it and play the system, they were not in the team. They had to fit into the system.'

Although Ireland failed to reach Euro '92, despite going through qualification unbeaten, they qualified again for the 1994 World Cup in America. By that time Tommy Coyne had joined the squad and, due to an unfortunate injury suffered by Niall Quinn, he boarded the plane to America: 'The opportunity to play for Ireland came about through Packie Bonner and Chris Morris. They were at Celtic with me, and they asked me if I had any relations of Irish descent. My grandmother from my mother's side was from Ballina, County Mayo, and as she had died at a young age it was a wonderful honour for me to represent Ireland in her memory.

'The decision to play for Ireland was very easy to make, and I had no hesitation in accepting the offer. The fact that a manager of a national side was interested in me was a massive boost to me and my career, and I think that I played the best football of my career during those years.

'Despite being a latecomer to the squad [Coyne was twenty-nine when he made his Ireland debut], and being on the periphery of the team, I managed to play three out of the four games at USA '94. It was a wonderful experience – one of the best of my career. I was very fortunate to be there, as Quinny had withdrawn due to a cruciate-ligament injury. Playing in the Giants' Stadium was amazing and very emotional.

'The spirit in the squad was fantastic. Everybody got on so well. Being in the Ireland squad, surrounded by players such as John Aldridge, Ronnie Whelan and Paul McGrath, really helped raise my game and take it to another level.

'I found Jack Charlton to be very down to earth and likeable, but I was in awe of him. He was a World Cup winner and had played at a very high level. He was unlike any manager I had played under. One time, we were in Dundalk before a game, and Jack showed me how to fly fish during a break in training. He had such a good manner, but it did not detract from his skills as a manager. In the years he was in charge he transformed Irish football.'

The first match in the Giants' Stadium saw one of the biggest upsets in World Cup history when Ireland beat Italy 1–0. Jack says, 'That was the highlight for me, that match against Italy in USA in 1994. You see, the rules had changed after Italia '90. Keepers could no longer pick up the ball from a pass-back, so we had to adapt our game. Our game was built on a pressing game, and our full-backs would play the ball over the head of their full-backs, which meant that they had to turn. This allowed us to get into good positions and attack. If the opposing full-back got to the ball before we did, he could play it back to his goalkeeper. That three, four or five seconds meant that we could regroup the players and get into shape again. However, with the introduction of the new rule, the keeper had to kick the ball, so there was less time to get our shape back and we had to adapt our plan. The players, as always, were very responsive, and we got the result that day.'

After the euphoria of the win over Italy, Ireland were brought back down to earth with a bang when they lost the next game to Mexico 2–1. The game is best remembered for two things, the first being Jack's pitch-side argument with the sideline official who was delaying a substitution. Jack was sent to the stands and later fined for his involvement as well as being suspended for the final group match in New York, where he was forced to watch from the stands. The second memorable event was John Aldridge's header that later ensured Ireland's qualification from the group on goal difference.

Ireland finished the group with a 0–0 draw with Norway, securing a second round match against Holland, where a poor display from Ireland saw them bow out 2–0. For the second World Cup in a row Ireland returned home as heroes and Jack's achievements saw him awarded the freedom of Dublin. However, following this things did not go so well and Ireland failed to qualify for Euro '96. Despite a strong start they finished as runners-up in their group and had to qualify via the play-offs. But against a strong Holland side they again lost 2–0 and the Charlton era drew to a close: 'Before the game I had already told the FAI I was going. At that stage I had been in charge for ten years, and I thought it was time for a change. Players get too used to you and the systems and ideas, and things need change. We had become predictable.'

Terry Phelan, who played under Charlton and later Mick

McCarthy, and is now a coach in New Zealand, recalls a man who was close to his players and loyal to them: 'He was a happy-go-lucky chap, a World Cup winner and a legend of the game. Everyone respected him, but he was jolly and liked a laugh. He was terrible with names, though. He was always calling me Chris or Paul or number three; all in good fun, though.

'The secret to Jack's success was his loyalty to the players. This was a team that was literally built by Jack, with the likes of Andy Townsend, Mick McCarthy, Ray Houghton and John Aldridge brought in by him. Once you were in the squad and performed, it became like a family. The older players really took you in. I remember in particular Gerry Peyton being a great help to the younger players in the squad.'

Gerry Peyton himself adds, 'Jack was very loyal to the players he had in the squad, but you had a job to do. Packie Bonner and I were very close, and we got on well together. Under Eoin we had been in and out of the squad, but under Jack it was very much Packie as first choice, with me as support. I was comfortable with that. As a player you need to be humble and accept decisions. Packie was playing in front of 50,000 people at Celtic, while I was playing to 12,000 in Bournemouth, so he was going to be first choice.

'Some players rock the boat and demand to play, but I made a decision to help Packie become a better player and pass my experience on to him. It's too easy to let your ego get in the way. Even today I preach that to the keepers at Arsenal. You need to help one another. As the saying goes, you're only as strong as your back-up players. I remember Jack picked me to play against Northern Ireland one time, and he said to me, "It doesn't matter whether it's you or Packie, as I know that neither of you will ever let me down." That kind of support is very important to a player.'

Terry Phelan says, 'Jack was such a big personality. He loved a laugh and a joke, and even though he would be dressed in a suit and shoes he would still get involved in training, sliding about with the team. That said, he loved his fishing and clay-pigeon shooting and was not averse to skipping sessions for some shooting or fishing. One time he took the team clay-pigeon shooting as a bonding session, and we were having a great old time of it until Jack started to get upset, as some of the boys were doing better than him. He threw down his gun and went off in a huff. We thought it was very funny.

'Training with Jack was very different, especially compared to nowadays. In his time there were no sports psychologists, no fitness coaches and no dietitians, but we were still successful. And Jack was in a league of his own tactically. While he is remembered for the brand of football that Ireland played during his era, his preparation for games could be just as interesting as some of the results he achieved. I can remember seeing Jack writing notes on cigarette packets, and another time when we were preparing for a big game against Austria, Jack put on a tape of the Australian Under-21 team. We all began to laugh, and Jack could not understand why. He was getting upset with us before Andy Townsend, I think it was, told him that we were watching a tape of the Australian side instead of the Austrian. Big Jack went into a huff and walked out of the room. It was a quirky approach, but it brought us success. He put us on the map. I mean you have to remember that Ireland was a small country, a small country that got decent results.'

Even though the game was changing, Jack would not.

Towards the end of his time in charge, teams had cottoned on to Ireland's approach, and the play-off match against Holland to qualify for Euro '96 was, in Jack's own words, 'a last throw of the dice'. He knew the road was coming to an end, and that 2–0 defeat to a strong, skilful and aggressive Dutch side signalled the end of his career.

His popularity in Ireland remains strong, some fourteen years since he last sat in the dugout for a match. Such is his standing in the country that in 1996 both he and his wife were granted honorary Irish citizenship. Charlton has the last word on his Ireland career: 'I loved my time with Ireland. We had a great time and some great players. During my time in charge we reached number six in the world rankings.

'It's rare that you leave a job and still have people respect you long after you leave. Even now when I meet people they still smile at me. The fans were very important to us, and we wanted them to be part of our success. After a big result we used to encourage the players to go out and have a drink in the places where the fans were. The public could almost have picked the team. They knew all the players. To this day I keep an eye out for Ireland's results and always have a smile when they get a good one.'

That sums up Jack Charlton. His time in charge was probably the closest the Irish public ever came to feeling part of the national team at any sport. The Ireland team under Jack embodied everything good about being Irish, especially punching above your weight.

JACK CHARLTON'S CLUB MANAGERIAL HONOURS RECORD:

One Division Two Championship 1974
One Anglo-Scottish Cup 1976

JACK CHARLTON'S IRELAND RECORD:

Total number of games in charge: 94
Total number of wins: 47 (ratio 50.00%)
Total number of draws: 30 (ratio 31.90%)
Total number of losses: 17 (ratio 18.09%)
Biggest win: 5–0 *v.* Israel and Turkey
Biggest defeat: 3–0 *v.* Portugal
Longest run without defeat: 12

JACK CHARLTON'S RESULTS AS IRELAND MANAGER:

Date	Home/ Away	Opponent	Score	Result	Type of Fixture
26/03/1986	Home	Wales	0–1	L	Friendly
23/04/1986	Home	Uruguay	1–1	D	Friendly
25/05/1986	Away	Iceland	2–1	W	Friendly
27/05/1986	Away	Czechoslovakia	1–0	W	Friendly
10/09/1986	Away	Belgium	2–2	D	Competitive
15/10/1986	Home	Scotland	0–0	D	Competitive

12/11/1986	Away	Poland	0–1	L	Friendly
18/02/1987	Away	Scotland	1–0	W	Competitive
01/04/1987	Away	Bulgaria	1–2	L	Competitive
29/04/1987	Home	Belgium	0–0	D	Competitive
23/05/1987	Home	Brazil	1–0	W	Friendly
28/05/1987	Away	Luxembourg	2–0	W	Competitive
09/09/1987	Home	Luxembourg	2–1	W	Competitive
14/10/1987	Home	Bulgaria	2–0	W	Competitive
10/11/1987	Home	Israel	5–0	W	Friendly
23/03/1988	Home	Romania	2–0	W	Friendly
27/04/1988	Home	Yugoslavia	2–0	W	Friendly
22/05/1988	Home	Poland	3–1	W	Friendly
01/06/1988	Away	Norway	0–0	D	Friendly
12/06/1988	Away	England	1–0	W	Competitive
15/06/1988	Away	Soviet Union	1–1	D	Competitive
18/06/1988	Away	Holland	0–1	L	Competitive
14/09/1988	Away	Northern Ireland	0–0	D	Competitive
19/10/1988	Home	Tunisia	4–0	W	Friendly
16/11/1988	Away	Spain	0–2	L	Competitive
07/02/1989	Home	France	0–0	D	Friendly
08/03/1989	Away	Hungary	0–0	D	Competitive
26/04/1989	Home	Spain	1–0	W	Competitive
28/05/1989	Home	Malta	2–0	W	Competitive
04/06/1989	Home	Hungary	2–0	W	Competitive
06/09/1989	Home	West Germany	1–1	D	Friendly
11/10/1989	Home	Northern Ireland	3–0	W	Competitive

15/11/1989	Away	Malta	2–0	W	Competitive
28/03/1990	Home	Wales	1–0	W	Friendly
25/04/1990	Home	Soviet Union	1–0	W	Friendly
16/05/1990	Home	Finland	1–1	D	Friendly
26/05/1990	Away	Turkey	0–0	D	Friendly
02/06/1990	Away	Malta	3–0	W	Friendly
11/06/1990	Away	England	1–1	D	Competitive
17/06/1990	Away	Egypt	0–0	D	Competitive
21/06/1990	Away	Holland	1–1	D	Competitive
25/06/1990	Away	Romania	0–0	D	Competitive
30/06/1990	Away	Italy	0–1	L	Competitive
12/09/1990	Home	Morocco	1–0	W	Friendly
17/10/1990	Home	Turkey	5–0	W	Competitive
14/11/1990	Home	England	1–1	D	Competitive
06/02/1991	Away	Wales	3–0	W	Friendly
27/03/1991	Away	England	1–1	D	Competitive
01/05/1991	Home	Poland	0–0	D	Competitive
22/05/1991	Home	Chile	1–1	D	Friendly
01/06/1991	Away	United States	1–1	D	Friendly
11/09/1991	Away	Hungary	2–1	W	Friendly
16/10/1991	Away	Poland	3–3	D	Competitive
13/11/1991	Away	Turkey	3–1	W	Competitive
19/02/1992	Home	Wales	0–1	L	Friendly
25/03/1992	Home	Switzerland	2–1	W	Competitive
29/04/1992	Home	United States	4–1	W	Competitive
26/05/1992	Home	Albania	2–0	W	Competitive
30/05/1992	Away	United States	1–3	L	Friendly

04/06/1992	Away	Italy	0–2	L	Friendly
07/06/1992	Away	Portugal	2–0	W	Friendly
09/09/1992	Home	Latvia	4–0	W	Competitive
14/10/1992	Away	Denmark	0–0	D	Competitive
18/11/1992	Away	Spain	0–0	D	Competitive
17/02/1993	Home	Wales	2–1	W	Friendly
31/03/1993	Home	Northern Ireland	3–0	W	Competitive
28/04/1993	Home	Denmark	1–1	D	Competitive
26/05/1993	Away	Albania	2–1	W	Competitive
09/06/1993	Away	Latvia	2–0	W	Competitive
16/06/1993	Away	Lithuania	1–0	W	Competitive
08/09/1993	Home	Lithuania	2–0	W	Competitive
13/10/1993	Home	Spain	1–3	L	Competitive
17/11/1993	Away	Northern Ireland	1–1	D	Competitive
23/03/1994	Home	Russia	0–0	D	Friendly
20/04/1994	Away	Holland	1–0	W	Friendly
24/05/1994	Home	Bolivia	1–0	W	Friendly
29/05/1994	Away	Germany	2–0	W	Friendly
05/06/1994	Home	Czech Republic	1–3	L	Friendly
18/06/1994	Away	Italy	1–0	W	Competitive
24/06/1994	Away	Mexico	1–2	L	Competitive
28/06/1994	Away	Norway	0–0	D	Competitive
04/07/1994	Away	Holland	0–2	L	Competitive
07/09/1994	Away	Latvia	3–0	W	Competitive
12/10/1994	Home	Liechtenstein	4–0	W	Competitive

16/11/1994	Away	Northern Ireland	4–0	W	Competitive
15/02/1995	Home	England	1–0	W	Friendly
29/03/1995	Home	Northern Ireland	1–1	D	Competitive
26/04/1995	Home	Portugal	1–0	W	Competitive
03/06/1995	Away	Liechtenstein	0–0	D	Competitive
11/06/1995	Home	Austria	1–3	L	Competitive
06/09/1995	Away	Austria	1–3	L	Competitive
11/10/1995	Home	Latvia	2–1	W	Competitive
15/11/1995	Away	Portugal	0–3	L	Competitive
13/12/1995	Away	Holland	0–2	L	Competitive

11

MICK McCARTHY

If ever there was a hard act to follow, it was Jack Charlton. Having transformed Ireland's fortunes during a ten-year spell, many people predicted that once he left the role Ireland would simply fall to pieces and return to the dark days of the 1960s and 1970s. However, the man given the task of replacing Jack could not have been more appropriate. Mick McCarthy's direct approach to the game epitomised the Charlton era. It was no nonsense and full of heart. Even more importantly, McCarthy had played at the major tournaments of world football, and he could guide players through the years ahead. It was as if the role had been made for him, and it completed a glittering Ireland career as player, captain and then manager.

Unfortunately, the Ireland job was becoming increasingly difficult. Mick had inherited an ageing squad that included many of the players he had played with, and he had to make the transition from teammate and friend to manager. And at thirty-six years of age 'Big Mick' was a managerial novice, having not yet managed a club in a top league, which meant there would be a lot of focus on how he did the job. It was a big challenge, but not for a man who appeared to thrive on pressure, and one who has since gone on to manage at the top level of English football.

His management career for Ireland had its ups and downs, and there were moments when lady luck deserted him. But McCarthy succeeded where others before him had failed, and in doing so he cemented his place in Irish football folklore when he became only the second Ireland manager to lead the country to a World Cup finals.

THE EARLY YEARS

Mick McCarthy was born in Barnsley, Yorkshire, in 1959, but qualified for the Irish team thanks to his father Charles, who was born in Ireland. Jim Iley was the manager who gave McCarthy his chance in the Barnsley team in 1977 at the age of eighteen, and he made his debut in a 4–0 win over Rochdale. But it was under the tutelage of former Leeds United striker Alan Clarke, who took the role of player-manager in 1978, and his successor Norman Hunter, another Leeds legend, that Mick and Barnsley flourished. Within three years, the club had moved up the divisions to Division 2 (now the Championship). Mick's reputation as a tough-tackling and no-nonsense defender was taking shape and his performances in the Second Division were catching the eye of other clubs, and in December 1983 Mick made the move from his Yorkshire roots to Manchester, signing for City.

Any doubts that Mick might have felt about the move were

soon removed as he helped City gain promotion to the First Division in his first full season. At the age of twenty-five 'Big Mick' was in the big time and able to show the footballing world that he was capable of playing at the highest level. In the following season he helped City avoid immediate relegation and they finished in a respectable mid table place. However, their luck did not hold and City ended the following season by being relegated. Mick did not get the chance to help City make an immediate return to the First Division as by this time his performances had caught the eye of Celtic and David Hay, who lured him to Parkhead in May 1987. Although he was signed by Hay, Mick never got to play under him, as the manager was replaced soon afterwards by Billy McNeill, an old acquaintance from McCarthy's City days. Despite the shock of being signed by one manager and then playing under another, it did not appear to be too much of a setback, and it was at Celtic that people really began to take notice of the centre-half. His first season in Scotland saw McCarthy pick up his first major silverware, as Celtic won the double under the new manager. The following season saw McCarthy once again savour success as he helped Celtic win another Scottish Cup, although the Parkhead club had to settle for a disappointing third place in the League.

Lex Baillie, a young player who was making a name for himself at Celtic when Big Mick joined the club, but who is now a sergeant in the Strathclyde police force, recalls his initial impressions of McCarthy: 'I was a young lad and had not played for the first team before, so I saw Mick as a rival, especially as he was a big signing from down south. I was of the view that he was depriving me of a first-team opportunity. We were of a similar mould and in direct competition as defenders, although I now realise that Mick had more ability, and at that time he had more experience.

'But he soon became a role model for me. I learned a lot from Mick. He was so driven and focused. He was a very strong character, with a sheer will to win, and there was a lot of intensity and competition in our training in those days. We had a lot of strong characters in the team, players such as Tommy Burns, and there were often training-ground bust-ups, although they were always left on the pitch.

'As a defender he was great to play alongside. He played to a very high standard and would push those around him to play to those standards. I remember in one of his first games he was playing against Falkirk, and he was up against a player by the name of Crawford Baptie, who was about six feet three inches. Well, Mick punched him in the mouth early on in the game after they clashed, and he just walked off. It was a red card, of course, but he knew he was going to be sent off so he just walked. Afterwards Mick admitted he had no idea what we were on about when we were talking about Crawford Baptie before the game. He thought it was a Scottish word he had not heard before.

'I think all the signs were there that Mick would become a coach. When I was coming through he was one of the senior players, and he had opinions and thoughts on the game, and he talked to a lot of people about football.

'A dozen of us from that 1988 team, together with our wives, met up last year in Dubai for a few days. I had not seen Mick in a few years prior to that. One of the things I noticed was that he seemed more relaxed and comfortable in himself. He has achieved a lot of things in football, and that seems to have mellowed him a bit. He was great company during the few days out there, and even though we were rivals before we were teammates, I don't have a bad word to say about him.'

After forty-eight appearances for Celtic, McCarthy was once again on the move, this time to France, where he joined Lyon in July 1989. The move to France did not work out as he had planned and the defender failed to settle in Lyon. Feeling that he might be damaging his international career, Mick made the decision to return to England, signing for Millwall on loan in March 1990. His arrival failed to inspire the Lions and they ended the season with relegation. However McCarthy had impressed enough to earn a permanent move. Injuries hampered his appearances over the following two seasons and his appointment as manager of Millwall in 1992 effectively brought an end to his playing career, with his final game coming in a Division One match against Southend.

IRELAND CAREER

As Mick's father, Charles, was born in Ireland, Mick qualified to play for Ireland under the parent rule, making his international debut against Poland in 1984. He soon became a first-choice player although it was under the management of Big Jack that his international career really took off. Like Jack, Mick was a no-nonsense defender and under the stewardship of the Englishman he went on to become captain of his national team, leading to the moniker 'Captain Fantastic'.

Mick played a major role in Ireland's qualification for Euro '88 and Italia '90. He played in all three games in Holland in

1988 and featured in all five games in Italy, captaining the country to quarter-final defeat to hosts Italy. Despite effectively retiring from playing when he took the player-manager job with Millwall, McCarthy continued to play for Ireland for another year and won the last of his caps in a 2–0 win over Portugal in Boston in 1992. He retired from international football with fifty-seven caps, having scored two goals.

MANAGEMENT – A FIRST GLIMPSE

As Mick's career as a player drew to a close, the leadership qualities that his playing evoked ensured that he would make the step into management. The change came at the club who had rescued him from his French nightmare and in March 1992 Mick was offered the change to become player-manager of Millwall, replacing Bruce Rioch. In his first full season at the club Mick led Millwall to a seventh place finish in the newly formed Division One (the formation of the Premiership in 1992 had led to a restructure of all the Leagues).

With injuries starting to take their toll, Mick made the decision to relinquish the player part of his job description and focus on the management part, and the decision seemed justified when he led Millwall to the 1994 play-off finals with a third place finish during the regular season. Sadly the club lost out to Derby County and instead of reaching the Premiership they now had another season in England's Division One to look forward to.

The following season saw Millwall fail to reach the play-off heights of the 1994 season and Mick saw his side finish in thirteenth position. The 1995–1996 season saw Millwall fly off the block and from October to December Mick's team led the division and seemed on track for promotion. Then in December 1995 Big Jack resigned from the Ireland job, a decision that would have a dramatic bearing on Millwall. Soon after Jack's resignation, Mick was linked with the Ireland job, and the speculation seemed to have an detrimental effect on the Lions as they slipped from first to eleventh position in the space of five weeks. The uncertainty at Dens Park was lifted in February 1996 when Mick was finally confirmed as the new Irish manager. He left Millwall in ninth position, fourteen points clear of relegation, but a poor run of form saw them win only three games over the coming months, culminating in their relegation to Division Two.

Former Millwall player Mark Kennedy was once the most expensive teenager in Premiership history when he signed for Liverpool in 1995 at the age of eighteen. His development began under McCarthy at Millwall: 'When I first started to travel over to Millwall as a fourteen-year-old, Bruce Rioch was the man in charge, but by the time I signed for them Mick had taken over as manager. I think I was one of his first signings. Mick was absolutely amazing for me. He really looked after me, like he did all his players, but I was just a young lad who'd moved away from home, so I think he put in that bit extra with me.

'I often stayed over at his house in those days. It was very surreal. Mick was a hero, an Ireland captain, and to be managed by him was amazing. While Mick helped me settle in to life in England, he also helped my football development in a big way. When I first arrived at the club I was a centre-forward, but Mick must have seen something in me, as he moved me to the left wing. He felt that I wasn't physical enough for a striker. That happens quite a bit in English football. A young player will arrive at a club having played in one position, and then the manager sees something that no one else has, and they try you in another position. A perfect example is Josh McGuinness. I visited Cardiff before moving there and watched the youth team play. Josh was in goal. By the time I signed for the club, Josh had moved to centre-forward.

'The chance to move to the left wing came about in pre-season. I remember Greg Berry had been injured, and Mick moved me out there. I was small in build, and Mick felt that I would be kicked to pieces up front, whereas out on the wing that might not happen as much. It was wonderful foresight, really, as seven months later I was signed by Liverpool as a winger.

'In those days all I wanted to do was play. However, my attitude to the game has changed over time. Although they affected me, I did not take defeats and wins the way I do now. I am thirty-three now, and I have a different mindset towards games and understand the importance of results.

'It was a great honour to play for Mick and Millwall. They were my first club, and it was not only Mick who was great for me. There was John Byrne, who also played for Ireland. He was a massive influence on my early years in the game.

'Before the move to Liverpool there were some rumours that Blackburn were interested in signing me, and I was worried that the club would not let me go. I was out for dinner one night, and I had a missed call from Mick. He just left a message to ring him. I knew something had come up, so I rang him, and he said to come over to his house. When I got there he told me that Liverpool had made an offer and I was to travel up the next day for a medical. I remember asking him, "What about Blackburn? Can I talk to them?" I had no agent then, and Mick said to me, "Get your arse up to Liverpool, will you." He was happy for me, though, and I was very grateful to Mick for helping me develop my game. He was the one who spotted the left-winger in me.

'Mick has great man-management skills, and I think you can see that by the way players speak about him. He has shown that he is a top manager. When I got into the Ireland squad towards the end of Jack's reign it was fantastic, but I only played a couple of games under Jack before Mick came in. There was so much talent in the squad, players such as Denis Irwin and Andy Townsend, who I actually thought would have made a great manager. Mick had a tough job, but he made the role his own. He treated the players as adults, but any problems were dealt with in Mick's way, and you wouldn't argue with him. International football is different from club football. If you are not in the first team, you can knock on a club manager's door and have a chat with him; however, with international football you are representing your country, so you can't kick up a storm.'

Richard Sadlier first came across the Ireland boss when McCarthy tried to sign him for Millwall: 'I first met Mick when I was invited over to Millwall in the Easter of 1995. I was only sixteen at the time, and he invited me to train with the first team. It was an amazing experience. I was in awe of him. He was a legend, a member of a team that had been to the World Cup, but he was down to earth and a really decent fella. When he became the Ireland manager he still lived in Bromley near Millwall's training ground, and as I also lived there we used to bump into one other quite often.'

THE IRELAND JOB

Despite being one of the loyal soldiers during Charlton's era Mick was determined to be his own man when he took over and set about rebuilding the side. A new and exciting crop of talented youngsters was about to make the breakthrough at international level; the likes of Robbie Keane, Damian Duff, John O'Shea and Richard Dunne would all go on to become household names. The player scouting system that had come to symbolise the Charlton days was put to ever further use, with players such as Paul Butler, who qualified for Ireland through his marriage to an Irish woman, and Clinton Morrison benefiting from the scouting of players with Irish connections.

McCarthy's first campaign was the 1998 World Cup qualifiers, in which Ireland were drawn with Romania, Lithuania, FYR Macedonia, Iceland and Liechtenstein, who had embarrassed Ireland in the final months of Jack's reign. There were to be no mistakes this time around, however, as Mick opened his competitive account with a good 5–0 victory. A further win over Macedonia put Ireland in control in the group. Then came the first signs of the rocky journey ahead when Iceland came to Dublin and got a draw. This was followed by two defeats, one to strugglers Macedonia, a shock 3–2 result, and a 1–0 loss to Romania. Ireland were at this stage behind Romania, who had won all their games to date. Ireland finished out the group with no more defeats and with wins over Lithuania, Iceland and Liechtenstein, as well as draws with Romania and Lithuania.

Ireland finished ten points behind Romania in the standings, but it was enough to secure a play-off game against Belgium. The first leg ended 1–1 after Luc Nilis cancelled out Denis

Irwin's opener. However, heartbreak was to follow in Belgium when Nilis again scored in the sixty-ninth minute to cancel Ray Houghton's leveller, so it was the Belgians who crossed the border to France '98 and left Mick with the task of rebuilding his side further.

It was around this time that McCarthy had a chance to return to his English footballing roots. Barnsley were interested in appointing him and his assistant Ian Evans to the coaching staff at the club. However, Barnsley failed to meet the FAI's compensation request. McCarthy was believed to have been interested in combining both roles, but nothing came of it, and he remained as Ireland manager.

Bernard O'Byrne was the chief executive of the FAI at the time that McCarthy was Ireland manager, and he recalls the backing and understanding that the Englishman received during the early days of his reign: 'Mick came into the role in early 1996, and I joined the FAI the following October. I found Mick to be straight as a die in my dealings with him. He was very fair and cooperative, and there was no manoeuvring from him. He was happy not to get involved in the politics.

'The first three years in the job were hard for Mick. It was a big task, and it was always going to be very hard succeeding Jack after what he'd achieved. I think Mick himself felt the pressure.

'I remember after the first qualifying campaign for France '98, when we lost to Belgium in the play-offs, there were some members of the FAI who wanted to replace Mick. However, Pat Quigley and I were allies of Mick and believed that he deserved a reasonable run in charge before he could be judged properly. We pushed to get a stay of execution for him, and before one board meeting we raised the subject and asked everyone in the room to stand up and support Mick. Our stance surprised a lot of people, and in the end they all opted to support him. From then on I think Mick went from strength to strength in the role.

'In my opinion one of the reasons that Mick struggled at the start was that he inherited an ageing squad that had lost a few players to retirement. However, that was not the only factor. His relationship with Ian Evans [assistant manager to Mick and Ireland Under-21 manager] was pivotal to Ireland's success. They had a big partnership. However, Ireland did not seem to be getting the full benefit of the partnership, as Ian was spending a lot of time with the Under-21s and not as much time with the senior side. We said to Mick that Ian needed to step back from his role with the Under-21 team and to get more involved with the senior side to help ease the workload on Mick. We decided that we needed someone to take over the management of the Under-21 side, someone who could work with Mick, and in the end we opted for Don Givens.

'Mick was very loyal to the players, and he stood by them. He would back them in public and would discuss any issues in private. He was a hero to a lot of the players. He was hugely respected. He had earned his war scars, so to speak, and the players believed in him.'

That loyalty was starting to get results, as qualification for the 2000 European Championship saw Ireland get off to the best possible start when they defeated Croatia 2–0. The Croatians had impressed at the World Cup in France and were one of the favourites to qualify from the group. However, goals from the United pair of Denis Irwin and Roy Keane got Ireland off to a perfect start.

That victory was followed by another win over Malta before

a 1–0 defeat away to Yugoslavia put the skids on Ireland's bid. The return game in Dublin saw Mark Kennedy net the winner as Ireland won 2–1. Croatia got their revenge with a 1–0 win in Zagreb, before old foes Macedonia scored in the ninetieth minute of the next match to deny Ireland the group and pushed them once again into the play-offs, where Turkey scraped in thanks to a 1–1 draw in Dublin.

The 2002 World Cup qualifying campaign finally saw Mick and his team excise the ghosts of the failure to reach France in 1998 and Holland in 2000. The team had matured and reached the levels that the public had come to expect. The results were improving, and having slipped down the rankings from fifteenth in the world, the team were slowly on the up again.

Drawn in a qualification group with Portugal and Holland, the task seemed onerous from the offset. However, two draws with Portugal home and away, as well a famous victory over Holland in Dublin, saw Ireland finish unbeaten and level at the top of the group with Portugal, only missing out on automatic qualification on goal difference.

Mick was displaying tremendous dedication to the job, but it must have been a difficult decision when he decided to manage the team for a game against Andorra following the death of his father. A few days earlier Mick had left the squad ahead of a game with Cyprus to be with his father, who was seriously ill at the time. His assistant Ian Evans deputised and saw Ireland win 4–0, with two from Roy Keane.

As it was, Ireland faced the prospect of a play-off for the third time under Mick. This time Iran were the opponents, and a 2–0 home victory followed by a 1–0 defeat was enough to send the green army to Japan and Korea for the 2002 World Cup.

With qualification secured, Mick set about finalising and experimenting with his squad, and friendlies with Russia, Denmark and the USA were arranged. Players such as Richard Sadlier, Colin Healy and Clinton Morrison were given their chance to stake a claim. As Sadlier recalled, 'I was called into the squad for a match against Russia in February 2002. Before that I remember thinking the call-up would never come, as it seemed that every time I had a stinker for Millwall someone would point out that Mick had been in the crowd. The full Ireland set-up was similar to the under-age set-up under Bruce Rioch. Everyone seemed close-knit, and there was a lot of respect for Mick within the group.

'Colin Healy, Steven Reid and Clinton Morrison were also making their debuts against Russia. I was sharing a room with Colin Healy, who started in the middle with Roy Keane. I remember being on the bus to the game and sitting next to Niall Quinn. He was so good to me. He kept playing down the importance of the occasion and told me there was nothing that I hadn't seen before. Then throughout the game, every time I came back from a stint warming up, Niall would elbow me towards Mick, as if trying to tell Mick to get me on. With twenty minutes to go Mick shouted over to me to get ready to go on. Afterwards Mick congratulated me and shook my hand.

'The World Cup was looming and at the Russian game the players were asked to fill out forms that would have been used for ticket allocation. I turned to Niall and asked him should I fill one out? I mean you had Robbie Keane, Damian Duff, Niall Quinn and Clinton Morrison in the squad. I didn't really think much of my chance. However, Niall said to me, "Shut up and fill it in. My back's in a bad way."'

In the end injury prevented Sadlier from going to the finals, and Mick took a calculated risk with Niall Quinn, one that reaped its rewards, most notably in the Germany game when his introduction caused havoc for the opposition's defence and helped create a goal for Robbie Keane. It was more than a risk. It was a measure of McCarthy's loyalty to the players who had helped the team qualify and a just reward.

With a good build-up behind them, Ireland appeared on course to have a relatively successful World Cup. Drawn in the same group as an ageing German team, Cameroon and Saudi Arabia, hopes were high that Ireland would once again reach the last sixteen stage of the tournament.

Ireland's preparations were thrown into disarray prior to the start of the tournament when Roy Keane and Mick McCarthy had their now infamous Saipan fall out, the result of which saw one of Ireland's greatest ever players opt to forego an appearance in the World Cup. Keane, used to the very best with Manchester United, felt let down by what he perceived as poor preparation and facilities, and not wanting to simply make up the numbers decided it was best to speak out. With Keane gone, all hope appeared to vanish, while the media attention and pressure this situation placed on the team was enormous. However, Mick managed to steady the ship and steer the team to the second round of the tournament. In Keane's absence Matt Holland and Mark Kinsella stepped up to the mark and helped balance the side, while Robbie Keane finally got the chance to show what a top player he was. Draws with eventual finalists Germany and Cameroon, followed by a victory over Saudi Arabia were enough to secure a second-round game with Spain. Despite the team playing out of their skin and managing to miss a penalty in normal time, they were eventually eliminated by Spain in a penalty shoot-out, thus narrowly missing out on a quarter-final place.

Instead of focusing on the achievements of a team that reached the second round at the World Cup, the focus shifted to what could have been had Keane been there. Indeed, the Saipan incident resulted in divided opinion countrywide and despite the credible results that Ireland had achieved, the public still did not fully back McCarthy. As soon as results started to turn against the team, the media and fans alike were on the manager's back and wanted him out the door.

The achievements of the World Cup were soon forgotten as Ireland made a poor start to their qualifying campaign for Euro 2004. Two opening defeats, a 4–2 away defeat to Russia and a 2–1 home defeat to Switzerland, saw the pressure on McCarthy begin to build and with the Saipan incident refusing to go away, Mick's position was becoming more and more untenable. In November 2002, Mick took the decision to resign.

The end of McCarthy's reign will always be remembered for the incident in Saipan. For Bernard Menton the whole thing is very simple. He recalls, 'Mick once said to me that Roy Keane could be very difficult, but he was always the first name that appeared on the team sheet, and I think that sums it up.'

LIFE AFTER IRELAND

Despite his much-hyped exit from the Ireland job, McCarthy did not remain out of the game for too long, and less than six months later, in March 2003, after sitting on the couches of TV studios providing commentary and insight, Mick returned to the dugout with Premiership side Sunderland. Joining the club after the sacking of Howard Wilkinson, it was a case of too little too late, as Mick could not help the club in their relegation battle.

The following season Mick picked the side up and led them to the Championship play-offs, where they lost to Crystal Palace on penalties. Sunderland had finished the regular season in third spot, seven points off the automatic promotion place. However, there was to be no mistake in 2005 when he led Sunderland to the Championship title, scoring twenty-nine victories and amassing ninety-four points along the way.

However, the Premiership proved to be a tricky proposition, and McCarthy struggled with a tight budget. During a season in which the Black Cats gathered only fifteen points and three wins, Mick found himself sacked in March with ten games to go. In an ironic twist Sunderland next turned to Roy Keane to revive their fortunes and provided him with a large transfer budget that would have made life a lot easier for his predecessor.

Management in the Premiership is at another level to the Championship – the Premiership is more skilful and tactical. It is where every football club in England wants to be, and the level of expectation and pressure, coupled with the riches on offer for success, means that the competition has proved to be the downfall of many managers. There seem to be men who will get you out of the Championship and men who will keep you in the Premier League. With McCarthy forging a reputation as a man of the Championship, it was no surprise when clubs outside of the top flight took an interest in him, and in July 2006, less than three months after the confidence-sapping season in the Premiership with Sunderland, McCarthy was back in management with Wolverhampton Wanderers, replacing former England manager Glenn Hoddle.

Wolves provided the perfect opportunity for McCarthy to rebuild his reputation once again, although he was not helped by a balancing of the books that saw an exodus of senior players, including big names such as Kenny Miller, Paul Ince, Mark Kennedy and Darren Anderton, who left the club when their contracts expired. The departure of Joleon Lescott in a big-money move to Everton, meant that the Wolves team needed to be rebuilt from scratch.

Wolves were seen as a sleeping giant with the facilities and history to be a Premiership club, but in need of a manager who could motivate players and was familiar with getting promotion out of the Championship. Mick was that man and he set about rallying the squad and creating a fantastic spirit within the team. The signing of Gary Breen, McCarthy's old stalwart from his Ireland days, helped bring stability to the team, and against all expectations they managed to make the promotion play-offs. The play-off semi-final saw Wolves pitched against midlands rivals West Bromwich Albion, but a 3–2 home loss, coupled with a 1–0 loss away, saw Wolves miss out on the play-off. The disappointment of the play-offs were soon put to the back of Mick's mind as that summer Steve Morgan took control of the club and brought with him the promise of investment. The 2008 season was one full of promise for the Wolves fans.

Wolves once again failed to live up to the expectations and for much of the season Mick's side failed to make an impact on the League. Mounting pressure was eased by a late run of results that brought Wolves within touching distance of the play-offs, but in the end goal difference saw them miss out. Despite the setback Mick managed to hang on to his job, and the ultimate reward was about to come for the Wolves faithful.

The 2009–10 season saw the club's best start to a campaign since 1949, and once they hit the top of the table for the first time at the end of August they never looked back, not leaving the automatic promotion spots thereafter. Promotion to the Premier League was finally confirmed on 18 April 2009 with a 1–0 win over Queens Park Rangers. A week later Wolves clinched their first divisional title since 1989, and Mick was back in the big time once again. Further confirmation of his talent arrived when Mick was named the Championship Manager of the Year.

McCarthy has shown a lot of faith in Irish players over the years, and the current Wolves squad contains some of the best young talent that Ireland has to offer: Kevin Doyle, Andrew Keogh, Stephen Ward, who has benefited from a positional switch instigated by McCarthy, and also young defender Kevin Foley. This faith in the Irish system has been coupled with a fantastic eye for lower League unknowns. McCarthy's ability to spot talent has seen stars such as Michael Knightly, Sylvan Ebanks-Blake, Christophe Berra, Andrew Surman and Richard Stearman thrive at Wolves and helped cement his reputation as a shrewd manager in the transfer market.

The 2009–2010 Premiership season saw Mick do something he had failed to do with previous clubs and keep them in the League. Wolves had been among the favourites for relegation, but against all the odds, Mick led the club to a fifteenth-place finish, their best finish since 1981.

In a career that has to date lasted four decades, McCarthy has shown himself to be man of honour and commitment, and above all loyal to a fault. He fully deserves his place as one of the heroes of Irish football.

MICK McCARTHY'S CLUB MANAGERIAL HONOURS RECORD:

Football League Championship 2005 & 2009

MICK McCARTHY'S IRELAND RECORD:

Total number of games in charge: 68
Total number of wins: 29 (ratio 42.65%)
Total number of draws: 20 (ratio 29.41%)
Total number of losses: 19 (ratio 27.94%)
Biggest win: 5–0 *v.* Liechtenstein (twice) and Malta
Biggest defeat: 4–2 *v.* Russia
Longest unbeaten run: 16 games

MICK McCARTHY'S RESULTS AS IRELAND MANAGER:

Date	Home/ Away	Opponent	Score	Result	Type of Fixture
27/03/1996	Home	Russia	0–2	L	Friendly
24/04/1996	Away	Czech Republic	0–2	L	Friendly
29/05/1996	Home	Portugal	0–1	L	Friendly
02/06/1996	Home	Croatia	2–2	D	Friendly

04/06/1996	Away	Holland	1–3	L	Friendly
09/06/1996	Away	United States	1–2	L	Friendly
12/06/1996	Away	Mexico	2–2	D	Friendly
15/06/1996	Away	Bolivia	3–0	W	Friendly
31/08/1996	Away	Liechtenstein	5–0	W	Competitive
09/10/1996	Home	Macedonia	3–0	W	Competitive
10/11/1996	Home	Iceland	0–0	D	Competitive
11/02/1997	Away	Wales	0–0	D	Friendly
02/04/1997	Away	Macedonia	2–3	L	Competitive
30/04/1997	Away	Romania	0–1	L	Competitive
21/05/1997	Home	Liechtenstein	5–0	W	Competitive
20/08/1997	Home	Lithuania	0–0	D	Competitive
06/09/1997	Away	Iceland	4–2	W	Competitive
10/09/1997	Away	Lithuania	2–1	W	Competitive
11/10/1997	Home	Romania	1–1	D	Competitive
29/10/1997	Home	Belgium	1–1	D	Competitive
15/11/1997	Away	Belgium	1–2	L	Competitive
25/03/1998	Away	Czech Republic	1–2	L	Friendly
22/04/1998	Home	Argentina	0–2	L	Friendly
23/05/1998	Home	Mexico	0–0	D	Friendly
05/09/1998	Home	Croatia	2–0	W	Competitive
14/10/1998	Home	Malta	5–0	W	Competitive
18/11/1998	Away	Yugoslavia	0–1	L	Competitive
10/02/1999	Home	Paraguay	2–0	W	Friendly
28/04/1999	Home	Sweden	2–0	W	Friendly
29/05/1999	Home	Northern Ireland	0–1	L	Friendly

09/06/1999	Home	Macedonia	1–0	W	Competitive
01/09/1999	Home	Yugoslavia	2–1	W	Competitive
04/09/1999	Away	Croatia	0–1	L	Competitive
08/09/1999	Away	Malta	3–2	W	Competitive
09/10/1999	Away	Macedonia	1–1	D	Competitive
13/11/1999	Home	Turkey	1–1	D	Competitive
17/11/1999	Away	Turkey	0–0	D	Competitive
23/02/2000	Home	Czech Republic	3–2	W	Friendly
26/04/2000	Home	Greece	0–1	L	Friendly
30/05/2000	Home	Scotland	1–2	L	Friendly
04/06/2000	Away	Mexico	2–2	D	Friendly
06/06/2000	Away	United States	1–1	D	Friendly
11/06/2000	Away	South Africa	2–1	W	Friendly
02/09/2000	Away	Holland	2–2	D	Competitive
07/10/2000	Away	Portugal	1–1	D	Competitive
11/10/2000	Home	Estonia	2–0	W	Competitive
15/11/2000	Home	Finland	3–0	W	Friendly
24/03/2001	Away	Cyprus	4–0	W	Competitive
28/03/2001	Away	Andorra	3–0	W	Competitive
25/04/2001	Home	Andorra	3–1	W	Competitive
02/06/2001	Home	Portugal	1–1	D	Competitive
06/06/2001	Away	Estonia	2–0	W	Competitive
15/08/2001	Home	Croatia	2–2	D	Competitive
01/09/2001	Home	Holland	1–0	W	Competitive
06/10/2001	Home	Cyprus	4–0	W	Competitive
10/11/2001	Home	Iran	2–0	W	Competitive
15/11/2001	Away	Iran	0–1	L	Competitive

13/02/2002	Home	Russia	2–0	W	Friendly
27/03/2002	Home	Denmark	3–0	W	Friendly
17/04/2002	Home	United States	2–1	W	Friendly
16/05/2002	Home	Nigeria	1–2	L	Friendly
01/06/2002	Away	Cameroon	1–1	D	Competitive
05/06/2002	Away	Germany	1–1	D	Competitive
11/06/2002	Away	Saudi Arabia	3–0	W	Competitive
16/06/2002	Away	Spain	1–1	D	Competitive
21/08/2002	Away	Finland	3–0	W	Friendly
07/09/2002	Away	Russia	2–4	L	Competitive
16/10/2002	Home	Switzerland	1–2	L	Competitive

12

BRIAN KERR

The best players do not always make the best coaches, nor do less accomplished players automatically make bad coaches. José Mourinho is the best modern-day example of this, having started out as a player before moving into coaching. Many club chairmen seem to think the bigger the player, the better the manager. The Premier League and the Championship in England are good examples of Leagues in which big personalities often start their management careers at the bigger clubs without first learning the traits and skills that make a good manager.

However, it can also be said that some people are simply born to play, while others are born to manage. Mick Meagan once said that he never actually liked managing, that he preferred to be one of the lads and that one of the hardest things in his life was finding out that he could not play any more. Brian Kerr, on the other hand, was destined to be a manager. Whether it is coaching Dublin inner city junior teams, Irish youth teams, League of Ireland teams or the Irish national team, Brian lives and breathes football – anyone who has met him will tell you that. More importantly for Irish soccer fans, he is also the only manager to have led an Ireland team to a win at a major tournament at any level.

EARLY YEARS

Brian Kerr was born in 1953 in Drimnagh, an area which over the years has been the birthplace of a number of famous sportspeople, including Kevin Moran and Tony Dunne who both played for Manchester United, 1983 Athletics World Champion Eamonn Coghlan and Olympic gold medal boxer Michael Carruth. In fact Brian's father was a coach with Drimnagh Boxing Club, but it was football that interested Brian the most and as a youth he played with Crumlin United, progressing to Leinster League football with Bluebell United. However, despite his love of the game and a determination to succeed at the top level of the game in Ireland, Brian failed to make the grade at League of Ireland level and instead made his mark on football in this country as a successful coach and manager. Kerr recalls those days well: 'In and around Drimnagh we would play in street leagues during the summer [these were games between other streets in the area]. I also played youth-team football for Rialto. The street leagues were for kids who were under thirteen and a half. While I was playing for the Under-13-and-a-half team, I also set up and managed an Under-11 team.

'I was a St Patrick's Athletic fan in those days, and I followed the managers of the team almost as much as the team itself. The likes of Charlie Walker, Jack Burkett, Barry Bridges and Gerry Dolan were gods to me and big influences. My dad coached boxing, and although I did not follow down that road, I think his passion and hard work transferred over to me. I loved managing players, and I loved the fact that I could influence teams and results. I played under a lot of coaches who were enthusiastic and dedicated, but I wanted more. I wanted more control.

'I was frustrated by the level I played at. Like all kids, I wanted to play professional football in England and for Ireland, and I think at about eighteen I realised that it was not going to happen. Thankfully, I was cute enough to have started my coaching badges at the age of sixteen, although in those days there were not a lot of courses around. I also got some lucky breaks along the way, from the likes of Gerry Moran and Liam Tuohy. Over the years I have been given opportunities, although generally those opportunities arose when there was no money or teams were struggling or both.'

When Brian took over as manager of St Patrick's Athletic in December 1986 they were one of the forgotten sides of Irish football and had not won a League title since 1956. However, under Brian, St Pat's was transformed and within three weeks the team won the Leinster Senior Cup. St Pat's continued to progress and a return to the heady days of the 1950s, when they'd won three titles, was on the horizon. For Brian the initial success was a dream come true and a sign that the tough work was starting to pay off, for as well as managing St Patrick's Athletic, Brian also had a day job at UCD where he was part of the technical staff of the Department of Food Science. Brian's job with St Pat's was even more remarkable considering the lack of resources that he had at his disposal. With a small budget Brian did not have the option to buy the best that the League of Ireland had to offer and instead he scoured junior and schoolboy football for hidden treasures. Curtis Fleming and future St Pat's manager John McDonnell were some of the success stories from Brian's transfer activities.

The 1988 season nearly saw St Pat's and Brian win the League when, in dramatic fashion, they drew 1–1 with Dundalk in the last game of the season – all that was required for St Pat's to claim the title was a win. The following season saw St Pat's finish fourth, losing only six games and having the best defensive record. Then in 1990 Brian delivered the League of Ireland crown to the Inchicore faithful, losing only three games in the process. While at St Patrick's Athletic in the early 1990s, he had a team that on paper should never have won the title from Shelbourne, but the mentality Brian instilled in the players ensured that they believed that they could win every match.

Despite the success that the club was enjoying on the field, off the field the club was in financial trouble and as a result Brian was forced to sell off the majority of the team he had created to raise money to keep the club afloat. In fact Brian went even further in his efforts to help the club, joining a group of investors who raised funds to save the club from liquidation in 1992. The financial troubles coincided with a return to mid-table mediocrity for St Pat's as Brian was faced with the task of rebuilding the side from scratch. However, by 1995 the club was showing signs of improving as they finished fifth in the League. The following season Brian once again showed his extraordinary talent for creating fairytales as his new look St Pat's side won the League by five points.

Dave Campbell, who was a member of the St Patrick's Athletic side that won the title under Kerr's stewardship in 1996, recalls: 'Brian was one of a kind. He was way ahead of his time. Looking back now they seem like simple things, but we had sports physiologists when nobody had them. He was very tactical, and his training sessions were never repetitive. I remember he was managing a League of Ireland representative side that was playing against Manchester United, and the evening before the game we were practising defending set-pieces. Brian was telling us, "Now Pallister, he likes to make his runs to the back post."

'Brian lives and breathes football. At training sessions he'd ask one of the lads, "Do you have the *Evening Herald* in the car?" When he got it he would open the fixtures page and plan out his weekend. And not just League of Ireland matches. If he heard there was a player playing in the junior leagues who had slipped under the radar but who with a bit of coaching could be a diamond, he was off to check him out. He would circle the fixtures and say, "If I leave that game at half-time, I can make this game" and so on. Pure dedication to the game.

'His preparation for matches was second to none. In the build-up to games he would get the local papers from where we were playing the following weekend and pull out quotes and put them on the walls, saying, "Do you see what they have been saying about us?" He really built us up for games. He lived football twenty-four hours a day and knew everything about every player. He could tell you the ones who might have had a pint during the week or the blind spot of a player who was making his debut and no one had ever heard of. That was his way.

'The season we won the League we lost only four games and, although we had good players, our success was more down to the sum of all the parts producing a good team, with the main part being Brian and his organisational skills. One time we were in Drogheda, and Brian started telling us a story. He had seen a play the night before, and the premise of the play was that a man was tied up in a room. Although he was tied up he could move himself a little bit. In the middle of the room there was a pair of scissors, and the man knew that if he got to them, he would be able to cut himself free. We were all thinking to ourselves, "What is he talking about? Has he been drinking?" Undeterred, Brian explained to us that the League was like a rope around us and only by winning it would we cut ourselves free. With that, Brian left the room. He came back a while later, and there was loads of laughter in the room, so he asked, "What's so funny?" He was getting pissed off, so one of the lads told him to look up. A pair of scissors were hanging from the ceiling. Brian shouted, "Ye fucking bastards" and stormed out of the room. He was good for a bit of banter and along with Noel O'Reilly, who was a great coach, they made an entertaining pair on the guitar for singsongs.

'One of the biggest gambles Brian took during the season we won the title was to persuade Liam Buckley, who he had signed to be his assistant, to also register as a player. Liam was about thirty-six or thirty-seven at the time, but, to his credit, he still had it and was an inspiration that season.

'Brian hated when anyone left the club. If you were playing against a former teammate and had the temerity to talk to him before the match, you would hear Brian's dulcet tones roaring at you, "Get away from him. If he wanted to talk to you, he wouldn't have left." When I left St Pat's he didn't speak to me for three years. That said, he is without a doubt the best manager I ever played for.

'He used to the treat the club's money as if it was his own. If we lost a game and one of the board members came in with the pay packets, Brian would take them off him and hold onto them until the following Tuesday. And so help you if you went over to him to ask him for yours. He'd give you a good tongue lashing, saying your performance didn't merit payment.

'My dad used to say to me, "If St Patrick's Athletic played Shelbourne or Manchester United, they'd win 1–0 or 2–1. However, if they played a First Division team from the League of Ireland they would only win 1–0 or 2–1 there, too." It seemed to be Brian's way. I suppose it holds true for the criticism he received while in charge of Ireland. There was always a perception that the team didn't push forward and always sat back a bit, although the same can be said of the current regime. There is also a feeling that luck was most definitely not with Brian.'

In December 1996 Kerr quit his post with St Patrick's Athletic to become the technical director of the FAI. It was the start of a golden era for Irish football. His new role meant that he was responsible for the Republic of Ireland sides from Under-16 to Under-20 level. His first major tournament was the 1997 World Youth Championships. Kerr stuck to his roots by including three players from the League of Ireland in his squad and in the process he showed his tactical ability by leading Ireland to a bronze medal position. The tournament saw a number of stars emerge into Irish footballing folklore, including a young Damian Duff. The next year he guided the Republic of Ireland to an unprecedented double, and to date Ireland's only international trophies, by winning both the Under-16 and Under-18 European Championships. A number of the players involved would go on to win full international caps, most notably Damian Duff and Robbie Keane, who have since become household names.

Former West Ham goalkeeper Alex O'Reilly was a member of the Under-18 team that won the European Championship in Cyprus under Kerr: 'The preparation was the most professional I had ever seen. I had not seen anything like it before, not even at West Ham. Brian would tell us what he wanted from us. He really knew what he wanted and how he wanted us to play. It was so in-depth. Nothing was a shock to us, as he knew every little detail about the opposition. We were never overwhelmed going out on the pitch.

'Brian had a great group of players within the squad. Everyone got on, and there was no one who was too big for his boots – it made Brian and Noel O'Reilly's jobs easier. England had a bigger pool of players than us, and they beat us 1–0 during the tournament, but we stuck together as a team. We would be down at the pool with Brian, Noel and a guitar, having a sing-song, so there was never any boredom to deal with. And no one was left out, no matter if you could sing or not. A lot of other teams' players would be in their rooms from about seven or eight, and this led to them getting distracted, so it was great that Noel and Brian kept it entertaining.

'Brian was not a ranter and raver. We played as a team, and he kept everything out in the open. I think the players really responded to it. Brian is definitely up there as one of the best managers I played under. I had great admiration for him and what he achieved.'

Jason Gavin was also a member of the Under-18 European Championship squad and later played at the FIFA World Youth Championships in Nigeria under Kerr. He remembers the camaraderie that existed within the squad, something that seems to have been a major part of any team that Brian has been involved with: 'Brian has a great ability to get players to like and trust him very quickly. He was a great motivator, and in Noel O'Reilly he had a great coach. The Under-18 team was fantastically prepared, and we all knew each other really well. A lot of us had played together from the age of twelve. Stephen McPhail, Richard Dunne, Robbie Keane, Alan Quinn and I were all very familiar with each other. It helps that the squad all got on well. Brian helped with that too. He was easy to speak to and have a laugh with, although he could easily switch into manager mode, too.

'The preparation was second to none. For the Under-18 Championships we were drawn in the same group as England, who at that time had an amazing youth team. I remember we headed over to Cyprus a few weeks early to acclimatise to the heat. The preparation and coaching off the pitch was just as important, and Brian was great in this area. We knew everything about the opponents, their strengths and weaknesses. Brian analysed them, and we would watch DVDs of them playing. It was spot-on preparation.

'Brian was very approachable, and you could have a talk with him if you weren't happy. I started the tournament on the bench and was obviously not happy, as I wanted to be playing. I came on against England and did well, and Brian said to me, "If you get in and do well, you'll stay in." And he was true to his word, as I started against Cyprus in the next game and then played all the way through to the final. He was a great manager to play and learn under.'

Colin Hawkins was a member of the youth side that captured

the Irish public's imagination in 1997: 'Brian was brilliant for me. I had just been released by Coventry, so as a young player it was a tough time for me. But Brian had named me in a forty-man training squad that assembled in Limerick. It was actually my first time meeting him, but I managed to make it into the final squad. It was a great show of faith by Brian in my abilities.

'We got together and started our preparations at the University of Limerick. Brian had really done his research. The main thing that the squad would struggle with in Malaysia, which is where the Championships were held that year, was the humidity, so Brian tried to prepare us for it. Firstly we would wear extra jackets when training and also when we were in the sauna. He also got us used to drinking loads of water, even though the weather in Limerick was obviously a lot different to what it would be like in Asia. We all thought he was crazy at the start, but those things definitely helped us over there, and we found it easier to cope with the heat. On his days off, Brian would go to watch the other teams, and he knew the name of all our opponents, so we were well prepared in that sense, too.

'Brian and his assistant Noel O'Reilly really built a great team spirit. We had a real siege mentality. A lot of the other teams didn't understand it when they saw us in the lobby of the hotel having a singsong. Before games we would form a circle, and Noel would often say a prayer. There was a real unity about us.

'We were not actually aware of the fuss that was being made of us in Ireland. We were too far away to realise. Brian really took the pressure off the team. He had us concentrate on our own game and told us not to worry about the opposition. This was especially true against Spain. We knew they would keep the ball all day, but Brian had that siege mentality instilled in us, and we were so prepared on the day. In the end we won thanks to a Trevor Molloy penalty.

'The semi-final was a tougher game again. Argentina had knocked out England and Brazil on their way to the semi-finals, and nobody fancied our chances, but we stuck to our jobs and only lost 1–0 in the end.

'Brian was a very good manager, and tactically he was excellent. He juggled the players around so that people got games while others were rested, and he also managed to keep the players fresh and happy, which is hard to do when you are away at a tournament like that.'

In the 1999 World Youth Championships, the Republic of Ireland team was knocked out by hosts Nigeria in the quarter-final. Kerr continued his excellent record in under-age youth football by once again leading Ireland to qualify for the 2003 World Youth Championships before leaving the role to take up the position of manager of the senior national side. And it was through his work with Irish youth teams that he made his name, which led to him replacing Mick McCarthy as manager of the senior team.

Former Millwall player Richard Sadlier played for Kerr at youth level and says, 'I became involved in the Under-18 team, and at the time the profile of the under-age set-up was at its highest. Brian was really down to earth, and the role suited him. I was only seventeen at the time, so I didn't have much experience of managers to compare him with, but there were no airs and graces about him. He was very meticulous and knew exactly what he wanted. Each coaching session had a specific aim, and plans were laid out. He liked everything to be perfect and could get cantankerous if they weren't. We were in Nigeria for the Under-20 World Championships, and the bus was running twenty minutes late to pick us up. Brian was getting annoyed. Then when we got to the training pitches the grass was up to his knees. Well, that tipped him over the edge.

'He was not afraid to make changes if they were needed. In Nigeria my teammate Robbie Ryan was told to get ready to go on. To our surprise we then realised that Brian was taking off a player who had just gone on. Before a game we would watch videos of our opponents and when the team line-up was announced for a game he would talk through individual roles and set-plays. He knew our strengths, and we were never outplayed.'

Although his tactics and preparation were the key to his success, Kerr also created a close-knit group of players, especially at under-age level, which helped Ireland prevail against more illustrious European opponents. At that time, Ireland youth players based in Ireland trained once during the week and once at the weekends with their clubs, while their English counterparts had the luxury of four or fives nights' training in a professional set-up.

When Brian eventually got his chance at the top job he had very big boots to fill. Mick McCarthy had had a successful World Cup campaign, although since then things had not quite gone to plan. After two defeats in the opening two Euro 2004 qualifying games, morale was low and the players' confidence needed to be improved. Mick McCarthy ultimately resigned from his post, paving the way for Kerr to take what many assumed was his natural role.

In January 2003 Kerr was appointed as the new manager of the senior team. In him, the FAI had a manager who had known the players before they all became rich and famous, and he had led them to success before. His appointment met with a very positive response, given his success with the under-age team. He was, however, left the massive challenge of reviving Ireland's bid to achieve qualification to Euro 2004. Brian had six games to save Ireland's 2004 qualification campaign and he began his competitive tenure with a 2–1 away win over Georgia. This was followed with a disappointing 0–0 away draw with Albania. Brian's first competitive game in Ireland was a nervy 2–1 win over Albania secured by a last minute own goal, before another home win over Georgia saw Brian with three wins and a draw from his opening four games. The autumn brought Brian a 1–1 draw with Russia in his first match against a top tier European side, but any hope Brian had of finishing his first campaign unbeaten were dashed as Ireland lost 2–0 away to Switzerland. In the end Ireland finished the group in third place, four points off qualification.

With Brian now familiar with the different pace of senior international football, hopes were high for the qualification campaign for the 2006 World Cup in Germany. Pitted against France, Israel and Switzerland, Ireland drew five and lost one game to finish the group in fourth place just three points away from an automatic place in Germany. Draws at home and away to Israel and Switzerland proved costly, especially as in three of the four games, Ireland were in the lead at some point. The initial optimism that had surrounded Brian's appointment was fading and his defensive tactics did not sit well with the media and critics. Brian's response to this criticism was a refusal to answer questions concerning his tactics and decisions. The stand-off did not have the desired effect, however, as it only increased the divide between the manager and the media who continued their campaign against him and his approach. Kerr himself concedes that the football Ireland played under him was conservative, but it was intended to win matches and get results: 'I was pushing the FAI to arrange friendly games against the top fifteen sides in the world, as I felt it was the only way to push the team forward. At the end of the season in June 2004 we played Nigeria, Jamaica and Holland over the course of a week, and we beat Jamaica and Holland and lost 3–0 to Nigeria, but we only had the bare bones of a team. Against Holland I had a midfield of Alan Quinn, Matt Holland, Graham Barrett and Liam Miller, and we won 1–0.

'I knew we were risking things taking on high-profile teams, but it was the only way to lead Ireland into the future. There was little benefit in playing countries lower than or the same as us in the rankings, as you learned very little from those games.'

Brian's preparation, his development of younger players and his ability to work on a limited budget were key to his rise up the footballing management ladder. As an Irishman who had enjoyed European success with Ireland's youngsters, the FAI, media and public all felt that Ireland had the right man for the manager's job. Despite the acrimonious parting of ways in the end, Brian's ascent up the footballing ranks in Ireland proves that in the modern era of football you do not have to be a former player or to have managed in England to reach the pinnacle of Irish football.

LIFE POST-IRELAND

Brian's tenure with Ireland came to an end with the failure of the FAI to renew his contract after the unsuccessful 2006 qualifying campaign. While he pondered his next move in football, Brian became involved in a directorial capacity with Sport Against Racism Ireland (SARI) and also provided regular analysis on football on radio, television and in the newspapers.

However, in March 2007, after almost eighteen months out of the game, the lure of everyday football proved too much for Brian to ignore, and he returned to former club St Patrick's Athletic, this time as director of football. However, the return to his old stomping ground was not the success everyone had envisaged and in May 2008 Kerr announced his resignation from the role.

St Patrick's Athletic defender Damian Lynch remembers Brian's second coming at Inchicore: 'I was there for the final seven months of his time there. I remember he brought some lovely small touches to the club. He had gained a lot of experience from international football, and as a club it was great to be able to call on this. Brian was willing to get involved, but he made sure not to overshadow John McDonnell, who was the man in charge.

'Brian wasn't too involved with the day-to-day coaching – that was left to John – but he would come up two to three times a week to watch us. His main role was to help bring in players and look at the overall set-up. A fitness coach was brought in, and these are the sorts of things that take clubs to another level. Brian was trying to build Pat's for the future, creating links with schoolboy clubs and establishing a strong youth set-up.'

Four years after losing his job as Ireland manager, Brian made a return to international management in April 2009 when he was appointed manager of the Faroe Islands national football team, a country with a population of 49,000 people and roughly the size of County Carlow in Ireland. The challenge of the Faroe Islands brought Brian back to his footballing management roots of no hope and very little budget, but in just five months in the job he had achieved the seemingly impossible and guided a team made up of fishermen, students and policemen to their first World Cup qualifying victory since 2001. His return to international football management with the Faroe Islands saw Brian re-capture the imagination of the Irish public once again, and his profile was enhanced further in a documentary entitled *Away with the Faroes* which covered Brian's week in the build up to the Faroe Islands' match with France. The Faroe Islands narrowly lost 1–0 to the French. Brian's reputation as a manager is back on track.

BRIAN KERR'S CLUB MANAGERIAL HONOURS RECORD:

League of Ireland: St Patrick's Athletic, 1989–90 and 1995–96

BRIAN KERR'S IRELAND RECORD:

UEFA Under-16 European Championship
UEFA Under-18 European Championship
Total number of games in charge: 33
Total number of wins: 18 (ratio 54.55%)
Total number of draws: 11 (ratio 33.33%)
Total number of losses: 4 (ratio 12.12%)

Biggest win: 3–0 (Canada November 2003 & Cyprus, September 2004)

Biggest defeat: 0–3 (Nigeria, June 2004)

Longest unbeaten run: 13 games

BRIAN KERR'S RESULTS AS IRELAND MANAGER:

Date	Home/ Away	Opponent	Score	Result	Type of Fixture
12/02/2003	Away	Scotland	2–0	W	Friendly
29/03/2003	Away	Georgia	2–1	W	Competitive
02/04/2003	Away	Albania	0–0	D	Competitive
30/04/2003	Home	Norway	1–0	W	Friendly
07/06/2003	Home	Albania	2–1	W	Competitive
11/06/2003	Home	Georgia	2–0	W	Competitive
19/08/2003	Home	Australia	2–1	W	Friendly
06/09/2003	Home	Russia	1–1	D	Competitive
09/09/2003	Home	Turkey	2–2	D	Friendly
11/10/2003	Away	Switzerland	0–2	L	Competitive
18/11/2003	Home	Canada	3–0	W	Friendly
18/02/2004	Home	Brazil	0–0	D	Friendly
31/03/2004	Home	Czech Republic	2–1	W	Friendly
28/04/2004	Away	Poland	0–0	D	Friendly
27/05/2004	Home	Romania	1–0	W	Friendly
29/05/2004	Away	Nigeria	0–3	L	Friendly
02/06/2004	Away	Jamaica	1–0	W	Friendly

05/06/2004	Away	Holland	1–0	W	Friendly
18/08/2004	Home	Bulgaria	1–1	D	Friendly
04/09/2004	Home	Cyprus	3–0	W	Competitive
08/09/2004	Away	Switzerland	1–1	D	Competitive
09/10/2004	Away	France	0–0	D	Competitive
13/10/2004	Home	Faroe Islands	2–0	W	Competitive
16/11/2004	Home	Croatia	1–0	W	Friendly
09/02/2005	Home	Portugal	1–0	W	Friendly
26/03/2005	Away	Israel	1–1	D	Competitive
29/03/2005	Home	China	1–0	W	Friendly
04/06/2005	Home	Israel	2–2	D	Competitive
08/06/2005	Away	Faroe Islands	2–0	W	Competitive
17/08/2005	Home	Italy	1–2	L	Friendly
07/09/2005	Home	France	0–1	L	Competitive
08/10/2005	Away	Cyprus	1–0	W	Competitive
12/10/2005	Home	Switzerland	0–0	D	Competitive

13

STEPHEN STAUNTON

Sometimes the right job comes about for the right man but at the wrong time. Depending on your point of view, international football can be a good entry point into management – a perfect example being Mark Hughes, who started his management career with Wales, before having success with Blackburn Rovers and Manchester City – or international football is for the more mature man, the man who has experienced all football has to offer, men such as England's Fabio Capello, Wales' John Toshack or Ireland's Giovanni Trapattoni.

From his very early days with the team it seemed that Stephen 'Steve' Staunton was destined for the role of Ireland manager. His status in the Ireland camp, his involvement with a successful Liverpool side in the early 1990s and his caps record all pointed to someone who was being groomed for the role. On paper he was the perfect man to motivate the players and show them how to play for your country.

Perhaps it was the wrong time for Staunton. He was unlucky in some respects, and in others his inexperience as a manager did not help. He tried to return Ireland to the glory days of Jack Charlton's time as manager and surrounded himself with people who would ultimately help him grow and develop in the role. However, it was sadly a case of too much too soon.

While Staunton's era was characterised by a mix of paranoia and poor results, it is very hard to point the finger at him. If anyone was offered money (or even no money) to manage their country, they would take it, that's the simple fact, whether or not they felt they were the right person for the job or qualified enough for the position. If the chance came along, wouldn't you take it? However, as Irish football pundit Eamon Dunphy put it to Bill O'Herlihy at the time of the appointment, 'Would you let him sit in your seat, Bill? Would you let him drive the train to Cork without any training, Bill? It's the same thing!' The point being that you need to have all the relevant qualifications and experience to do any job you are hired to do.

International managers do not require coaching badges, unlike in the Premier League, for example. However, they are an essential qualification for any football manager to have. To do the best job, you need to have all the tools to hand.

Staunton was not ready for the Ireland job, but he made the right moves with his appointments to the back room staff. Terry McDermott and the late Sir Bobby Robson were inspired appointments on paper, although sadly for football, and Ireland in general, illness meant that Staunton could not count on Sir Bobby as much as he would have liked.

STAUNTON THE EARLY YEARS

Staunton was born in January 1969 in Drogheda, County Louth. In his early years he showed promise at a variety of sports, and as well as playing soccer he also played Gaelic football for Louth, appearing in the Under-21 GAA Championship. However, it was his performances for Dundalk that prompted the interest of Liverpool manager Kenny Dalglish, and in September 1986 he signed for Liverpool in a £20,000 deal.

Turlough O'Connor was the manager of Dundalk in those days, and he recalls the fair-haired kid who would one day play for and manage his country: 'He was a super fella. He was very enthusiastic and also a very good listener. He wanted to be a success. He was a credit to Dundalk. He played Gaelic and local soccer before he got into the second team under Tommy Connolly. We played Stephen as a left midfielder in those days. He had a lovely left foot. In the game before he went to Liverpool for the trial he scored a lovely free-kick from outside the box.

'After two weeks over at Liverpool they had seen enough and they wanted to sign him. They were coming to Cork for their pre-season, and we travelled down to meet them and agreed a fee. It was marvellous for Dundalk and marvellous for Stephen, who was ambitious and wanted to play in England. I remember I met him when he was manager of Ireland, and I said to him, "You probably didn't realise it at the time, but the money we got for you kept the football club going for a good few years." It was a great deal for Dundalk. There were a number of clauses in the deal whereby we got a bonus if he made a certain number of appearances, if he played for Ireland and if they ever sold him.'

His first two seasons were spent at Liverpool in the reserves and on loan to Bradford, learning the trade. However, it would not be long before he finally made his debut for the club, coming on as a substitute in a 1–1 draw with Tottenham Hotspur in September 1988. His performance that day ensured that he made the bench again a few days later, coming on against Arsenal in the semi-final of the centenary trophy, and over the course of the season he continued his integration into the team. Typically a defender, Staunton showed his scoring skills in 1989 when he replaced Ian Rush during a League Cup tie at Wigan and scored a second-half hat-trick.

He soon became a vital part of the line-up and was a member of the Liverpool side that was hit by tragedy in the FA Cup semi-final at Hillsborough in 1989. However, he rallied to help his side win a memorable final 3–2. He was also a member of the side that won Liverpool's most recent League title in 1989–90, some twenty years ago.

Despite his part in Liverpool's success, Staunton failed to make an impression on the new manager in charge, Graeme Souness, and he was sold to Aston Villa in August 1991 for £1.1 million. However, he put the disappointment behind him and became an instant hit at Villa Park by scoring during his debut game, in an away fixture at Sheffield Wednesday. The solid start helped him settle well into life at Villa Park and in his first season there he helped his new club to a seventh place finish, just behind his old club. In 1994 Staunton, who had been joined in the Villa team by former Liverpool players Ray Houghton and Dean Saunders, helped the club to a League Cup win over Manchester United and in the process Steve completed his collection of domestic medals. After his starring role in the 1994 League final, Steve added another League Cup winners' medal to his collection in 1996, although this time he was an unused substitute in Villa's 3–0 win over Leeds. Two years later Steve left the club to make a shock return to Liverpool on a Bosman (free) transfer, but he did not have the same impact he had on his first stint with the club and was largely a squad member. His two years back at Anfield, which included a loan spell at Crystal Palace, saw Steve reach 147 League games for Liverpool. At the end of his second stint at Anfield, Steve made the move to another previous club, when he returned to Villa Park for a two-year stint. His playing career then wound down with spells at Coventry and Walsall. It was at Walsall that he got his coaching career off the ground, becoming assistant manager at the Bescot Stadium. However, the following January he got a call from the FAI, and Staunton's world was turned upside down.

STAUNTON THE INTERNATIONAL LEFT-BACK, CENTRE-BACK AND MIDFIELDER

Just a month after Staunton made his debut for Liverpool, and still not having completed a full ninety minutes for his club side, he also made his debut for Ireland, playing the full game and setting up a last minute goal for Tony Cascarino in a 4–0 win over Tunisia. A month later, in November 1988, he made his first competitive start for Ireland in a World Cup qualifying loss to Spain. Over the coming year, Staunton started to cement his place in the team and at the age of twenty-one, with thirteen caps to his credit, he was selected for the 1990 World Cup squad, starting in Ireland's opening game against England. He played the full ninety minutes in all of Ireland's games at Italia '90, with his only substitution coming during extra time in the second round match with Romania.

Post-Italia '90, Staunton continued to be an important part of the Irish line-up and four years later he made his second appearance at a World Cup tournament. Once again he featured in all of Ireland's matches. Despite missing out on the World Cup in France 1998, he was a senior member of the 2002 squad. His four appearances in Japan in 2002 meant that Steve Staunton is the only Irish international player to have played in all of Ireland's 2002 World Cup games. His appearance in the group game against Germany was his hundredth game for his country. Despite his record appearances at World Cup tournaments, he never got to play in a European Championship, as Ireland failed to qualify for Europe's biggest competition during his international career. This was the only blot on a successful international career. In all Staunton won 102 caps for Ireland, calling time on a thirteen-year international career after the 2002 World Cup.

STAUNTON THE GAFFER

Just a year after retiring from professional football, Steve Staunton became the second youngest manager in the history of Irish football, when at the age of thirty-six he was picked as the successor to Brian Kerr, who had paid the price for his failure to guide the team to the World Cup in Germany. Prior to his appointment Staunton was assistant manager at Division

Two side Walsall. He was a surprise appointment by the FAI, which, after the departure of Brian Kerr, had promised that a world class manager would be appointed. The organisation took the step of appointing a three man committee to oversee the selection process. Despite being one of Ireland's greatest players, Steve was not the world class manager promised; in fact, Steve's journey on the managerial road was just beginning. However, the FAI's reasoning was clear. Staunton was a Division One and FA Cup winner with Liverpool and a double League Cup winner with Aston Villa. He was used to success, and he was going to be working in tandem with Sir Bobby Robson, a manager of the highest calibre who had managed Barcelona, Newcastle, PSV Eindhoven and England with great success.

Staunton quickly surrounded himself with experienced coaches, appointing former Aston Villa reserve-team coach Kevin McDonald. However, his and the FAI's biggest gamble was the appointment of an ageing Sir Bobby Robson in the role of International Consultant. Sadly, Sir Bobby soon began a fifth battle with cancer and as a result had little interaction with the Ireland set-up.

Staunton's reign became a constant battle with the media, although he struck the first blow himself at the start of his reign when he publicly declared himself the 'Gaffer'. Although not quite in the 'I am the special one' vein of José Mourinho, Staunton's self-proclaimed title earned him ridicule in the media and was the first of many such incidents with the press.

Any doubts as to his appointment were put to the back of people's minds when in his first game in charge, with Robbie Keane as his new captain, Staunton led Ireland to a 3–0 win over Sweden. The impressive start was soon forgotten, however, and doubts reappeared as Ireland lost their next two matches to Chile and Holland. The 4–0 defeat at home to Holland was Ireland's biggest home defeat since a similar 4–0 loss to West Germany in 1966.

Staunton's first competitive game in charge was a European Championship qualifier, and the heavy defeat at the hands of Holland was put to the back of people's minds as Ireland produced a spirited display, managing to restrict Germany to a 1–0 home win. However, once again Steve's inexperience as a manager was evident as a kicked water bottle, a reaction to his own frustrations, landed on the pitch and the referee reacted by sending Steve to the stands. It would be a costly mistake for the team as Steve was forced to watch Ireland's next game, away to Cyprus, from the stands. With Kevin McDonald in the dugout, Ireland was on the end of an embarrassing defeat, losing 5–2 to one of Europe's smaller sides. With the pressure mounting, Steve needed a run of results to appease the fans and critics alike. A 1–1 draw with the Czech Republic at Lansdowne Road, followed by a 5–0 win over San Marino, finally gave him some breathing space.

The return match against San Marino saw a return to the struggling autumn performances with Ireland needing an injury-time goal to come away with a 2–1 win. The team's poor away results coupled with their inconsistent displays meant that Steve was under constant pressure. Successive 1–0 wins over Slovakia and Wales did little to inspire the nation, but despite this, Ireland remained in contention for qualification. Four games in September and October ultimately decided Steve's fate, as a defeat away to the Czech Republic was followed by successive draws with Slovakia, Germany and Cyprus (who before the campaign had never taken any points from Ireland). Ireland would not be on a plane to the European Championship finals in Austria and Switzerland. Despite finishing the group in third place, Ireland were twelve points behind the Czech Republic.

Confusion about Staunton's role surfaced thereafter, as the FAI refused to back their beleaguered man while Staunton refused to resign, the manager stating that he intended to see out the remainder of his four-year contract. However, in the end the FAI and Staunton bowed to public pressure, and his twenty-one month reign as international manager came to an end.

BACK TO BASICS

With his reputation seemingly in tatters following the Ireland job, it was a case of back to basics for Staunton. It was crucial for him to remain in football and lessen the damage done by his time with Ireland. Thankfully, his first opportunity for redemption arrived in the shape of the assistant manager's role with Leeds United under another former Liverpool teammate, Gary McAllister. The move back to day-to-day coaching was essential to his redevelopment, and although he was sacked along with McAllister following a poor run of form, his reputation was not further damaged by the Leeds appointment.

During Staunton's time at Leeds he worked with Alan Sheehan, a former Ireland Under-21 defender: 'He was a massive influence on my game. He came to Leeds as assistant to Gary McAllister, and one of his main duties was to work with the defenders. As I am a left-back like him he really looked after me a lot. He passed a lot on to me, and he definitely helped my development as a defender. He'd work on defending exercises with us, and I found that he had a lot to give as a coach. When it came to games Gary would say his piece beforehand, and Steve would also get involved. The day-to-day involvement seemed to work for him. They were unlucky in the end at Leeds. A couple of bad results cost them in the end.'

His old Ireland teammate Mick McCarthy offered Staunton a coaching role with Wolves. During this time Staunton completed his coaching badges and took the opportunity to watch St Kilda, an Australian rules team, train in an effort to get an insight into other sports and their methods.

In October 2009 he returned to club management when he accepted the manager's job at Darlington, who at the time were the ninety-second club in League football, rooted to the bottom of League Two. It was a big job for the manager, but he did not have to wait long for a morale-boosting victory, which came in his second game in charge. Taking the job with Darlington could be viewed as an attempt by Staunton to take things back to grassroots level. That was how Paul Ince, for example, had started out, and success with a small club, struggling with budgets and cash, can catch the eye of money conscious chairmen around the country.

When Staunton took over at Darlington they were at the bottom, and the only way, or so it seemed, was up for both club and manager. However, the remit of saving the team from relegation proved too difficult, and in March 2010 he was sacked from the role, with Darlington still rooted to the bottom of the League.

While he might not be recognised as one of Ireland's greatest-ever managers, it is hard to dispute what Steve Staunton has given to Irish football over the last twenty years. While his reputation might have been tarnished by his time spent in the Ireland hot seat, with his growing experience he will have the opportunity to become a great manager in time.

STEVE STAUNTON'S CLUB MANAGERIAL HONOURS RECORD:

No management honours

STEVE STAUNTON'S IRELAND RECORD:

Total number of games in charge: 17
Total number of wins: 6 (ratio 35.29%)
Total number of draws: 6 (ratio 35.29%)
Total number of losses: 5 (ratio 29.42%)
Biggest win: 5–0 *v*. San Marino
Biggest defeat: 4–0 *v*. Holland
Longest run without defeat: 9 games

STEVE STAUNTON'S RESULTS AS IRELAND MANAGER:

Date	Home/ Away	Opponent	Score	Result	Type of Fixture
01/03/2006	Home	Sweden	3–0	W	Friendly

24/05/2006	Home	Chile	0–1	L	Friendly
16/08/2006	Home	Holland	0–4	L	Friendly
02/09/2006	Away	Germany	0–1	L	Competitive
07/10/2006	Away	Cyprus	2–5	L	Competitive
11/10/2006	Home	Czech Republic	1–1	D	Competitive
15/11/2006	Home	San Marino	5–0	W	Competitive
07/02/2007	Away	San Marino	2–1	W	Competitive
24/03/2007	Home	Wales	1–0	W	Competitive
28/03/2007	Home	Slovakia	1–0	W	Competitive
23/05/2007	Away	Ecuador	1–1	D	Friendly
26/05/2007	Away	Bolivia	1–1	D	Friendly
22/08/2007	Away	Denmark	4–0	W	Friendly
08/09/2007	Away	Slovakia	2–2	D	Competitive
12/09/2007	Away	Czech Republic	0–1	L	Competitive
13/10/2007	Home	Germany	0–0	D	Competitive
17/10/2007	Home	Cyprus	1–1	D	Competitive

14

DON GIVENS

Collins Dictionary describes a caretaker as 'a person employed to look after a place or thing', and on two separate occasions that is exactly what Don Givens has done for the Irish football team. Despite knowing that the role was only temporary every time he took it, he has managed the team in a professional manner, and the performances under him have been in line with what is expected of an international coach. Don has stepped in and helped his country whenever he has been called upon, whether in the dugout or on the pitch.

Imagine a striker who played at the top level of English football and was top scorer for his country for over nine years, and no, I am not talking about Robbie Keane or John Aldridge. Don Givens might be more familiar to younger readers as the Ireland Under-21 boss, but his goal-scoring feats for Ireland were the stuff of dreams. Over the years Ireland have been blessed with some fantastic strikers, from the great Jimmy Dunne in the 1930s and 1940s to Frank Stapleton, John Aldridge, Tony Cascarino, Niall Quinn and the current strike pair of Kevin

Doyle and Robbie Keane, all fantastic players, and, although they weren't strikers, Noel Cantwell and Gerry Daly had impressive scoring records for Ireland. However, during the dark days of the 1970s Don Givens was a shining light for Ireland, and his exploits endeared him to the fans of the day.

He has a higher profile today, especially as a result of his time spent managing the Under-21s and his stints as caretaker boss of Ireland. And whereas Giovanni Trapattoni is known as 'the Italian', Givens will always be remembered as 'the Caretaker', for it seems likely that he will always be the bridesmaid and never the bride, although perhaps he would be better described as the best man, as he is still an essential part of the Ireland set-up, overseeing the FAI's UK-based scouting network.

There is no doubt that Givens can be very proud of the role he has played in Irish football, from his goal-scoring displays as a striker to his more recent roles, including being on the panel that helped select the current Ireland manager, not to mention his role in developing future talent while manager of the Under-21 side. He has given himself fully to the cause and deserves his rank as a legend of the game in Ireland.

Born in Limerick in 1949, Givens the footballer started his career as a seventeen-year-old with Manchester United, arriving at the club in 1966 in one of the most glorious chapters in the team's history. Givens was surrounded by and learned from players such as George Best, Denis Law and Bobby Charlton, although it was two years later before he would make his debut for United. His time at the club was short-lived, and he only made a handful of appearances for the Red Devils before making the switch to Luton in a £15,000 deal. He spent two seasons with Luton, scoring nineteen goals in eighty-one games, before he transferred to Queens Park Rangers.

Gordon Jago was the manager at QPR at the time, and he was faced with the challenge of replacing Rodney Marsh. He recalls, 'QPR had sold Rodney Marsh in March 1972 for £200,000. However, my instruction from the club chairman was that we would not buy any new players until after the season had ended. Other clubs knew about the money we'd received for Rodney and would tend to place a higher price on any players who were of interest to us. I was to consider new players, and we would make enquiries during the summer months.

'I had seen Don play against us and was very impressed. He was a highly skilled player in control of the ball, quick and ice cool in front of goal. We knew that we would need two or three forwards to replace Rodney, and Don was my first choice. We contacted Luton Town in the summer to enquire if he was available. Fortunately for us they were in need of money, and we agreed a price of £40,000. Don was away playing for the Republic of Ireland in South America, so we had to wait until he returned before we could speak to him and discuss his terms. It was a nail-biting wait, for we were sure that other clubs would get to hear about our deal with Luton and there would be competition for his signature. Fortunately, we met with Don on his return, and he signed for us. Before the start of the new season we also signed Stan Bowles from Carlisle for £100,000, and not long into the season we added Dave Thomas from Burnley for £162,000. The new forward line was complete, and we won promotion to the First Division that season.

'Both Stan and Dave were excellent players, but Don was the best buy when you consider the prices paid. He played forty-one games, only missing one League match and scoring twenty-three goals. He went on to play 293 games for QPR and scored 101 goals.

'Not only was he a very good player, he was a first-class person. A quiet man who trained hard, he was very disciplined, always pleasant and a first-class role model for the young players at the club. He was exceptionally fit, and he would do extra training most days to practise his shooting and penalty taking. He was the club's penalty taker in those days. Even though he was quiet he was very popular with the other players and was well liked, and, you know, I don't recall ever subbing him in a match.

'I was so fortunate to have him with the club and will always be indebted to him for the major part that he played in bringing success to QPR. I followed his later career, trying to contact him during his coaching spell in Switzerland, unfortunately without success, and I am just as pleased about his achievements as a coach.'

Givens settled into the team very quickly and soon became an integral part of the club. His finest season for QPR came in 1975–76 when he helped QPR to a second-place finish behind Liverpool in the First Division, losing out on a winner's medal by one point.

After six years in London, Givens moved to the midlands with Birmingham before winding down his career in English football with a loan spell at Bournemouth and a short period with Sheffield United. His time at Sheffield United was marred by a missed penalty in a key winner-takes-all match against Walsall, which ultimately saw the Blades suffer relegation to the bottom tier of English football, the old Fourth Division.

However, his career did not end there. Instead, he moved to the football outpost of Switzerland and to Neuchâtel Xamax. At a time when Irish players were making their mark on English football, and to some extent on the American soccer scene, making the move to a European club was rare, and when it did happen it was often for a short period only. However, Givens settled in to life in Switzerland and spent five seasons with the club. It was while there that he won his only top-level medal, winning the National League A in 1987 at the age of thirty-seven.

INTERNATIONAL CAREER

At the age of twenty, Don made his debut for Ireland under Charlie Hurley, playing the full ninety minutes in a 2–0 loss to Denmark. In his second match for Ireland, Don scored his first goal for Ireland, in a 2–1 World Cup qualifying loss to Hungary. Three months later, in September 1969, he scored the first goal of Mick Meagan's reign as team manager, to take his tally to two in three games. A year after this debut for Ireland, Don had become an integral part of the line-up, having scored four goals in his seven games.

Two of Don's finest performances in an Irish shirt came during the 1970s under the management of Johnny Giles. In October 1974, Don overshadowed the debut of Liam Brady when he scored a hat-trick as Ireland beat the Soviet Union 3–0 and then a year later he went one better, scoring all the goals in a 4–0 win over Turkey. His achievement was the first time an Irish player had scored four goals in a game in forty years, emulating the feat of Paddy Moore, who scored all four in a draw with Belgium in 1934. Those goals took Don's international tally to fifteen goals in just thirty-one games for Ireland. In May 1976, Givens scored two goals to first equal and then break Noel Cantwell's Irish goal-scoring record of fourteen goals. He added further goals against Bulgaria, Denmark, the USA and Switzerland to set an international record of nineteen goals, a record that lasted until 1990 when it was broken by Frank Stapleton. In an international career that lasted twelve years and six different Ireland managers, Don bowed out of international football in a 3–2 win over France. In all he won fifty-six caps. Such is his legacy that Don still stands fourth on the list of all time top Irish goal scorers.

GIVENS THE MANAGER

Switzerland might have afforded Givens an Indian summer to his career, but it also led to him getting his first break in club management. Once his playing days came to an end he became a youth coach at Neuchâtel, but he quickly got a break and was given the top job in 1993 when he replaced former Switzerland manager Uli Stielike as head coach. Givens managed to save the club from eventual relegation in his short spell but failed to make an impression on the Xamax hierarchy, who replaced him with their former coach Gilbert Gress for the following season. Gress was the person who had originally signed Don, and he had also previously led Neuchâtel to League Championships in 1987 and 1988. As a former player and manager he was well known to the club's directors.

Givens remained out of the game until his old friend Liam Brady helped him get involved with the youth set-up at Arsenal in 1997. He took charge of the academy players, and in his first season he led the Under-18s to the FA Premier League Academy Under-18 title. With a career being forged in youth development Givens did not make any further impact on the management scene until he was appointed manager of the Republic of Ireland Under-21 side in 2000. The appointment was part of a restructure of the Ireland international set-up intended to enable Ian Evans to help Mick McCarthy with the senior side. At the time Don decided to maintain his involvement with the Arsenal youth side, and he combined the two roles for two years before taking on the Ireland Under-21 job full-time.

In November 2002 he briefly became caretaker manager of the senior squad following Mick McCarthy's departure, managing the team for a goal-less draw against Greece. His tenure ended with Brian Kerr's appointment as manager in January 2003.

He was once again appointed as caretaker manager in October 2007, following the departure of Steve Staunton, and he was in charge for the final European Championship qualifier against Wales, which once again ended as a draw. In February 2008 he experienced his first defeat as caretaker manager when Ireland lost 1–0 to Brazil. In three games as caretaker manager he never tasted victory.

GIVENS THE UNDER-21 MANAGER

While Givens has been a great servant to Irish football, both as a player and as a caretaker manager, it is for his most recent role as manager of the Ireland Under-21 team that he is best known. He spent ten years in the role after taking over from Ian Evans in 2000 and stepping down in March 2010. His position with the youth set-up at Arsenal meant that when the FAI was looking for a new man to take over from Ian Evans,

Givens seemed the perfect choice. A former internationalist, who was a record goal-scorer and part of the Arsenal backroom staff, should have no problem earning the respect of the players. Sadly, during his reign the Under-21 team under-achieved, especially when compared to the glory days of the Liam Tuohy and Brian Kerr's youth teams.

Young players with the necessary talent are often fast-tracked into the senior squad, the prime examples being Damian Duff and Robbie Keane, who were under-age stars from the Brian Kerr days. However, while Ireland currently has some very skilful young players in the English Premier League and Championship, such as Seán Scannell at Crystal Palace, Owen Garvan at Ipswich and Jay O'Brien at Birmingham getting game time at big clubs, more recently we have seen less and less make the transition through the ranks to the senior side as the latest manager Giovanni Trapattoni looks to make a more immediate impact on the team with more established and mature players.

Another damaging aspect of Given's reign as Ireland Under-21 manager was the often very public spats between him and the players, with some youngsters being dropped from squads never to return. Ireland, as a footballing nation has a small pool of talent to choose from and cannot afford to stop the international development of young players. Success at youth level can have an important impact on the senior side. The set-up of the Under-21 team should be as similar as possible to the senior side so the players can make an easier transition if and when a first-team call comes. Despite the problems, Givens oversaw the transition of John O'Shea, Steven Reid, Andy O'Brien, Colin Healy, Gary Doherty, Aiden McGeady and Kevin Doyle from the Under-21 side to the senior side.

Swansea City defender Marcos Painter was one of the kids who was guided by Don in the Under-21 team: 'I was seventeen and playing in the reserves at Birmingham when Keith Bertschin, who was the reserve-team manager, told Don I had Irish connections, as my grandmother was from Kildare. Don was based in Birmingham at the time, and he came to see me play a couple of times. He had a chat with me, and I was eventually called into the Under-19 squad for a tournament in Portugal.

'I played at Under-19 and Under-20 level before I was called into the Under-21 group. I played for two seasons with Don at that level, and I found him to be a very calming influence. It gives you great confidence as a player when a coach who is well respected within the game has faith in you, and with Don you had a manager who was genuine and had also played at a high level. He never put pressure on the players, and he solely focused on the Under-21 team. There was never any mention of the senior squad, so in that respect it took away the distraction and helped us concentrate on the game.

'He made the players feel very welcome and part of the group. When I was making my debut against Switzerland the fact that Don wanted me was a good confidence booster, especially when I started. Don created a good environment with the Under-21s. It wasn't just him, though, as he also had some very good support staff around him.'

In March 2010 Don stepped down from his role as Irish Under-21 manager, but remained on the FAI payroll, taking up a new role overseeing the FAI's UK-based scouting network. It ensures that a relationship that started forty-one years ago, and has seen Don progress through the FAI ranks from player to backroom staff, continues. While Don is an integral part of Ireland's future building programme, his place in Irish footballing history will never be forgotten.

DON GIVENS' CLUB MANAGERIAL HONOURS RECORD:

No management honours

DON GIVENS' IRELAND RECORD:

Total number of games in charge: 3
Total number of wins: 0 (ratio 0.00%)
Total number of draws: 2 (ratio 66.66%)
Total number of losses: 1 (ratio 33.34%)
Biggest win: none
Biggest defeat: 1–0 *v.* Brazil
Longest run without defeat: 2 games

DON GIVENS' RESULTS AS IRELAND MANAGER:

Date	Home/ Away	Opponent	Score	Result	Type of Fixture
20/11/2002	Away	Greece	0–0	D	Friendly
17/11/2007	Home	Wales	2–2	D	Friendly
16/02/2008	Home	Brazil	0–1	L	Friendly

15

GIOVANNI TRAPATTONI

Despite the difference in world rankings and the pool of talent available, the Ireland and England national football teams have shared many similarities over the years. The most recent of these is the appointment of an Italian as the national manager. Whether or not the FAI were inspired by England's appointment of Fabio Capello, one of the most successful coaches in Europe, is not known. However, the committee that was appointed to bring inspiration to the nation's football team definitely followed England's lead when they selected Giovanni Trapattoni, then Red Bull Salzburg manager, as the replacement for Steve Staunton.

A former manager of the Italian national team, Trapattoni is a highly regarded manager who, during a management career that started in the 1970s, has won a remarkable nine League titles and six European trophies in Italy, Germany, Portugal and Austria. His profile and experience were exactly what the FAI required to restore confidence both in the national team and their own organisation after the perceived debacle with the previous regimes.

The reigns of Brian Kerr and Steve Staunton had failed to inspire the nation, and with Ireland's rugby team on the up and enjoying international success, soccer was once again in danger of being left behind. The appointment of Trapattoni has brought about a period of stability and an improvement in performances for the Irish team.

EARLY YEARS

Giovanni Trapattoni was born in the small town of Cusanio in the province of Milan on 17 March 1939. As a footballer he made his name with AC Milan, joining the team at the end of the 1950s. His father worked in a factory and encouraged Trapattoni to abandon football and follow the same road he had taken, seeing football as a hobby only and not to be taken seriously, as did a lot of fathers at the time. Trapattoni worked in a factory after school six days a week, but travelled to watch Milan, the team he supported, train and play whenever he had free time.

In 1958 a nineteen-year-old Trapattoni fulfilled a dream when he pulled on AC Milan's red-and-black shirt for the first time, making his debut in an Italian Cup match against Monza – the only problem on what was almost a perfect day was that he had to play with a 38.5°C fever. Two years later, on 24 January 1960, Trapattoni made his Serie A debut, AC Milan beating Spal 3–0. It was a bitter-sweet debut for Trapattoni, as his joy was overshadowed by the death of his father Francesco ten days beforehand.

Trapattoni soon became an integral part of the Milan line-up, and as a defensive holding midfielder who often operated at centre-back, his job was to tidy up play and help the more attack-minded players concentrate on just that. In modern-day football, Claude Makélélé, Javier Mascherano and Lassana Diarra have made a similar role their own. Not renowned for their scoring abilities, these footballers break up play, win the ball and act as a shield in front of the back four. In a diamond formation the role works very well. However, most midfield pairings work with a defensive and attacking split.

His time with AC Milan came during a very successful period for the club, coinciding with the appointment in 1961 of Nereo Rocco as head coach, starting a trophy-laden era for the *Rossoneri*. With Rocco on board, Milan won two Italian Championship titles, one Italian Cup, two European Cups, one Cup-Winners' Cup and one Intercontinental Super Cup. After Milan, Trapattoni eventually ended a successful playing career with A.S. Varese 1910. Varese, who currently play in the fourth tier of Italian football and were footballing neighbours of Milan, were a midtable Serie A club in those days, and Trapattoni ensured their status would last another season before he decided to retire from the game and concentrate on coaching.

Trapattoni also played for Italy, appearing in seventeen international matches over a four-year period from 1960 to 1964, scoring his only goal when he claimed the winner in a 1–0 success over Austria in Vienna in 1963. The highlight of his Italy career was the 1962 World Cup in Chile, although Trapattoni failed to start a match and the team only won one game, limping out of the tournament at the first hurdle.

FOOTBALL MANAGEMENT

Trapattoni is the rarest of managers, one who has enjoyed success wherever he has managed, with very few exceptions. He has won the League Championship in four separate countries (Italy, Germany, Portugal and Austria), only the second man to do so, after Austrian Ernst Happel.

Trapattoni began his management career in the early 1970s with the club he had given great service to as a player, AC Milan. Taking control of the youth team he managed the senior side for a period of six matches in 1973–74. The following season saw his ascent up the ranks as he was promoted to the position of assistant coach and became first-team coach in 1975. They finished ninth in Serie A in his first season in charge.

In 1976 Trapattoni made the short trip from Milan to Turin to take charge at Juventus, and so began ten glorious years of success. In his first season with Juventus, Trapattoni led the team to the League title, and he repeated the feat a year later. A treble of titles followed in the early 1980s, and Juventus soon came to dominate Italian football. Trapattoni also led the team to a trio of European triumphs as they won the European Cup, the Cup-Winners' Cup and the UEFA Cup. The European Cup victory will forever be etched in the minds of football fans, as the 1–0 win at the Heysel Stadium in Belgium was overshadowed by events off the field that led to the deaths of thirty-nine football fans.

Despite the disaster, Juventus had finally claimed the European crown that many felt they deserved. In Michel Platini they had the best player in world football at that time, confirmation of which came when he won the European

Footballer of the Year title during the peak of Trapattoni's success with Juventus, from 1983 to 1985. The 1984 Super Cup and the Intercontinental Cup (now the World Club Championship) in 1985 confirmed Trapattoni as a manager who was at the top of his profession.

His last season with Juventus brought yet another title before Trapattoni decided to move to Inter Milan. He spent five years with that team but failed to reach the dizzy heights of his Juventus days, as a Diego Maradona-inspired Napoli and a resurgent AC Milan challenged the upper tier of Italian football. That said, he did win the Serie A title in 1989 and yet another UEFA Cup in 1991 when Inter won an all-Italian final against Roma 2–1.

They say you should never go back once you leave a club, but the lure can be too strong for some managers. Juventus had declined in the period since Trapattoni had left them, and having seen the rise of the Milan teams, the aforementioned Napoli, and Lazio and Roma, it was inevitable that they would turn to their former manager to return them to the glory days. Sadly, the second coming was not the success many had envisaged, with a single UEFA Cup the only major success, although this did provide further proof of Trapattoni's abilities beyond domestic football.

In 1994 Trapattoni set off on a road that would eventually lead to Ireland. At the age of fifty-five he decided to accept the role as manager of Bayern Munich. However, his first season in Germany did not go to plan, and at the end of the campaign he decided to return to Italy with Cagliari, having seen the Bavarians finish without a trophy. His return to Italy did not last long, however, and he only managed twenty-one games for Cagliari before the lure of the world outside Italy proved too much. In 1996 he returned to Bayern. His second term in charge was much more successful, as the team won the German Championship in 1997 and the German Cup in 1998. Despite winning the Cup, his second season was largely perceived as a failure, as he lost the Championship title to newly promoted Kaiserslautern.

During this time his relationship with the players became strained. In a well-documented outburst, directed at the team and delivered in broken German, he announced that the players were like an empty bottle. The pressure of managing the German giants was becoming too much for Trapattoni, and following the loss of the title it was no surprise when he left the club for a second time.

A two-year stint with Fiorentina saw the club secure a Champions League group place, when they managed to claim victories over Manchester United and Arsenal. The club had finished third in his first season in charge, but their League position was not as impressive as their Champions League results, and at the end of the season Trapattoni was once again looking for work.

The next port of call was the top job in Italian football and completed the cycle for Trapattoni, from player to manager of his beloved Italy. Dino Zoff had resigned from the job, having led the country to the final of the 2000 European Championship, which they lost due to two late goals. The new style of open and attacking football was a change for Italy, and the future was looking rosy. Under Trapattoni Italy qualified ahead of Romania in group eight for the 2002 World Cup in Korea and Japan, where they opened with a win over Ecuador before losing in controversial circumstances to Croatia. The result against Croatia derailed Italy, and they failed to recover. The defeat angered the Italians, as they felt they were the victims of some poor refereeing that cost them two goals. They regained their composure to draw late on with Mexico, but the damage was done, and they were beaten in the second round by co-hosts South Korea, who came from behind to defeat them, thanks to Ahn Jung Hwan's golden goal.

At the 2004 European Championship, Italy once again failed to impress. They drew with both Denmark and Sweden, leading to an unexpected early exit from the competition at the group stage, despite being undefeated, ousted on goal difference after all three teams finished on the same points total. In June 2004 Marcello Lippi was named as Trapattoni's replacement.

Trapattoni was not long out of a job, and he set off for pastures new to rebuild his reputation. His port of choice on this occasion was Benfica in Portugal. A renowned powerhouse in European football, Benfica was a sleeping giant and had not won the domestic League title for eleven years. The job had seen some of the biggest names in management try and fail to break their main rival Porto's dominance in the Portuguese League: Jupp Heynckes, José Mourinho, Graeme Souness and José Antonio Camacho had all failed to lead them to success. However, in his first and only season in charge Trapattoni brought home the title. The club were also runners-up in the Cup, but despite this success Trapattoni felt Portugal was too far from Italy, and he decided that he needed to be nearer his family in northern Italy. He resigned the post shortly after the conclusion of his successful year. However, instead of returning to Italy, he took a role in Germany with Stuttgart amid much fanfare. Negative results and open criticism from players saw him last only seven months there.

Country number four was soon on the horizon, and in May 2006 Red Bull Salzburg announced they had signed Trapattoni as their new director of football, along with one of his former Inter Milan players, Lothar Matthäus, as coach. History was made when Red Bull won the League, adding another title to Trapattoni's record.

With the sacking of Steve Staunton, Ireland needed a big name to appease both the media and fans. Staunton's reign had seen Ireland's reputation diminish, and they needed an experienced manager to rebuild the squad. The FAI had never moved outside of Ireland or England in their search for a manager, and the likes of Terry Venables and Graeme Souness were the favourites for the job. However, to the surprise of everyone in the country, the FAI delivered one of the biggest names in football when in February 2008 they announced that Giovanni Trapattoni had agreed to become the country's new manager.

THE IRELAND JOB

With such a big name on board, wages were always going to be an issue for the FAI, but they had a knight in shining armour in the shape of Denis O'Brien. O'Brien, an entrepreneur who formed Esat Digifone in the 1990s, agreed to part fund the appointment of Trapattoni, and a new chapter in Irish football history was about to begin.

Trapattoni's first game in charge, a friendly against an up-and-coming Serbia on 24 May 2008, ended in a 1–1 draw. Andy

Keogh was the hero for the new coach, scoring an injury-time equaliser that won the FAI goal of the year. Trapattoni did not have to wait long to get his first victory, as five days later in another friendly, against Colombia, Ireland's talisman, Robbie Keane, scored the winner in a 1–0 win.

Trapattoni's team then went unbeaten during the qualifiers for the 2010 World Cup, winning four and drawing six of their ten group games. The pick of the results were four draws with Italy and Bulgaria. The 2–2 home draw with Italy was a return to the golden days, and were it not for a last-minute goal Ireland would have taken the group right down to the wire. The wily Italian also managed to scare the daylights out of Marcello Lippi in Bari when ten-man Italy was left clinging on for a much-needed point, despite taking an early lead. His tactical abilities were in evidence that day, as the introduction of Caleb Folan led to Robbie Keane scoring.

Giovanni Trapattoni has come under criticism from some factions of the media for his perceived lack of interest in watching new players. The Italian has been seen to be very loyal to the players he has used so far and in his defence, an unbeaten qualifying campaign is a good building block for any team.

The League of Ireland has largely been ignored by international managers, with Jason Byrne and Glen Crow the last League players to be capped by Ireland at international level, in 2006 and 2004 respectively. Before that it had been sixteen years since a League of Ireland player had appeared for the national side when Shamrock Rovers' Pat Byrne got a cap. However, Bohemians goalkeeper Brian Murphy was called into the squad for the France play-off match that followed Ireland's second-place finish in their World Cup qualifying group. This and the fact that players such as Noel Hunt and Kevin Doyle both started their careers in Irish football and have gone on to make an impact on the English and international stage, gives League of Ireland players some hope.

However, St Patrick's Athletic defender Damian Lynch reckons that at the moment the League of Ireland is not in a position to aid the national team too much: 'It's hard to argue with what Trapattoni has achieved with Ireland. He has done a tremendous job. In terms of League of Ireland players in the squad, obviously it would be great to see, and there are players here who are capable of playing at that level, but the League does not help itself, especially with clubs in difficulties and players not getting paid. You can't blame Giovanni Trapattoni for not attending matches. The financial cloud that has been hanging over the clubs for the last eighteen to twenty-four months has meant that teams are struggling.

'The likes of Keith Fahey and Jay O'Shea are great talents who have started to catch the eye of the Ireland set-up now that they have moved to England, but, being honest, and this is my opinion, the standard over here is not as good. In the League of Ireland you get six weeks of the year in Europe to show how good you are, but week in week out you are not getting to the same level as you would in the Championship. That said, there are some great players in this League, some of whom are capable of making the grade with Ireland.'

While Trapattoni's reign has been well received by the fans, the man himself is really enjoying the challenge that Ireland offers: 'Ireland is a small country, but it has good players with a lot of heart. The last decade has shown us that in international football everything is possible if a team is well organised with a good structure. Greece showed everyone that when they won the European Championship in 2004, and the USA have showed it too with their good performance at the Confederations Cup, beating Spain in the process. With Ireland I have brought in a system that has helped the players believe in themselves and obtain good results.

'One of the first things I did was that I told the players that they must believe, and they responded very positively. The squad improved progressively during the 2010 World Cup qualification campaign, with results against Montenegro, Cyprus, Bulgaria, then Italy and lastly France. With each new challenge the players rose to the task and have grown in stature.

'Managing Ireland is different to managing Italy in that Italy is a very big country in world football, so the size of the squad and the number of options available to the manager is a fundamental difference. When I started with Ireland it was a small squad, and we did not have that many options, so injuries and suspensions were always a concern. During the campaign, however, we have introduced many new players, and this has given the squad more depth, something that I hope to continue.

'Fans in both countries have a real impact on their team's performances, and I have been genuinely impressed by the Irish fans. They have been very supportive of me. They really made a huge difference at decisive moments in so many of our games.

'When Ireland played Italy it was of course an emotional experience, but I have always preferred to keep these things simple. When you are playing cards with your friends do you want to win or lose? You always want to win, of course. That is the answer. In terms of the results against Italy it was disappointing not to win, but over two legs to go unbeaten against the 2006 world champions was a great result for our players and they should be proud of their performances. Managing Ireland means a lot to me. The welcome I have received in Ireland has been exceptional, and when we are playing I am very proud to accept the responsibility of representing the Irish people.'

Trapattoni has also shown that despite not having the strongest grasp of the English language he is not afraid to make tough decisions. The manager has courted negative publicity for omitting Andy Reid from the squad on a regular basis, while he has also found disfavour with Sam Allardyce by commenting on Steven Reid's ongoing injury problems. And Clinton Morrison, Lee Carsley and Steve Finnan have all been left out in the cold by Trapattoni as he battles to put his own stamp on the squad, although, with an emphasis on the future, the likes of Glenn Whelan and Leon Best have come into the squad.

Despite the team starting to take shape during the qualifiers, the football played was reminiscent of the Italian style, with Trapattoni happy to sit back and defend, and it is significant to note that Ireland's biggest win under Trapattoni came in his twenty-first game in charge, a 3–0 win over Algeria; prior to that 2–1 had been his biggest victory. There appeared to be a certain lack of confidence in the abilities of the players, but as the campaign went on, belief increased in both the management and on the field, and the football became that bit more expressive. The highlight of the campaign was during October 2009 at Croke Park in the Italy match, which showed that when the reins were taken off, the team could perform and entertain. However, the draws in previous qualifying matches cost Ireland dear, and they needed to slip through the back door if they were going to make it to South Africa for the 2010 World Cup.

PLAY-OFF HEARTBREAK YET AGAIN

As we have seen throughout this book, the Ireland team do not like play-offs, especially when they are against European teams. From Spain in 1965, Holland in 1995 and Belgium in 1997 to Turkey in 1999, history has shown that we do not win when the going gets that bit tougher. However, after going through a qualifying campaign unbeaten against Italy and Bulgaria, the hopes of a nation were high.

Two weeks before the end of the group matches, FIFA suddenly announced that there would be seeding for the play-offs. This had a massive impact on Ireland's chances. Being a smaller footballing nation in terms of success, Ireland would not have the benefit of the seeding and as such were faced with the possibility of a play-off game against either Portugal, France or Russia, three of Europe's big guns. The reward for finishing second in their group meant that Ireland would eventually be paired with France, a side that was rumoured to be disjointed and fraught with internal bickering under Raymond Domenech. In what would become a tale of perceived rough justice against Ireland, they had to play the former world champions at home first, handing the advantage to France.

The first leg was a game of two halves, with Ireland showing the tactical awareness that had become a trademark of the Trapattoni reign, dominating their opposition from the start.

However, the second half saw France come out of their shell, and a deflected goal saw them home 1–0.

So with their backs to the walls the time had come for Trapattoni to show the nation just why he was so well paid. What happened in the second leg will no doubt become part of Irish folklore. Trapattoni changed his cautious approach and arranged for the team to play higher up the field. This was the first time that the team had really been allowed the freedom to play, and they pushed France all the way to extra time before a tragic goal, that would have Diego Maradona smiling, settled the affair. Thierry Henry was the villain in the piece as he controlled the ball with his hand in the box to cross for William Gallas to head home. The goal was a result of a simple free kick into the box by Florence Malouda from just inside the halfway line. The ball was not dealt with by the Irish defence, but was heading out of play when Henry intervened. It was a hugely disappointing end to what had been one of Ireland's finest away performances in a competitive match. The goal stood, despite the protests of the Irish players, and Ireland would not be going to the World Cup. Instead Trapattoni and the team would have to switch their focus to the European Championship in 2012. Trapattoni has agreed to remain with the team for that campaign and carry on the good work that has been done since his appointment.

Despite its unfortunate outcome, the France game helped restore public faith in the Ireland team. The game in this country had stagnated after Japan 2002, and the France match could well turn out to be a turning point for football in Ireland. While we might have failed to qualify, the manner of defeat was treated as a victory by many football purists, as Ireland outplayed France for almost 120 minutes.

Football and the economy hardly work in tandem with one another – the share prices of the Bank of Ireland and Élan are not dependent on whether Ireland win, lose or draw – but at a time when the country is going through a tough patch and people have little to cheer about, the performances of the Ireland team under Trapattoni have restored some much-needed pride and belief. Under Trapattoni, Irish football appears to be on the up again.

GIOVANNI TRAPATTONI'S CLUB MANAGERIAL HONOURS RECORD:

Juventus:

Six Italian Serie A titles: 1977, 1978, 1981, 1982, 1984 and 1986

Two Italian Cups: 1979 and 1983

One European Cup: 1985

Two UEFA Cups: 1977 and 1993

One UEFA Cup-Winners' Cup: 1984

One European Super Cup: 1984

One Intercontinental Cup: 1985

Inter Milan:

One Italian Serie A title: 1989

One UEFA Cup: 1991

Bayern Munich:

One Bundesliga title: 1997

One German Cup: 1998

S.L. Benfica:
  One Portuguese League title: 2005

Red Bull Salzburg:
  One Austrian League title: 2007

GIOVANNI TRAPATTONI'S IRELAND RECORD:

Number of games played: 21
Total number of wins: 8 (38.10%)
Total number of draws: 10 (47.61%)
Total number of losses: 3 (14.29 %)
Biggest win: 3–0 *v.* Algeria
Biggest defeat: 3–0 *v.* Australia
Longest run unbeaten: 6 games

GIOVANNI TRAPATTONI'S RESULTS AS IRELAND MANAGER:

Date	Home/ Away	Opponent	Score	Result	Type of Fixture
24/05/2008	Home	Serbia	1–1	D	Friendly
29/08/2008	Away	Colombia	1–0	W	Friendly
20/08/2008	Away	Norway	1–1	D	Friendly
06/09/2008	Away	Georgia	2–1	W	Competitive
10/09/2008	Away	Montenegro	0–0	D	Competitive
15/10/2008	Home	Cyprus	1–0	W	Competitive

19/11/2008	Home	Poland	2–3	L	Friendly
11/02/2008	Home	Georgia	2–1	W	Competitive
28/03/2009	Home	Bulgaria	1–1	D	Competitive
01/04/2009	Away	Italy	1–1	D	Competitive
29/05/2009	Away	Nigeria	1–1	D	Friendly
06/06/2009	Away	Bulgaria	1–1	D	Competitive
12/08/2009	Home	Australia	0–3	L	Friendly
05/09/2009	Away	Cyprus	2–1	W	Competitive
08/09/2009	Home	South Africa	1–0	W	Friendly
10/10/2009	Home	Italy	2–2	D	Competitive
14/10/2009	Home	Montenegro	0–0	D	Competitive
14/11/2009	Home	France	0–1	L	Competitive
18/11/2009	Away	France	1–1	D	Competitive
25/05/2010	Home	Paraguay	2–1	W	Friendly
28/05/2010	Home	Algeria	3–0	W	Friendly

EPILOGUE

LET'S TALK STATS

People love to talk about football; they love to discuss tactics, their favourite teams, favourite players, the price of players and their favourite managers. Football fans enjoy the banter that these often heated discussions generate. Passion and statistics form a large part of any football fan's arguments. Fans take great pride in supporting their favourite team and their national football side. Unlike club football, international team organisations cannot buy players to make them a footballing force, but they can pay managers big money to make sure that the players they have at their disposal bring the country success.

Although this book is a celebration of the men who have managed Ireland, it is still worthwhile debating the relative merits of each manager, and the tools needed for such a debate are statistics. It is also informative to look at the money each manager earned when in charge of the national team.

One of the main reasons football enthrals people is that over the years it has constantly reinvented itself and evolved. From the European Nations Cup of the 1960s to the modern-day

European Championships to World Cups in America, Asia and Africa, football has shown itself to be a truly global sport. Likewise the structures of Irish football have had to change to incorporate these world changes, and one of the key elements of change is money. Not a lot can be achieved without money, and when it comes to the management of Ireland, a country that has come to demand high standards from the FAI, the cost of these demands has increased as the years have progressed.

Such is the changing face of Irish football and football in general that the price of success increases with each management cycle. When Mick Meagan became the first manager to select an Ireland team, he did so on a wage that started at IR£35 a game. Compare that to current manager Giovanni Trapattoni, who earns a mind-boggling €250,000 per match. Put more simply, after two matches Mr Trapattoni could effectively take a break from the touchline, sub-let his job and hire out the footballing brains and talents of Jack Charlton and Mick McCarthy. The only men to bring Ireland to the ultimate stage in world football, the FIFA World Cup, started on salaries of IR£35,000 and IR£175,000 respectively. In the twelve years since Mick McCarthy's appointment, the wages have increased at a phenomenal rate and the current manager, Giovanni Trapattoni will earn a whopping two million euro a year under his deal with the FAI. In their defence, the FAI do have the financial help of Denis O'Brien, who has agreed to help fund the post from his own pocket.

When you compare the salary of Trapattoni with the managers of the 1970s and early 1980s you get a real sense of how much money has changed the game of football. One of Ireland's greatest players, Johnny Giles, received just IR£6,000 a year for his stint in charge, while his successor Eoin Hand, the youngest man ever to manage Ireland, earned IR£17,500 a year. The appointment of Jack Charlton as the manager in 1985 might have caused a stir in the footballing world, but his starting salary was only IR£35,000, double that of his predecessor. While this might have been large at the time, no amount of inflation could account for the jump to two million in just twenty-three years. When Liam Tuohy took over from Mick Meagan in the 1970s he managed to bag himself a retainer of IR£500. However, he was paid the same match fee as Mick at the end of his tenure. (He started on IR£35 a game and moved up to IR£50 by the end of his time in charge.) Although Tuohy now had full control of the squad and team selection, he also worked as a manager with HB Ice Cream and managed Dundalk. As you can imagine it was a busy time for the man. Both Johnny Giles and Eoin Hand were at the lower end of the wage scale, although neither were in it for the money – it gave them a sense of pride to manage their country. It was the patriotic thing to do, and you get a sense that these men would have done it for free if they had had to.

Once Jack Charlton had vacated the Merrion Road office it was the turn of his foot soldier and Ireland's very own 'Captain Fantastic', Mick McCarthy, to take the stage. By then the Premiership was in full swing, and the FAI could no longer hand out the paltry figures that McCarthy's predecessors were paid. Despite coming from unfashionable Millwall, at the time a second-tier club, albeit one on the up, McCarthy surpassed Big Jack's final wage and started on a more impressive IR£175,000. By the time he left in 2002, the year the euro was introduced, his salary had gone up to around €300,000 a year.

Having seen previous League of Ireland managers take the hot seat for pocket money, Brian Kerr became the highest paid manager ever in 2002 when he accepted the role on a deal worth approximately €350,000. Unlike Big Jack or McCarthy, Kerr had never managed at English club level, but he had made a big impression, first with St Patrick's Athletic and then with the Ireland youth sides.

The big bucks just kept on coming, as next up Steve Staunton was given the job on a starting salary of €450,000, and that is excluding the money that was paid to Sir Bobby Robson in his supporting role as football consultant. The money on offer was not buying managerial experience in this case. On this occasion the FAI's gamble failed, and Staunton did not enjoy the success he yearned for and deserved.

Giovanni Trapattoni has taken the Ireland manager's job to a different level financially. His large salary certainly buys experience and, judging by his results so far, it seems he has provided an added bit of luck that has eluded some of the other managers. One thing is for certain in the new money-conscious Ireland: he will be expected to deliver value for money.

Moving on to the statistics of Irish football since Johnny Carey became coach in 1953, the national team have played a total of 390 matches. Of these they have won 155 of the games they have played, or 39.74 per cent, drawn 112, or 28.72 per cent, and lost 123 games, or 31.54 per cent. Of these games, 196 have been away from Irish soil, with 194 games played in Ireland, at Dalymount Park, Lansdowne Road, Croke Park and, under Giovanni Trapattoni, Thomond Park in Limerick.

But how does Ireland fare in competitive games versus friendly games? Do the players step up to the table for an essentially meaningless match in an effort to show that they are good enough to be selected for competitive games, or does a competitive game really show the winner in us? Of the 390 games played, 219 have been competitive. The level of competition has ranged from World Cup and European Championship qualifiers to actual World Cups and European Championships. Of the 219 competitive games that Ireland has played they have managed to win eighty-four of them, or 38.36 per cent, a slight drop on the overall record. They have drawn seventy-one games, or 32.42 per cent, an increase on the overall results, and lost sixty-four, or 29.22 per cent, which is a drop on the overall level. In friendly matches they have played 171 and won seventy-one, or 41.52 per cent, which is higher than the overall average, drawn forty-two games, or 24.56 per cent, and lost fifty-eight games, or 33.92 per cent.

So when it comes to competitive games versus friendly games Ireland has a greater win rate in friendly matches but a lower percentage of defeats in competitive games. For a country of just four million people, with a small pool of players to call upon, to have a win average in both competitive and friendly matches greater than your loss average is a fantastic achievement. When it comes to friendly matches it is worth noting that their main opponent is Poland, who they have played nineteen times.

But how does Ireland fare when it comes to playing countries in the FIFA top ten? Looking at the FIFA top ten (West Germany figures have been added to those of the unified Germany team) in November 2009, Ireland has played thirty-eight games. Of those they have won twelve (31.57 per cent), their biggest result coming in a 4–1 away win over Holland in Johnny Carey's second match as team manager. Seventeen of the games (44.74 per cent) have ended in defeat for Ireland, with Brazil leading the way with a 7–0 victory in 1982, while in 2006 Ireland suffered their second-largest defeat to a top-tier nation when Holland avenged an earlier loss with a 4–0 win in Dublin.

But this is about the managers and their individual records as manager of the Irish national team. When it comes to the less important fixtures, Alan Kelly senior tops the bill, although given that he was only in charge for one game his 100 per cent record is open to debate. A more realistic choice would be Brian Kerr, as he won 64.71 per cent of his friendly matches, followed closely by Jack Charlton on 59.46 per cent, with Johnny Carey also thereabouts with a 45.45 per cent win ratio. Mick Meagan and Eoin Hand top the losing ratios, with Mick losing three out of every four friendly games he managed, while Hand's loss record is slightly better at 64.71 per cent. The Noel Cantwell–Charlie Hurley combination never coached a winning XI side in a friendly match, and they share this record with Mick Meagan, Seán Thomas and the caretaker Don Givens.

When it comes to competitive matches the man who you would want managing Ireland would be Mick McCarthy, who with a 47.50 per cent win ratio is Ireland's most successful manager. Unsurprisingly, there is little between him and his old boss Jack, who comes in second with a 43.86 per cent win ratio. It really is no surprise that these two men top the pile, although Brian Kerr can count himself unlucky, as he ran Jack close, but in the end he comes home in third with a 43.75 per cent win ratio.

Eoin Hand comes in fourth, winning 39.13 per cent of his competitive games, while Giovanni Trapattoni looks to have given himself a very good chance of reaching the targets set by Mick and Jack, as he is already in fifth spot with a win ratio of 38.1 per cent, and has only suffered one defeat in a competitive game to date. Meagan, Kelly and Givens never won a competitive game for Ireland, although in fairness to Alan Kelly, he never managed a team in a competitive match.

The stats also show that since the 1980s, Ireland's results have greatly improved in competitive football, although to be fair to the pre-1980s managers there are now more countries involved in the qualifiers as a result of the fragmentation of Europe, leading to more games against smaller nations.

As football has evolved into the commercial sport that it is today, the importance of playing at home has become all the more apparent. In qualifying tournaments the teams with the best home form generally qualify for the major events. Ireland have played 101 competitive matches at home and have won more than half of them, winning fifty-four (53.47 per cent), drawing thirty-three (32.67 per cent) and losing only fourteen (13.86 per cent).

King of the home matches is Johnny Giles, who never achieved qualification to a major tournament as a player or manager, but won 66.67 per cent of his matches on Irish soil. In fact, Giles never lost a home competitive match in Ireland in his time in charge, winning six of the nine games he had and drawing the rest.

Jack Charlton has the second-best home win ratio at 63.64 per cent, while Mick McCarthy is third with a 61.11 per cent win ratio. Eoin Hand also had an impressive record on Irish soil, winning 58 per cent of his games, losing just two out of twelve games.

Steve Staunton had his critics, but he never lost a competitive fixture at home, despite Ireland moving from the familiar surroundings of Lansdowne Road to Croke Park during his tenure. His win ratio is 50 per cent though, as he drew half of his competitive games in Ireland. Giovanni Trapattoni is also currently unbeaten at home, but like Steve Staunton he has been in charge for a plethora of draws.

When it comes to competitive away matches, the figures change completely. Ireland have played 118 games away from home, winning only thirty of them and losing fifty. The early managers top the pile here, with Mick Meagan losing all the matches he played away from Dublin, while Johnny Carey lost 75 per cent of his away games. In third spot is Johnny Giles, whose away form was why he failed to guide Ireland to a major tournament. He lost 70 per cent of his games and won only one match away from home. In fact, between Ireland defeating Czechoslovakia 2–1 in 1967 under Charlie Hurley to the win over Cyprus in 1980 they did not win any away games in competitive football.

Brian Kerr is the king of tactics, as more often than not he returned from an away game with a point. He lost only 12.5 per cent of his games, suffering only one defeat. Charlie Hurley and Noel Cantwell have the highest win ratios, 50 per cent. However, they only oversaw two competitive matches. Kerr has the next best win ratio at 37.50 per cent, while 50 per cent of the games he managed away finished in a draw. In the five away games Giovanni Trapattoni has been involved in, he has shown his class, winning 33.33 per cent of them and drawing the other 67.67 per cent, and he is yet to suffer defeat. Mick McCarthy is ahead of Jack Charlton, winning 36.36 per cent versus 31.43 per cent, and despite his impressive home record Steve Staunton only won 20 per cent of his away games.

When it comes to friendly matches Ireland have shown themselves to be more than competitive. Alan Kelly can boast a 100 per cent record, winning his only home friendly. Liam Tuohy never had the luxury of playing a home friendly. Brian Kerr always took every game seriously, and his win ratio of 66.67 per cent is the best, although Johnny Giles runs him close with a 62.50 per cent win ratio. Jack Charlton won 59.09 per cent of his friendly games. Giovanni Trapattoni has shown himself to be a master of the competitive game, and as his reign has gone on and he has become more familiar with the team, he has seen his success ratio increase to 50 per cent in friendly games at home. However, he has overseen two defeats for Ireland in games outside Dublin, the venture to Thomond Park in Limerick not providing a winning formula. The Charlie Hurley–Noel Cantwell project can claim never to have lost a friendly at home. However, neither did they win, drawing both games.

Brian Kerr and Jack Charlton share the spoils in the away friendly matches, both men winning 60 per cent of their games, while Johnny Carey won 44.44 per cent to take second place and Liam Tuohy with a 40 per cent win ratio is third. Eoin Hand lost 75 per cent of the friendly games he played away from Dublin, and his poor friendly record is highlighted with an 8.33 per cent win ratio overall, the lowest.

The perfect manager for Ireland would be a blended mix of all the men who have been in charge. If you had a friendly at home, Brian Kerr was your man. If that friendly was away, you'd be better off with Jack Charlton at the helm. However, if you needed to qualify for a tournament, you'd want Johnny Giles to manage the team for the home games, and Giovanni Trapattoni,

Charlie Hurley, Noel Cantwell and Brian Kerr for the away matches. But if it's consistency you want, Mick McCarthy is the manager for you.

Ireland has been truly blessed by the men who have managed the team over the decades. These men have given themselves to the role and helped Ireland develop into the footballing nation that we are today. The loyalty and pride that each man has taken in the job is a testament not only to their character but also to the players and fans of Irish football.

INDEX